SURROGATE MOTHERHOOD AND THE POLITICS OF REPRODUCTION

SURROGATE MOTHERHOOD AND THE POLITICS OF REPRODUCTION

Susan Markens

University of California Press Berkeley Los Angeles London

University of California Press, one of the most distinguished university presses in the United States, enriches lives around the world by advancing scholarship in the humanities, social sciences, and natural sciences. Its activities are supported by the UC Press Foundation and by philanthropic contributions from individuals and institutions. For more information, visit www.ucpress.edu.

University of California Press
Berkeley and Los Angeles, California

University of California Press, Ltd.
London, England

Library of Congress Cataloging-in-Publication Data

Markens, Susan, 1967–.
Surrogate motherhood and the politics of reproduction / Susan Markens.
p. cm.
Includes bibliographical references and index.
ISBN 978-0-520-25203-5 (cloth : alk. paper)
ISBN 978-0-520-25204-2 (pbk. : alk. paper)
1. Surrogate motherhood. 2. Surrogate mothers—Legal status, laws, etc.—United States. 3. Surrogate motherhood—United States—Social aspects. I. Title.

HQ759.5.M37 2007
306.874'3—dc22 2006029089

Manufactured in the United States of America

15 14 13 12 11 10 09 08 07
10 9 8 7 6 5 4 3 2 1

This book is printed on New Leaf EcoBook 50, a 100% recycled fiber of which 50% is de-inked post-consumer waste, processed chlorine-free. EcoBook 50 is acid-free and meets the minimum requirements of ANSI/ASTM D5634–01 (*Permanence of Paper*).

For my mother, Ella Markens

CONTENTS

ILLUSTRATIONS

FIGURE

TABLES

ACKNOWLEDGMENTS

This book is the result of a long period of gestation and labor. Consequently, its writing was at times exciting and stimulating and at times tedious and arduous. Along the way many people helped me through the process of producing it. During the period of conception, I had a supportive dissertation committee—Carole Browner, Laura Gómez, Gail Kligman, and Ruth Milkman—that helped nurture both me as a feminist sociologist and the dissertation that was the first version of this work. Much later in the process, as I pulled apart the original dissertation and worked on putting it back together, Éva Fodor read some of my first revised chapters and gave me confidence that I was on the right track. Both Jonathan Markovitz and Ellen Reese read the entire manuscript as I revised it, a chapter at a time, and gave me very useful feedback and advice as well as the encouragement and support that every book writer needs. Later on, Linda Blum and Sherri Grasmuck, along with anonymous reviewers, also read the manuscript in its entirety and provided insights on how to make it even stronger. I am grateful to all these readers for taking time to read each chapter carefully and provide me with their feedback. I know the advice they generously shared made this a better book, and of course whatever weaknesses remain in the book are my own responsibility.

At various stages of research and writing I had the help of research assistants—Megan Howe, Elizabeth Halen, Stephanie Gabis, and most crucially Jason Martin—who aided me in big and small ways. I would also like to thank Kim Goyette, who helped me create my first SPSS data set while I am sure she had her own papers to write. And toward the end I had the crucial help of Bruce Markens, Paul Markens, and Joanna Cohen, who helped watch my daughter as I made my final push to get the manuscript to the press. I would also like to acknowledge the eleven interviewees who generously gave their time for me to talk to them. I am also very grateful to Kathy Mooney for her help in editing and revising the manuscript, to Elisabeth Magnus and Chalon Emmons for their aid during the copyediting and production phase at the press, and to Naomi Schneider for her support of this project.

The writing of this book was made possible by a large cadre of friends, spread over many cities (and sometimes continents), who kept me sane and optimistic. For nights out on the town, dinner parties, e-mail exchanges, long phone conversations, and even gentle prodding and useful discussions about my work I have many people to thank. They include Lisa Askenazy, Kate Auerhahn, Maria Bardach, Carole Browner, Mark and Monica Carnesi, Tina Collins, Jen and Paul Crowe, Amy Denissen, Sharon Fagen, Kerry Ferris, Éva Fodor, Kim Goyette, Lisa Handler, Jessica James, Eric Kaldor, Joanna Kempner, Dustin Kidd, Catherine Lee, Naomi Levitsky, Bill Maclehose, Jonathan Markovitz, Joanie Mazelis, Mike Miller, Lynne Moulton, Alex Muentz, Emily and Joe Navetta, Rebecca Berman Phelps, Julie Press, Jo Pritchard, Phil and Jerry Ratcliffe, Kevin Reardon, Ellen Reese, Julia Rodriguez, Jill Rodstrom, Benita Roth, Silke Roth, Sophia Tsakraklides, and Jocelyn Williams.

Finally, I could not have written this book without the unconditional love and support that I have received from my family my whole life. Although he used to call me a "geek," my brother Paul Markens has always put family first. I see this now in the fabulous uncle that he is. And although he teased me about how long it took me to get my PhD and then to finish this book, I know that he has always admired my accomplishments and is proud of me. Although they are now a continent away from me, as they were during my childhood years, my aunt and uncle, Nancy Ehrlich and Michael Floyd, have always been extended family I could count on. I particularly appreciated their proximity during the near-decade I lived in California. And most recently, the birth of my beautiful daughter Sophie has reminded me once again of the importance of family, as well as the meaning of motherhood—if not the difficulty of finishing a book while breast-feeding! Last, and not least, I am grateful to my parents, Bruce and Ella Markens, who raised me to be a strong and intelligent woman and who have supported me (in every way possible!) in my endeavors. Although they too could not resist asking when I was going to finish my book, I always knew that they had confidence that I would. The only disappointment in seeing this book come to fruition is that my mother died too young to see it in print. This book is dedicated to her.

INTRODUCTION

Unfamiliar Families?

John and Luanne were married in May 1989. On March 30, 1995, John filed a petition for dissolution of marriage. He alleged that the couple separated in September 1994, and there were no minor children.

Luanne filed her response April 20, 1995. Instead of agreeing with John that there were no minor children, she asserted that the "[p]arties were expecting a child by way of surrogate contract" and that the doctor indicated the birth would be about May 5. Luanne attached a copy of the surrogacy contract to her response.

The surrogacy contract was signed by John, Luanne, a woman named Pamela, and Pamela's husband, Randy. Under the terms of the contract, Pamela was to be "implanted with the embryo(s) created with donated genetic material, unrelated to any of the parties. The child [was] to be taken into the home of the Intended Father and Intended Mother and raised by them as their child, without interference by the Surrogate [Pamela] or her husband, and without retention or assertion by the Surrogate and her husband of any parental rights."

Jaycee B. v. The Superior Court of Orange County (1996)

The case of *Jaycee B. v. The Superior Court of Orange County* was heard by the Fourth District California Court of Appeal in 1996.[1] Unlike the dozen or so other court battles involving surrogacy that had taken place up to that point, this was not a dispute over child custody.[2] Instead, Luanne B. was requesting child support from her ex-husband for a child conceived via a surrogate parenting arrangement. None of the four adults involved was genetically related to the baby, Jaycee. John and Luanne's marriage had dissolved prior to Jaycee's birth. John contended that he did not owe any child support because he did not meet the criteria typically used to establish paternity: (1) his wife had not given birth to the child; (2) he was not genetically related to the child; and (3) he had never formally adopted the child.[3]

This case clearly illustrates how surrogacy and new reproductive technologies challenge our notions of family and relatedness. As anthropologist Sarah Franklin points out, "Not only are new individuals being conceived [through new technologies], but new conceptions of kinship and relations are also 'born.'"[4] When the process of conception changes, what do the social categories of "woman," "mother," and "family" mean? Can we rely on existing cultural values, laws, and beliefs to guide our choices, or are new understandings and legal frameworks required? These and other similarly fundamental social questions lie at the center of the debates over surrogacy that have flared, faded, and flared again over the last two decades of the twentieth century.

Jaycee B. v. the Superior Court of Orange County also indicates how far we have come, technologically speaking, since 1978, when Louise Brown, the first "test tube" baby, was born. Fertilizing biological parents' embryos outside the womb seems straightforward in comparison to the more recent scenario of "gestational motherhood" evident in cases like Jaycee's.[5] In this form of surrogacy, the birth mother is not genetically related to the child, nor is she intending to raise the child as her own. Moreover, the case reminds us that the practice of surrogate parenting has changed dramatically since 1987, when the Baby M custodial dispute (discussed below) reached the New Jersey high courts. At that time, most surrogates were "merely" artificially inseminated with sperm. Finally, the legal tussle that gestational motherhood generated in Jaycee's case suggests that in the United States social policy has advanced much more slowly than the burgeoning field of new reproductive technologies and surrogacy arrangements.

Indeed, legislative response to the challenges that new reproductive technologies and surrogacy pose to traditional notions about the rights, responsibilities, and definitions of family has been sluggish and incongruous.[6] This book explores the divergent ways two "mega-states," New York and California, responded to the issue of surrogate motherhood in 1992.[7] The analysis addresses three overlapping questions: (1) What accounts for the emergence of surrogate motherhood as a social problem worthy of public and legislative attention in the 1980s? (2) What accounts for the continued slow and inconsistent policy response to surrogacy in the United States? and (3) What do the debates about surrogate motherhood tell us with regard to cultural assumptions about and conflicts over gender, mothers, and families at the end of the twentieth century?

SURROGACY IN THE UNITED STATES: BABY M AND BEYOND

Because families, and mothers in particular, are believed to play an essential role in creating and socializing future citizens, reproductive issues, practices, and policies are central to how nations view themselves and their prospects for the future.[8] American society is so pronatalist that those who choose to remain childless often have to defend that decision.[9] Moreover, even nontraditional prospective parents, from gays and lesbians to professional single women, frequently are encouraged to have children.[10] At the same time, it is precisely this explosion of diverse family formations and gender relations that many have viewed as threatening to "the" family. As a result, in the late twentieth and early twenty-first centuries, scholars and the public at large have questioned what makes a family, who should and can be a parent, how important mothering is in women's lives, and what responsibility the state has in encouraging and sustaining particular family forms.

In the midst of these debates over the future of the family and mounting concerns about changing gender relations, a new social issue—surrogate motherhood—seized the public's imagination. In 1987, a bizarre custody case in New Jersey gained national prominence. The dispute was over who should get custody of a baby girl, popularly known as Baby M, who was the product of a contractual arrangement between William and Elizabeth Stern and Mary Beth Whitehead. Baby M was genetically related to both Mary Beth Whitehead and William Stern. According to the contract, after the birth of the child, Mrs. Whitehead was to relinquish parental rights and custody of the baby to the Sterns. She was to receive a $10,000 fee for her services. Mrs. Whitehead decided she wanted to keep the baby and the infamous custody case ensued.

The Sterns were both professionals; he was a biochemist, she a pediatrician. Elizabeth Stern had a mild case of multiple sclerosis and was afraid pregnancy would affect her condition. Mary Beth Whitehead was a married working-class woman with two children. After several attempts at artificial insemination, she was successfully impregnated with William Stern's sperm. When Mrs. Whitehead realized she could not give up the baby, she informed the Sterns of her decision and declined the $10,000 fee. The Sterns went to court to gain custody of the child. Mary Beth

Whitehead and her family fled to Florida, where she was eventually apprehended, and the Sterns were given temporary custody of the baby. After a lower-court trial, a New Jersey judge upheld the surrogacy contract, thereby validating the termination of Mary Beth Whitehead's parental rights and giving custody of Baby M to the Sterns. A year later, the New Jersey Supreme Court invalidated the surrogacy contract. However, using the legal standard of "the best interests of the child," it assigned permanent custody to the Sterns. Mary Beth Whitehead retained her parental rights and was awarded visitation privileges.[11]

The Baby M case engendered both public uproar and widespread uncertainty concerning the legal status of surrogate parenting.[12] Nevertheless, the number of surrogate-born children in the United States continues to increase each year. In 1988, there were an estimated 600 surrogacy births nationwide. By the mid-1990s, roughly 6,000 babies had been born as the result of such arrangements, with approximately 250 surrogate births per year occurring in California alone. At the beginning of the twenty-first century, surrogacy births per year in the United States number around 1,000.[13] A large portion of these involve gestational surrogacy (the surrogate is not genetically related to the child she bears).[14]

Few state legislatures have kept pace with the growing popularity of surrogacy. As of 1992, five years after the Baby M case had gained national prominence, only fifteen states had enacted laws specifically addressing surrogacy,[15] and only Washington, D.C., and two states have passed legislation since then. Moreover, these states' surrogate parenting policies differ.[16] The responses of New York and California in 1992 are representative. The New York legislature passed a law that essentially banned commercial surrogate parenting and disallowed the legal enforcement of surrogacy contracts. The California legislature passed a bill that allowed for state regulation of surrogacy (a veto by then-Governor Pete Wilson prevented the bill from becoming law). These two legislative approaches diverged in fundamental ways. New York's policy was constructed to discourage surrogate parenting; California's proposed policy was designed to regulate the practice in order to allow it to continue with as few problems as possible. More specifically, New York expanded its laws on adoption and the prohibition of baby selling to cover surrogate parenting arrangements, whereas California's approach to surrogacy was an explicit attempt to accommodate this new reproductive practice by circumventing existing adoption law.[17]

In this book, I use these two states' divergent legislative responses to surrogate motherhood as the basis for a comparative exploration of the complementary and competing ways social actors and institutions came to define, and thus respond to, the problems of surrogate parenting transactions.[18] One important aim of the study is to critically evaluate common assumptions about the U.S. legislative response to surrogate motherhood in particular and to new reproductive and genetic technologies more generally. For instance, using the findings from these two comparative cases, I question two widely accepted explanations for the lack of regulatory response and overall policy inertia regarding surrogate parenting: that they stem from a "culture war" of competing values and beliefs and that they issue from the uncritical embrace and dominance of commercial values and the free market in the United States.

A second goal of the book is to make the case that social theory must take reproduction seriously. As Engels noted over a century ago, reproductive relations that constitute the "production of human beings themselves" are fundamental to the social organization of any society.[19] As a result, reproductive politics can provide an unusually clear view of the ideological and structural foundation of societies as well as insight into the basis of specific social conflicts. The analysis of policy debates over surrogate motherhood presented in this book demonstrates the utility of a "sociological imagination" that can link the "personal troubles" of the seemingly private and mundane issue of procreation to the "public issues" of reproductive politics.[20]

RESEARCH ON SURROGACY AND NEW REPRODUCTIVE TECHNOLOGIES

The emergence and proliferation of new reproductive and genetic technologies have drawn the attention of feminist sociologists and anthropologists, who rightfully see these developments as providing an important site for examining change in cultural norms around gender, parenthood, and the family. Studies of women (and their partners) involved in and making decisions about reproductive interventions—from in vitro fertilization (hereafter IVF) and prenatal testing to fetal surgery and neonatal intensive care—show the internalization and transformation of women's and men's gender identities vis-à-vis their ability (or inability) to reproduce.

These ethnographic observations and qualitative interviews also reveal the role that cultural ideologies of selfless maternal responsibility toward would-be children play in both individual identity construction and the judgments made by others—whether medical experts or laypersons. At the same time, these constructs are necessarily race and class specific, given both the groups of people who predominantly use these technologies and, consequently, the white middle-class focus of most research. Furthermore, the ethnographic literature often provides insight into how these technological developments and interventions shape and are shaped by cultural values and norms about scientific knowledge and practice. Overall, this scholarship has added to our understanding of how reproductive practices become "renaturalized"; how we come to (re)define the facts of life and personhood; why women are increasingly experiencing what are termed tentative pregnancies; the effects of the "never-enough" quality of technology that compel its usage; and the normalization of medical routines such that decisions about their use become nondecisions.[21]

Most scholarship on assisted reproductive technologies has focused on the people involved in and making decisions about various techniques. There is, however, an emerging literature on policy debates about new reproductive and genetic technologies, from the status of embryos and infertility research to genetic engineering and human cloning. This body of social policy-oriented work is small, tends not to address the United States, and pays little or no attention to the role of ideologies about gender and motherhood, let alone race, in shaping public debates and reaction to developments in reproductive medicine.[22] Instead, like the ethnographic research in this area, these studies usually focus on cultural views of and reactions to science and technology. Research ranges from examining definitional debates about when life begins and the moral status of embryos, to exploring the rhetorical features of the debate that express fears of and hopes for scientific advances, to evaluating the degree of "thickness" or "thinness" of arguments depending on the professions and social actors involved.

Empirical research on surrogacy, particularly work from a policy and social problems perspective, lags significantly behind ethical and legal work on surrogate parenting.[23] Most studies have been conducted on a micro level, with an interactionist focus similar to that of much of the scholarship on new reproductive technologies discussed above.[24] These ethnographic and anthropological investigations of surrogate parenting participants have contributed a nuanced understanding to the motivations behind surrogacy arrangements, demonstrating empirically the contradictory definitions of the situation held by the parties involved. In particular, these studies reveal the ways in which both surrogate mothers and the couples who employ them simultaneously challenge and reinforce prevailing notions of the family and motherhood. But the micro focus of this work leaves us without much understanding of the broader social, cultural, and political implications of surrogacy arrangements. In this book I draw on the valuable contributions of existing scholarship, but I broaden the research focus beyond the realm of individuals to encompass the policy arena. And, unlike most policy-level studies, this book places gender at the center of the analysis, while necessarily paying attention to implicit and explicit racial ideology as well. Surrogacy practices affect and are affected by continuing social conflicts over reproductive choice, mothers' versus fathers' rights, definitions of parenting and motherhood, racialized fears, and the importance of the nuclear family structure. All of these issues demand a feminist and gendered analysis, as well as an approach sensitive to the ways these conflicts overlap and interrelate (i.e., an intersectionality perspective). This study's examination of the political struggles over surrogate parenting legislation succeeds on both counts. The debate over surrogacy illuminates the social and cultural forces that produce social problems; the legislative response captures the symbolic, gendered, and racial nature of policy battles and discourses that form and inform the politics of reproduction.

CONCEIVING SURROGACY: THE CONSTRUCTION OF SOCIAL PROBLEMS AND THE DISCURSIVE AND GENDERED POLITICS OF REPRODUCTION

In the last few decades, a sociological perspective has emerged that emphasizes the constructed nature of social problems.[25] From a constructionist perspective, an issue's emergence as a problem is connected not to objective conditions but rather to subjective claims-making activities.[26] This insight is important when it comes to studying surrogate motherhood. Only a few people are directly affected by or involved in surrogacy, yet in the closing decades of the twentieth century it was claimed as a social problem in the public arena, as measured by both the media and legislative attention given to it.[27] In this sense, surrogacy is like adoption, a topic that also has received far more media attention than warranted by its incidence alone.[28] Each taps broader societal concerns linked to the meaning of motherhood and anxieties about the future of white families. Thus the politics of surrogacy can be viewed as a form of symbolic politics—debates that reflect underlying social tensions and concerns during an era of transformation in gender and familial relations, as well as ongoing racial anxieties.

Taking a constructionist approach to understanding social policies requires paying attention to the rhetorical tools used to define a given social problem. These definitional activities include the use of a *discursive frame* that gives the problem its particular meaning. As William Gamson and Andre Modigliani explain, "A frame is a central organizing idea or story line that provides meaning to an unfolding strip of events, weaving a connection among them. The frame suggests what the controversy is about, the essence of the issue."[29] The purpose of a frame is to provide a causal story regarding the origin of a social problem and to propose a potential solution.[30] The result of what has been called "frame work" and "discursive politics" is the presentation of policy alternatives in light of the issues named and the claims made. In the case of social movements, frames provide the scaffolding in which politics occurs; struggles over definition are thus the primary place in which political debate and strategy develop and unfold.[31]

Subsequent chapters draw on this constructionist concept of framing to understand and explain the legislative responses to surrogacy in New York and California. The diverse interpretations of surrogacy this book explores are further evidence of the cultural and political processes that imbue a given issue with specific meaning. The analysis shows that the meaning of surrogacy and related technologies was (and remains) flexible and not predetermined but that competing visions of surrogate parenting both drew on and reinscribed traditional notions of family, gender, race, and motherhood. In particular, the book's remaining chapters reveal the tension between ideals of reproductive freedom and empathy toward the infertile and concerns about the commodification of reproductive practices and children (i.e., worries over the rise of baby selling).

Additionally, with its comparative analysis of divergent policy responses, this book contributes to an emerging literature. Recent comparative work on social problems from abortion politics to sexual harassment to embryo research demonstrates the importance of illuminating how contextual, contingent, cultural, and institutional factors can affect the discursive frames that become dominant at the same point in time at several different sites.[32] This kind of approach reduces the likelihood of overdetermined accounts of how social problems become framed; it focuses attention instead on the presence and role of fluid and contingent possibilities. Finally, an examination of the political and cultural debates about surrogacy confirms the symbolic politics that are enmeshed in the definition of new social problems and thus highlights the integral role of discourse and language in shaping the politics of reproduction.

BIRTHING SURROGACY: THE ROLE OF CONTEXTUAL FACTORS

Constructionist research on social problems often focuses on why a given issue becomes defined as a social problem at a particular point in time or on how definitions change over time.[33] This suggests that an understanding of surrogacy and the debate that surrounded it cannot be separated from a broader analysis of the particular historical moment in which it captured the public's imagination. Surrogacy's emergence as a publicly perceived social problem can be viewed as a product of two separate but interrelated developments in the late-twentieth-century United States: (1) changes in family structure and in the roles of and ideologies about women and mothers; and (2) the rise of an infertility "epidemic" and debates about the development of new reproductive technologies. In the remainder of this chapter, I consider each of these interrelated developments. I begin by outlining the contextual factors that affected the emergence of surrogate motherhood as a social problem in the mid-1980s; then I turn to the key issues that came to frame public debate about surrogacy in the years to come.

The Transformation of American Families and the Politics of Motherhood

By the mid-1980s, many changes had occurred in American families. Surrogate motherhood's entrance into the public spotlight with the Baby M case captured the concerns and tensions over the trends of the preceding two decades. While some praised the diversity of new family forms, others bemoaned the breakdown of the family and the changing status of motherhood.[34] Baby M, in a new way, came to symbolize changing and competing notions of kinship relations and mothering. Indeed, the challenge surrogacy posed to who and what constitutes family both was produced by and contributed to the larger debates about the future of American families.[35] What was occurring in American families to prompt such attention and alarm?

First, between 1960 and 1979, there was more than a twofold increase in divorce rates.[36] Second, there were marked changes in childbearing trends. Despite a slight increase in the late 1980s, the fertility rate for women had fallen from its peak in the mid-1950s.[37] At the same time, the rate of childlessness for women had risen.[38] This simultaneous increase in divorce and decrease in fertility rates caused fears not only about the deterioration of marriage but also about the preservation of the American family. A related—and, for some, more alarming—concern was the huge increase in out-of-wedlock births. In 1990, over 25 percent of births were to unmarried women, compared to only 5 percent in 1960.[39] Connected to the climbing rates of divorce and out-of-wedlock births was an increase in single-mother families. Between 1960 and 1992, the proportion of children living in mother-only families almost tripled (from 8 percent to 23 percent). In the early 1990s, it was estimated that by the time they reached age sixteen, half of all children would have lived in a single-parent family at some point. The shift in the composition of the American family evident toward the close of the twentieth century provoked questions regarding the rights and responsibilities of parents, in particular fathers, and generated public anxiety over the "future of the family." These concerns were racialized, however. Cultural discourses about declining fertility generally were focused on white, middle-class women, while cultural discourses about out-of-wedlock births, and in particular teenage pregnancies, usually were focused on women of color. These simultaneous concerns about over- and underfertility demonstrate the combination of gendered and racial anxieties embedded in reproductive politics.

Changes in divorce and fertility rates and the rise in single-mother families in turn are tied to transformations in the roles of women and mothers. While the overall rate of female labor force participation had risen substantially since the middle of the century, it was the great increase in rates of working mothers that was most remarkable. By 1992, 68 percent of married women with children under eighteen were working; the comparable statistic for 1960 was 28 percent. Even more stunning was the increase in the labor force participation of married women with young children. Between 1948 and 1991, the figure rose from 11 percent to 60 percent. By the early 1990s, almost one-half of all women were back in the paid labor force after the birth of their first child. These trends indicate a shift in the understandings and experience of motherhood. As more and more women with young children spent a greater percentage of their time in paid labor, they increasingly found their identities outside their homes and apart from their children. The transformation of work-family roles was particularly significant for white women, since their labor force participation rates traditionally had lagged behind those of black women. So, again, we have evidence of a racial component to the gender anxiety that was a key contextual factor in the reproductive politics that characterized the 1980s and early 1990s.

The last decades of the twentieth century also involved increasing expectations and greater social control of women as mothers. These developments included the medicalization of pregnancy and mothering, expectations regarding "supermoms," and ideologies of "intensive" and "exclusive" motherhood.[40] Alongside such unrealistically high expectations of mothering emerged various categories of "bad" mothers, from welfare cheats and crack moms, to new mothers who did not breast-feed or who were so depressed postpartum that they thought they might (and sometimes did) hurt their babies, to women who delayed childbearing or chose not to be mothers at all.[41] The changing roles of women, specifically as mothers, and the accompanying changes in expectations provided the backdrop to the diverse responses to surrogate parenting. Racial anxieties as well as gender anxieties are evident in the reproductive discourses and politics of the period. Which women can and want to breast-feed and which are targeted as prenatal drug users have a racial component. Racialized discourses also influence which mothers/women are targets of intensive mothering ideologies and are culturally reprimanded about delayed childbearing. This is not surprising. In the last several decades, feminist scholars of intersectionality have convincingly shown that the experience of gender cannot be untangled from the experiences of race, class, sexuality, and other social statuses in the contemporary United States.[42] This insight is equally applicable to the politics of reproduction and motherhood.[43]

Indeed, scholars of reproduction have noted that throughout American history reproductive politics—from birth control to abortion—has been shaped by the interplay among a variety of factors. These include cultural assumptions regarding the relation among womanhood, motherhood, and equality; the role and the needs of the state and nation; and race-based anxieties.[44] For example, in her exemplary history of the birth control movement in the United States, historian Linda Gordon reveals how diverse feminist groups of the late nineteenth century—suffragists, moral reformers, and free-lovers—all agreed on the strategy of "voluntary motherhood" as the way women could control their reproductive lives. At the same time, the ideology of voluntary motherhood was steeped in notions of the traditional family and conceptions of motherhood as a woman's natural and essential role, ideologies drawn from the white, middle-class experience of most of the female activists involved in these earlier campaigns.[45]

Research on abortion politics has also demonstrated that both women's social location and prevailing gender ideologies have a profound effect on the reasons why women mobilize in the political arena. Sociologist Kristin Luker's classic research on prochoice and prolife activists in California highlights how the diverging worldviews of women on each side of the abortion debate stem from their views about gender roles and their understandings of the meaning of parenthood. These views, in turn, are shaped by their social position and location.[46] Anthropologist Faye Ginsburg's study of the abortion debate in one Midwest community draws some similar conclusions. Like Luker, Ginsburg argues that the conflict over abortion is based on conflicting interpretations of gender. At the same time, though, she finds that prolife and prochoice activists similarly base their politics on female experience, particularly that of nurturance.[47]

The history of birth control and abortion regulation also reveals the pivotal issue of race. For instance, nineteenth-century limitations on birth control and abortion in the United States can be linked to concerns about the declining fertility of white middle-class women, which in turn fanned fears of "race suicide." Birth control pioneer Margaret Sanger's success in promoting contraception has been amply documented as stemming from her alignment with early-twentieth-century eugenicists. Eugenic campaigns in the United States targeted poor and minority populations who were thought to be overproducing and thus diminishing the "quality" of the population as whole. One result of these campaigns was the forced sterilization of thousands of politically powerless people (mostly women). Astonishingly, this practice continued until the 1970s, targeting mainly black, Latina, and Native American women. White, middle-class women, on the other hand, frequently were denied access to both abortion and sterilization. This history reveals a race-based hierarchy for determining the value of women's mothering.[48]

Welfare state scholars who focus on issues of social reproduction also emphasize the importance of gender ideology and racialized discourses in shaping reproductive politics and social policies.[49] For instance, in the early decades of the twentieth century, white, middle-class, female social reformers from the General Federation of Women's Clubs and the National Congress of Mothers successfully lobbied for mothers' pensions.[50] Both groups fought for women's entitlements from the state, but they saw "equality in difference."[51] In particular, these white female reformers wanted to "honor motherhood." In their view, mothers' pensions would allow women to fulfill their natural roles as mothers by creating conditions that permitted them to care for their children rather than joining the labor force.[52] Meanwhile, African American female reformers accepted women's employment and unsuccessfully fought for programs such as child care that would make life easier for working mothers.[53]

These studies show that a complex, contradictory, and sometimes surprising terrain of discursive politics surrounds the politics of reproduction. Prevailing understandings of gender and family are not monolithic, uncontested, or even consistently applied. For instance, traditional notions of motherhood are often used *by* women to promote women's interests.[54] At the same time, more feminist notions of equality can exist side by side with seemingly more traditional and conservative notions of and arguments about gender, mothering, and family.[55] Or, as Ginsburg's work on abortion politics indicates, activists on opposite sides of the debate may hold different positions but share many of the same values and utilize similar discourses.[56] These contrasting *and* overlapping discourses about gender and reproduction are, as subsequent chapters will show, a key characteristic of the debates over surrogacy as well. Likewise, reproductive politics in the United States cannot be separated from racial politics. Studies of welfare activism and the history of fertility policy make clear the extent to which racist assumptions and agendas have informed and even motivated population policies.[57] The category of women considered fit to be viewed or promoted as the "honored mothers" of the nation, for instance, clearly had (and continues to have) a race and class component. Just as gender ideologies underlie political discourses about surrogate parenting, so do racialized notions of "good" or "natural" mothering.

The politics of reproduction is thus enmeshed in gender politics, the politics of motherhood, and racial politics. Public debates and interest in mothering practices also reflect larger cultural anxieties and concerns about groups of women considered to be "good" or "bad" mothers.[58] Not surprisingly, when questions about the actual biological act of reproduction are raised, these larger cultural anxieties are more likely to boil up into the public arena. As sociologist Elizabeth Armstrong writes, "Pregnancy crystallizes concerns about gender, female identity, motherhood, and work, as well as hopes and fears of children—the next generation, the 'future' of society."[59] The context of social change and anxiety surrounding race, gender, and familial relations at the end of the twentieth century combined to create conditions under which surrogacy emerged as a social problem worthy of sustained public and legislative attention. And, as the chapters that follow explain, these concerns shaped the discursive politics of reproduction about surrogate motherhood.

The Infertility "Epidemic" and Debates about New Reproductive Technologies

Trends affecting marriage and divorce, labor force rates, and out-of-wedlock births certainly transformed the look of American families in the latter half of the twentieth century. But a different problem, emerging in the early 1980s, seemed to threaten the very possibility of families: infertility among married couples. Objective evidence of an upturn in infertility rates during the past thirty years is lacking, and most experts concluded that there was no new "epidemic."[60] But the fact that infertility rates had remained fairly stable in the United States for the last half of the century did not dispel the *perception* of an alarming climb in infertility.[61]

Concern over an infertility epidemic was partially the result of two social trends discussed in the previous section. First, the increased presence of women in the labor force meant that more women delayed having children until they had established their careers. Fecundity decreases with age, so this delay increased the likelihood of infertility among childbearing couples. Since many of the women who had delayed having children were from the large baby-boom cohort, even though more women were seeking medical help, the overall incidence of infertility among the population remained the same.[62] The size of the baby-boom cohort thus partially accounts for the dramatic increase in the absolute number of office visits for infertility (up from 600,000 in 1968 to 1.6 million in 1984), just as surrogate motherhood was beginning to gain attention in the social arena.[63] Second, with the increasing social acceptance of single mothers, as well as the legalization of abortion, there were fewer infants, particularly white, healthy babies, available to be adopted. As adoption became increasingly difficult, more couples pursued medical remedies for their infertility. The increased demand for and advancements in medical solutions led, in turn, to an increased visibility of involuntary childlessness.[64]

Other factors contributing to the social construction of an infertility epidemic included media attention to infertility and to biomedical techniques and technologies as possible solutions.[65] For instance, sociologist Arthur Greil found that "[i]n the decade prior to 1978, a total of eighteen popular articles on infertility appeared; but in 1978 alone, sixteen infertility articles were published, and on average thirteen articles a year have been published since 1978."[66] The proliferation of new reproductive technologies also probably added to the growing concern over infertility. The birth of Louise Brown in 1978 via IVF is often seen as a watershed event in reproductive medicine.[67] But although there has been an increased demand for treatments and a proliferation of physicians and clinics specializing in such services, infertile couples today are not much more likely to conceive than they were a few decades ago.[68]

In the end, it was not a real climb in infertility that prompted social concern but rather the volume and range of attention that "made infertility problems more salient for both the public at large and couples planning to have children."[69] This new worry over (some) couples' inability to have biological children was one more factor disrupting notions of normative family life. As chapter 3 explains, surrogate parenting pits sympathy for infertile couples against discomfort with the techniques, transactions, and costs used to produce "miracle children." If couples cannot have a child the "natural" way, the question debated is to what length they should go to have genetic offspring. The availability of a wide variety of new reproductive technologies makes answering that question increasingly pressing—and difficult.

Procreative technologies, such as IVF, that disrupt traditional reproduction pose serious challenges to the meaning of family, parenting, and motherhood. These techniques potentially separate genetic parenthood from social parenthood and, in the case of IVF, separate conception from the womb. Issues of maternity as well as paternity become muddled when more than one man and one woman are involved in the reproductive process. Assisted reproductive technologies also make biological (and social) parenthood possible for categories of people who previously had few options for genetic parenthood, including gay and lesbian couples and single women. Of course, the rise of such non-normative families outrages some people as much as it pleases others. Finally, the focus on gametes and genetics affects the weight we accord to sex and gender in the determination of parental rights. Thus, as the meaning of motherhood, parenting, and kinship expands and changes, concerns arise over how to balance the state's right and responsibility to legislate family and reproductive relations with its duty to protect people's reproductive freedom.

Second, reproductive technologies—from sperm banks to IVF treatments—introduce commodification into reproduction: explicitly commercial transactions are used to create family relations.[70] High-tech reproduction is not cheap. In the 1990s, rates for egg donation ranged from $1,500 to $3,000; a single attempt at IVF cost $8,000 to $10,000, with an average cost of $72,000 for an in vitro birth; and couples hiring surrogates paid $28,000 to $45,000 in fees.[71] This represents a move away from a notion of the family as private to one associated with the marketplace.[72] The intrusion of pecuniary concerns into familial relationships, women's mothering capacities, the value of gametes, and the status of children are thus central to debates about new reproductive and genetic technologies more generally.

Efforts to construct legislative policy in response to developments in assisted reproductive technology are stymied by the lack of societal consensus. Concern over the commodification of reproductive practices and changes to "natural" family relations must be balanced against empathy for those who desire to have children and support of reproductive freedom. These cultural tensions are equally evident in feminist responses to surrogate motherhood, which range from supporting regulation to calling for a ban on all surrogate contracts.[73] One view, typified by FINRRAGE (Feminist International Network of Resistance to Reproductive and Genetic Engineering), pessimistically appraises new reproductive technologies/practices in general, and surrogacy in particular, as indicative of male attempts to control and regulate women.[74] FINRRAGE asserts that assisted reproductive technologies exploit women's bodies, including, in the case of surrogacy, using women's wombs as empty vessels.[75] They draw links between prostitution and surrogacy; some envision the practice of surrogacy resulting in "reproductive brothels."[76] For this camp of feminists, the only acceptable response by the state to the practice of surrogacy is to ban it (i.e., make all surrogacy contracts invalid and thus legally unenforceable).

Another feminist perspective maintains that surrogacy reflects class exploitation, an arrangement by which upper-class men and women take advantage of poor women.[77] This is seen as further evidence of the commodification of social life, in this case the commodification of children and women's bodies. Furthermore, these feminists argue that as the use of a woman to gestate a fetus that is not genetically hers becomes more feasible, more poor women of color and women from Third World countries will be sought as surrogates, thus increasing the exploitative (and racist) potentials of surrogacy arrangements.[78] Consequently, this group of feminists also advocates the banning of commercial surrogacy arrangements.

However, not all feminists oppose surrogacy. For instance, liberal feminists and their supporters defend a woman's right to use her body as she chooses, even if that means being a surrogate. For these feminists, to prevent women from entering into surrogacy contracts is to deny them both democratic and reproductive freedom. This perspective casts surrogate parenting as no different from any other wage labor contract. Therefore, according women special treatment in this area would only undermine their autonomy and equality as citizens.[79] At the same time, liberal feminists recognize the problems and confusions that can arise when surrogacy is handled under existing adoption laws that were not written to deal with the particular nuances of surrogate parenting (e.g., intentional conception). Therefore, while such feminists advocate making surrogacy legal, they also endorse regulating the practice.

A final group of feminist scholars has argued for a more complex and less polemical understanding of surrogacy. This approach recognizes the simultaneously reactionary (e.g., privileging the heterosexual nuclear family) and radical (e.g., making parenthood feasible for gay and lesbian couples and for single women) potentials of surrogacy and new reproductive technologies for redefining what family, women, motherhood, and responsibility to children mean.[80] As they are aware of both the liberating and oppressive potentials of surrogacy, these feminists advocate regulating surrogacy so that its worst aspects are eliminated and its best ones retained.[81]

Given the potential that procreative technologies have to create and redefine families, responses to these techniques and to surrogate motherhood resonate with larger debates about women, gender, and family, from the changing roles of mothers to the commercialization of family relations. Different interpretations of these issues contribute to diverse policy responses to surrogate parenting. However, one of the key—and unexpected—findings presented here is that advocates and opponents of surrogacy, rather than holding distinct worldviews or engaging one another in a culture war of diametrically opposed values,[82] generally are in ideological agreement on the sanctity of family. This unexpected overlap in ideology is revealed through a careful examination of the familiar frames and overlapping discourses that shaped the politics of reproduction surrounding surrogate motherhood legislation.

ORGANIZATION OF THIS BOOK

This introduction shows that public reaction and political responses to surrogacy are immersed in ongoing societal debates about women, mothers, fathers, and families. Chapter 1 turns to public policy. It begins with a brief overview of legislative responses to surrogate parenting on the international, national, and state levels. The remainder of chapter 1 is devoted to describing the different policy responses to surrogacy devised by the New York and California legislatures from 1980 to 1992. Chapters 2 and 3 locate the issue of surrogate motherhood in contemporaneous reproductive and racial politics, and debates about the future of the family, as a way of understanding how and why surrogacy emerged as a publicly recognized social problem. Each chapter examines the different ways surrogacy was represented and framed by supporters and opponents of the practice, while at the same time exposing underlying similarities underpinning the arguments both for and against surrogate parenting. In chapters 4 and 5, the focus shifts to explaining the divergent ways surrogacy came to be defined and responded to in New York and California. Chapter 4 follows the framing approach to social problems used in the previous chapters, paying particular attention to the media's role in how the public came to understand the problem of surrogacy. Chapter 5 continues the exploration of factors that affected New York and California's diverse policy responses. After describing the political cultures and tendencies in each state, the chapter examines the impact of the history and reputation of the task forces that produced reports on surrogate parenting in the two states, as well as the role sponsors and interest groups played in determining the success of different legislative approaches to surrogacy. Chapter 6 is a concluding chapter that reviews the study's main findings regarding the social and cultural factors that shaped societal responses to surrogate parenting at the end of the twentieth century and discusses how the discourses on gender, motherhood, parenting, family, children, race, genetics, and choice that shaped public debates about surrogate motherhood may also inform current conflicts over other issues concerning reproductive medicine and biotechnology.

Chapter I | THE NEW PROBLEM OF SURROGATE MOTHERHOOD

Legislative Responses

Surrogate motherhood can be viewed as a classic social problem in that its life history can be measured by the rise and fall of attention given to it. Media coverage is the first clear indicator of surrogacy's arrival as a social problem in the mid- to late 1980s. In the early 1980s, newspaper stories about surrogate parenting appeared only intermittently. The combined coverage provided by the *New York Times, Los Angeles Times,* and *Washington Post* totaled 15 articles in 1980, 19 in 1981, 8 in 1982, and 25 in 1983. News coverage dipped for the next two years until halfway through 1986, when Mary Beth Whitehead changed her mind and took Baby M from the Sterns. In that year, these three national papers published 41 articles on surrogacy. In the following year, during the Baby M custody trial, coverage of the issue peaked at a dramatic total of 270 articles. And in 1988, when the New Jersey Supreme Court handed down its decision on the case, although the count dropped, coverage was still relatively high, at 99 articles. Media attention ebbed and flowed in the following decade, staying at mostly pre–Baby M rates, except for 1990, when 41 articles were published among these three papers (see figure 1).

National public opinion polls indicate the impact of the Baby M case in etching surrogacy indelibly onto the national consciousness. A Gallup poll conducted during the 1987 trial found that 93 percent of those surveyed had heard of the Baby M case; 79 percent of the respondents in a

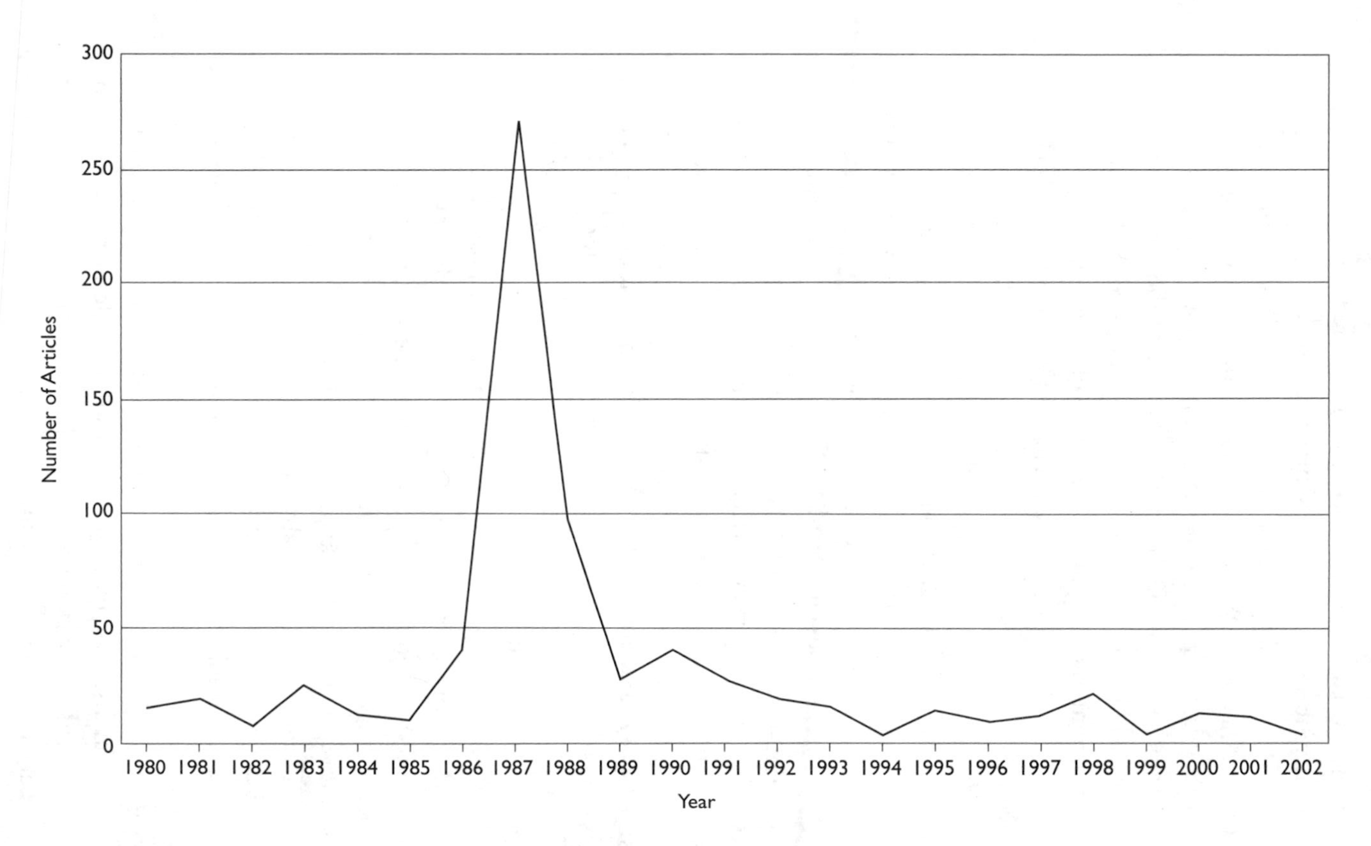

Figure 1. Coverage of surrogacy in the *New York Times, Los Angeles Times,* and *Washington Post,* 1980–2002.

Roper poll claimed they had read or heard enough about the case to feel they knew what it was about. Polls also captured the public's contradictory and ambivalent response to surrogate motherhood, both with regard to Baby M and more generally. For instance, a CBS/New York Times poll and a U.S. News & World Report poll found that most respondents favored William Stern receiving custody of the baby (74 percent and 75 percent, respectively); at the same time, when asked about whether such contracts should be legal or whether it was right or wrong for a woman to be a surrogate mother, respondents were evenly divided.[1]

The rise and fall of surrogacy as a national social problem can be gauged by more than the news coverage the issue received. Legislative attention provides an important index as well. In 1987, the year of peak news coverage of surrogate motherhood, twenty-six state legislatures introduced seventy-two bills on the topic. In the following two years, twenty-seven states introduced seventy and sixty-three bills. By 1990, however, the number of states introducing legislation dropped to ten and the number of bills to twenty-eight; by 1992, seven states had introduced a total of thirteen bills. Over the next thirteen years, no more than nine states in any given year introduced surrogacy legislation—on average from four to seven states pursued the issue in any year—with as few as one bill introduced in both 1998 and 2002 and none in 2000. In addition to prompting an increase in the number of proposals for dealing with the problem of surrogate motherhood, the Baby M case influenced the type of policy responses proposed in the years immediately following the dispute. In 1987, bills were split fifty-fifty on whether to permit or prohibit the practice, but the proportion of bills that sought to prohibit the practice rose to 57 percent in 1988, 66 percent in 1989, and 64 percent in 1990. By the mid-1990s, though, the vast majority of bills in state legislatures had taken a more accepting regulatory approach.[2]

This chapter treats the Baby M case as a dramatic event that focused political as well as public attention on surrogacy and initially helped define it as a social problem (see also chapter 4, which examines the media's role in framing surrogacy as a problem, and chapter 5, which looks closely at surrogacy policy-making constraints and opportunities). Moreover, as a key critical discourse moment, this custody battle shaped the controversies and tensions over appropriate policy solutions for several years after the trial ended.[3] Since the political arena represents an important institutional space where solutions to social problems are formed and debated, this chapter first surveys the range of legislative responses to surrogate motherhood, both here and abroad. Then, to better clarify why U.S. policy making in this area has lagged, the focus narrows to two representative states, New York and California, to trace the history of the process by which surrogacy as a social problem was discovered, defined, and (sometimes) resolved at the institutional level. The remainder of the chapter examines these two states' efforts to address the challenges presented by surrogate motherhood through public hearings, bill proposals, and floor debates, from shortly before the Baby M case through 1992.[4]

POLICY RESPONSES TO THE PROBLEM OF SURROGACY ON THE INTERNATIONAL, NATIONAL, AND STATE LEVELS

Most industrialized nations have rejected or greatly restricted the practice of surrogate parenting. Australia, Canada, Denmark, France, Germany, Great Britain, Italy, the Netherlands, Norway, Spain, Sweden, and Switzerland all have national laws that prohibit or discourage the practice (see table 1). The United Kingdom and Germany impose criminal sanctions as well.[5] The seriousness other nations have accorded the issue is also attested to by the fact that several countries have sponsored national commissions to study this new social problem. The reports prepared by these bodies frequently have served as guidelines for the national laws eventually enacted.[6]

In contrast, in the United States there is no national-level legislation regarding surrogate parenting arrangements. The lack of consensus in the United States, and the ambivalence it represents, is thus singularly American and may be accounted for chiefly by two deeply ingrained national characteristics: our simultaneous exaltation of individual rights and laissez-faire approach to the marketplace and our protective stance toward families. An additional likely influence is the contentiousness of abortion politics in the United States. Some believe this factor is largely responsible for the United States' overall lack of federal regulation in the area of assisted reproductive technologies.[7] In this regard, the lack of comprehensive surrogacy legislation parallels the country's legislative lacunae with regard to all assisted and genetic reproductive technologies.

TABLE 1. International Laws on Surrogacy, 2004

	Legality			*Parental Rights*		*Regulation*
	Bans Contracts	Bans Payment to Surrogate	Prohibits Payment to Third Parties	Intended Parents Are Legal Parents	Surrogate and Husband Are Legal Parents	Regulates Unpaid Surrogacy
Australia		x	x		x	
Austria	x					
Canada		x				
Denmark		x				
Egypt	x					
France	x					
Germany	x					
Hong Kong		x	x	x		x
Israel				x		
Italy	x					
Japan	x					

Netherlands	x		
Norway	x		
Russia			x
Spain	x		
Sweden	x		
Switzerland	x		
UK		x	

SOURCES: Kepler and Bokelmann (2000); East Coast Assisted Parenting (2000); Surrogacy UK, "Registering the Birth of a Surrogate Child and the Law," www.surrogacyuk.org/legalities.htm, and "Surrogacy Arrangements Act 1985," www.surrogacyuk.org/surrogacyact1985.pdf (both accessed October 3, 2006); Taylor (2003): Ruppe (2003); Government of South Australia, "Reproductive Technology: Legislation around Australia," 2006, www.dh.sa.gov.au/reproductive-technology/other.asp (accessed October 2, 2006); T. Smith (2004); Hong Kong Department of Justice, "Prohibition against Surrogacy Arrangements on Commercial Basis, Etc.," Bilingual Laws Information System, www.legislation.gov.hk/blis_ind.nsf/0/6497234f26732f184825696200330659?OpenDocument (accessed October 3, 2006); Center for Genetics and Society (2004); Teman (2003a, 2003b); Kahn (2000).

As in other countries, however, there have been national hearings on surrogacy, such as the one held in 1984 on procreative technologies by the House of Representatives Committee on Science and Technology, Subcommittee on Oversight.[8] In 1987, but after the close of the Baby M trial, another House-sponsored hearing was held. This time the Subcommittee on Transportation, Tourism, and Hazardous Waste of the Committee on Energy and Commerce called the hearing, in response to a bill introduced by Representative Tom Luken (D-Ohio). Luken's bill, HR 433, known as the Surrogacy Arrangements Act of 1987, proposed to "prohibit making, engaging in, or brokering a surrogacy arrangement on a 'commercial basis'" and to "prohibit advertising of availability of such commercial arrangements."[9] Fifteen people testified at this hearing, and most who spoke opposed the practice. Then, in 1989, in an unusual cross-party alliance, House members Barbara Boxer (D) and Henry Hyde (R) introduced legislation that would have banned surrogate parenting.[10] These national-level attempts to outlaw surrogacy parallel the dominant international response. But in the United States, unlike other countries, none of these activities produced either national legislation or influential advisory research reports.

The absence of national legislation on surrogacy in the United States can be explained largely by our federal system of government, which reserves to individual states power over certain areas, including family law. Only one attempt was made to produce a unified, state-level response to surrogacy in the 1980s. The National Conference of Commissioners on Uniform State Laws drafted the Uniform Status of Children of Assisted Conception Act in 1988.[11] The act specified two alternative legislative options for states: (1) judicially regulating surrogacy—so that if a surrogate agreement is not approved by a court it is void; or (2) making all surrogate motherhood agreements void. The act was designed primarily to regulate the status of children born by assisted conception. However, even as a guideline to state legislatures, it was of limited influence. Only two states adopted either option. The legislative alternatives the act proposed merely captured the conflicting societal and political responses to surrogacy in the United States.[12] The continuing lack of consensus was evident in 2000, when the act was replaced by the Uniform Parentage Act. The only policy recommendation proposed in the 2000 act recognized and regulated gestational agreements, but the section was made optional, without even a recommendation for or against its adoption. The act's authors were quite aware of the contentious and controversial nature of gestational surrogacy; they hoped an optional approach would increase the chances that states would adopt the act in its entirety.[13]

Because so few states have developed legislation, disputes over surrogate parenting often end up in court. That most existing laws, all originally designed for other transactions (e.g., adoption; donor insemination), are inadequate for guiding decisions in cases involving surrogacy arrangements is obvious in the opinions handed down by most judges. For example, in the early 1980s, before most of the public had even heard about surrogate motherhood, a judge in Arcadia, California, who was presiding over a custody dispute involving a surrogacy arrangement urged the legislature to "consider coming out with a policy statement or legal guideline" that could be applied in similar suits in the future.[14] In the Baby M case, Judge Harvey Sorkow stated that "many questions must be answered . . . [and] the answers must come from legislation."[15] As recently as 2004, a judge in Pennsylvania, one of the many states still without legislation that specifically deals with surrogate parenting, ended a ruling on a gestational surrogacy custodial dispute with a further plea for legislative intervention: "It is . . . the court's hope that the legislature will address surrogacy matters in Pennsylvania to prevent cases like this one from appearing before the courts without statutory guidance."[16] Nevertheless, state legislatures generally continue to respond very slowly to the problem of surrogate motherhood. And the laws that do exist at the state level reflect a range of positions on the issue.

In 1992, over five years after Baby M catapulted surrogate parenting into the national spotlight, only fifteen states had enacted laws pertaining to surrogacy.[17] Of these laws, two-thirds can be classified as prohibiting and banning surrogacy and one-third as permitting and regulating surrogacy (see table 2). In 1993, the District of Columbia also passed legislation prohibiting surrogacy and declaring such contracts unenforceable. It was not until 1999 that legislation was again passed on the state level. That year, Illinois enacted regulations that recognized parental rights under gestational surrogacy transactions.[18] Since then, most legislatures have not addressed the issue. Texas is a recent exception. A law passed there in 2004 allows for and regulates surrogate parenting arrangements. In general, though, at the beginning of the twenty-first century, states' most common response to surrogate motherhood remains a lack of legislation.

TABLE 2. State Laws on Surrogacy, 2005

	Legality				
	Bans Contracts	Bans Payment to Surrogate	Bans Payment but Allows for Services	Prohibits Payment to Third Parties	Permits Payment for Lawyer Services
Arizona	x				
Arkansas					
District of Columbia	x				
Florida*			x*	x*	x*
Florida**			x**	x**	x**
Illinois*					x*
Indiana					
Kentucky		x		x	
Louisiana					
Michigan		x		x	
Nebraska					
Nevada			x		
New Hampshire			x	x	x
New York			x	x	
North Dakota					
Texas*					
Utah		x		x	
Virginia			x	x	x
Washington			x	x	x

*Laws apply specifically to gestational surrogacy.

**Laws apply specifically to traditional surrogacy.

***Law declared unconstitutional in court.

SOURCES: National Conference of State Legislatures, "Surrogacy Statutes," March 4, 2005, in author's files; Brandel (1995); "Table IV: State Laws on Surrogacy," www.kentlaw.edu/isit/TABLEIV.htm (accessed May 12, 2004); American Surrogacy Center, "Legal Overview of Surrogacy Laws by State," 2002, www.surrogacy.com/legals/map.html (accessed January 24, 2005).

Enforceability		*Parental Rights*			*Regulation*	
Voids Paid Contracts	Voids Unpaid Contracts	Intended Parents Are Legal Parents	Intended Parents Are Legal Parents, but Time to Change Mind	Surrogate and Husband Are Legal Parents	Regulates Unpaid Surrogacy	Regulates Paid Surrogacy
x	x			x***		
		x				
x*		x*				
x**			x**			
		x*				
x	x					
x						
x**						
x	x					
x						
		x				
			x		x	
x	x					
x	x			x		
		x*				
x	x			x***		
x			x		x	
x						

Among those states that have implemented specific laws, the dominant policy response is similar to that found on the international level, namely policies that ban and/or do not recognize surrogacy contracts. This contradicts the common assumption that the United States, unlike most other nations, uncritically embraces new reproductive practices such as surrogate motherhood.[19] At the same time, the range of state-level legislation institutionalized thus far signals a diverse political response to surrogate motherhood. Additional evidence of the lack of consensus that surrounds surrogate parenting is present in the scores of bills introduced but never passed. Between 1987 and 1992, for instance, 208 bills on surrogacy were introduced into state legislatures. Fifteen were enacted. During this same period, fifty-five bills to form study commissions were introduced; the vast majority of these proposals didn't make it out of their respective legislatures. This relative standstill and inability to reach consensus has continued past the peak period of legislative attention to surrogate parenting. In the ten years between 1993 and 2003, fifty-one more bills on surrogacy were introduced into state legislatures, and only three were signed into law.[20]

Furthermore, within the groupings of states broadly categorized as prohibiting or permitting surrogacy, there are many variations at the level of specific provisions. Of the states prohibiting surrogate parenting, some, like Louisiana and Nebraska, merely claim surrogacy contracts as void and unenforceable; others, like Kentucky and Washington, further specify that payments to surrogates are prohibited. Of the states with a prohibitory surrogacy approach, only Michigan criminalizes the practice.[21] The states with a more permissive approach to surrogacy likewise exhibit a variety of legislative responses. Nevada, for instance, bans payments but provides limited guidelines for contracts. Both New Hampshire and Virginia provide extensive regulatory schemas for contracts. In New Hampshire, only contracts preapproved by the court are legally recognized. And although New Hampshire and Virginia allow and regulate surrogacy contracts, surrogates may be compensated only for medical and legal costs.[22]

Emblematic of the schism in state responses, and of the general ambivalence and contradictions evident nationally, were the policy approaches to surrogate motherhood pursued by the New York and California legislatures in 1992. The former took a prohibitory approach and the latter a regulatory one. The remainder of this chapter provides a descriptive history, beginning in the early 1980s and ending in 1992, of the two states' legislative proposals pertaining to surrogate motherhood. This background provides the broad context for the two different bills passed by their respective legislatures in 1992. (See chapter 5 for a detailed look at the specific forces that shaped legislators' actions.) Equally important, New York and California's experiences are representative of the trends in state legislatures across the country and of the types of political actors that characterized this instance of reproductive politics. Thus comparing the different responses to this newly identified social problem in these two specific political arenas (the New York and California legislatures) may help clarify some of the reasons behind the varied and lethargic policy response to surrogate parenting in the United States more generally.

THE LEGISLATIVE RESPONSE TO SURROGACY IN NEW YORK AND CALIFORNIA

Pre–Baby M Legislative Attention to Surrogacy: 1980–86

In the early 1980s, most people in the United States were unaware of the phenomenon known as surrogate motherhood. In 1980 and 1981, news reports appeared regarding Elizabeth Kane, the first known surrogate mother, but this coverage was nowhere near as overwhelming as the media response to the Baby M case, which began in 1986. (See chapter 4 for details regarding media coverage of Baby M.) The general inattention to surrogacy did not prevent California Assemblyman Mike Roos (D) of Los Angeles from introducing a bill in 1981 that specifically addressed the practice. Roos's involvement began when he was invited to speak at a forum on surrogate parenting held in Los Angeles and organized by Whittier Law School.[23] This exposure to the issue led Roos to conclude that surrogacy needed regulation to prevent those who participated in such arrangements from being taken advantage of, particularly the supposedly growing numbers of infertile couples.[24] Around the same time, attorney Bill Handel, director of the Center for Surrogate Parenting in Los Angeles, guest-lectured at Whittier and had the students in the class draft a model regulatory bill.[25] Roos agreed to sponsor this legislation.[26] In the 1981 and 1982 legislative sessions, he introduced two versions of the bill.[27] These proposals represented some of the first in the country to deal with surrogate motherhood. (See table 3 for a summary of California bills.)

TABLE 3. Introduction of Surrogacy Legislation: California Legislature, 1981–92

Year	*Bill #*	*History*	*Sponsor*	*Summary*
1981	AB 365	Died in Senate Judiciary	Roos	Provides for the approval of a petition incorporating a contract in which a woman agrees to be inseminated by the sperm of a man whose wife is unable to bear a child and to relinquish all legal rights to any child resulting from that insemination to the husband and wife, upon its birth, and for the enforcement of such a contract.
1982	AB 3771	Died in Assembly Judiciary	Roos	Same as AB 365 (1981).
1985	AB 1707	Died in Senate	Duffy	Authorizes the procedure by which infertile couples become parents through the employment of the services of a surrogate or through the use of a donated egg and the execution and the judicial enforcement of contracts with regard thereto, as specified.
1987	AB 2404	Died in Assembly	Longshore	Declares that contracts whereby a woman receives consideration for an agreement to undergo specified prenatal diagnostic testing or procedures for other than stated purposes and those whereby a woman receives consideration for an agreement to abort, or to consent to the abortion, of her child are contrary to public policy and are void and unenforceable.
1988	AB 2606	Died in Senate Judiciary	Montoya	Provides that contracts to terminate parental rights to, or consent to an adoption of, any person, whether or not the person has been conceived, and those transferring the custody, control, or possession of any person, whether or not the person has been conceived, are contrary to public policy, void, and unenforceable. Misdemeanor and criminal sanctions.

1988	AB 2607	Died in Senate Judiciary	Montoya	Provides that a parent-and-child relationship may be established by proof of a woman's having given birth to the child, without regard to the child's genetic makeup.
1988	AB 3200	Died in Senate Judiciary	Mojonnier	Provides that any contract to bear a child is against public policy and is void and unenforceable. Criminal sanctions.
1988	ACR 171	Signed	Mojonnier	Creates the Joint Committee on Surrogate Parenting and directs and authorizes the joint committee to ascertain, study, and critically analyze the facts related to commercial and noncommercial parenting.
1988	SB 2635	Died in Senate Judiciary	Watson	Provides for the establishment of the parent-and-child relationship in situations where a woman agrees to bear a child for a husband and wife, subject to specified requirements, including written agreement. This bill would authorize an action to be brought by a birth mother to establish the mother-and-child relationship and custody within ten days of the birth. Only payment of expenses allowed.
1989	AB 2100	Died in Assembly	Mojonnier	Any contract to bear a child is against public policy and is void and unenforceable.
1991	SB 937	Vetoed	Watson	Declares that surrogate contracts are not against sound public and social policy and regulates the process by which infertile persons become parents through the employment of the services of a surrogate or through the use of a donated ovum.

Both versions were known as the Surrogate Parenting Act, and each "would have established the legality, enforceability and regulation of surrogate parenting contracts."[28]

In response to Roos's legislative advocacy, in November 1982 the California Assembly Judiciary Committee held a public hearing at Whittier Law School. Twenty-six people testified at this hearing, including nine lawyers, four surrogate mothers, and five people from a center that arranged surrogacy contracts.[29] At this point, most people were not ready to support the idea of surrogate parenting, but neither was there much opposition to it, except from some religious organizations. Yet this small bit of opposition was enough to prevent the bills' smooth journey through the legislative process. Opposition from antiabortion groups was reported in the news as an important factor in the failure of Roos's bills.[30] The first bill died in the Senate; the second never made it out of the Assembly Judiciary Committee. Roos became frustrated when what he had perceived as a straightforward issue became increasingly complicated. He did not attempt to introduce further legislation on surrogate parenting.[31]

The lack of significant political or popular interest or concern regarding surrogacy in California continued. No other legislator became involved with the issue again until 1985, when Assemblywoman Jean Duffy (D) introduced AB 1707, the Alternative Reproduction Act of 1985. The Family Law Section of the State Bar of California was a sponsor of AB 1707, an early indicator of some institutional support for and approval of the practice in California.[32] Duffy's bill, like Roos's earlier ones, would have recognized and regulated surrogate parenting arrangements. It passed in the Assembly but died in the Senate. These three bills aimed at regulating surrogacy were the extent of the involvement by the California legislature prior to the national attention that the Baby M custody trial brought to the practice.

In New York, legislation on surrogate motherhood also was introduced into the legislature before the publicity surrounding Baby M. Assemblyman Patrick Halpin (D) sponsored bills in the 1983–84 and the 1985–86 legislative sessions. (See table 4 for a summary of New York bills.)[33] Halpin's early involvement in surrogate parenting was prompted by a case in Michigan in which neither party took responsibility for a physically handicapped child born via a surrogacy arrangement. This baby was not claimed by either of the parties involved until a blood test showed that

TABLE 4. Introduction of Surrogacy Legislation: New York Legislature, 1983–92

Year	*Bill #*	*History*	*Sponsor*	*Summary*
1983	A 5537	Died in Assembly Judiciary	Halpin	Provides for certain requirements imposed upon all parties to surrogate parental agreements. Criminal sanction impact.
1985	A 3774	Died in Assembly Judiciary	Halpin	Same as A 5537 (1983).
1987	A 2403	Died in Assembly Judiciary	Halpin	Same as A 5537 (1983).
1987	A 4748/ S 1429	Died in Assembly Judiciary/Died in Senate Child Care	Koppell/ Dunne-Goodhue	Provides that a child born in fulfillment of a surrogate parenting agreement shall be the responsibility, from birth, of the intended parents, including rights to inheritance; further provides for informed consents to be judicially approved and for enforcement of such judicially approved agreements.
1987	A 5529	Died in Assembly Judiciary	Schmidt	Prohibits any consideration for a surrogate parenting agreement but permits payments by the intended parents of all reasonable, actual, and necessary expenses of the surrogate mother rendered in the connection with the birth of the child or incurred as a result of her pregnancy.
1987	A 6277	Died in Assembly Judiciary	Barnett	Defines "surrogate motherhood" and "in vitro pregnancies" and provides that any contractual arrangements entered into for such purposes are void and unenforceable.

TABLE 4. (*continued*)

Year	*Bill #*	*History*	*Sponsor*	*Summary*
1988	A 8852/ S6891	Died in Assembly Judiciary/Died in Senate Judiciary	Proud/ Marchi	Prohibits the practice of surrogate motherhood, whether accomplished by artificial insemination or in vitro fertilization, wherein the surrogate mother agrees to surrender the child, regardless of consideration or the lack of it.
1988	A 9857	Died in Assembly Judiciary	Hevesi	Same as A 5537 (1983).
1988	A 9882	Died in Assembly Judiciary	Faso	Declares surrogate parenting to be against public policy and makes any agreement or contract providing therefore void and unenforceable.
1988	A 10851/ S 9134	Died in Assembly Judiciary/Died in Senate Judiciary	Weinstein/ Marchi	Declares surrogate parenting contracts void and unenforceable; prohibits compensation in connection with such contracts except for certain medical and legal fees; provides for certain rights of birth mothers in legal proceedings. Governor's Program Bill.
1988	A 11607	Died in Assembly Judiciary	Rules Committee	Defines "surrogate parenting contract" and prohibits its formation; penalizes violations for arranging or assisting in the formation of such contracts; makes such contracts void as contrary to public policy. Criminal sanction impact.
1989	A 994	Died in Assembly Judiciary	Schmidt	Same as A 5529 (1987).
1989	A 3467	Died in Assembly Judiciary	Faso	Same as A 9882 (1988).

1989	A 3558/ S 2884	Died in Assembly Judiciary/Died in Senate Rules	Weinstein/ Marchi	Provides that surrogate parenting contracts are void and against public policy and prohibits payment or receipt of compensation in connection with a surrogate parenting contract. Criminal sanctions impact. Governor's Program Bill.
1989	A 4205	Died in Assembly Judiciary	Barnett	Same as A 6277 (1987).
1989	A 4471	Died in Assembly Judiciary	Proud	Same as A 8852/S 6891 (1988).
1991	A 1138	Died in Assembly Judiciary	Schmidt	Same as A 5529 (1987).
1991	A 3945	Died in Assembly Judiciary	Barnett	Same as A 6277 (1987).
1991	A 4060	Died in Assembly Judiciary	Faso	Same as A 9882 (1988).
1991	A 7367/ S 1906	Signed	Weinstein/ Marchi	Establishes surrogate parenting contracts as void and against public policy and prohibits payment or receipt of compensation in connection with a surrogate parenting contract. Governor's Program Bill.
1992	A 11994	Died in Assembly Judiciary	Rules Committee	Grants the family and surrogate courts concurrent jurisdiction over petitions for review and approval of surrogate parenting agreements and sets forth the venue for court hearings; declares that any surrogate parenting agreement that does not receive judicial approval shall be considered null and void and unenforceable by the courts; requires that a surrogate parenting agreement include specific provisions; makes related provisions.

the genetic father of the child was the husband of the surrogate mother—a fact revealed on the *Phil Donahue* TV talk show. Concerned about the plight of "unwanted children" born through such arrangements, Halpin wanted legislation that would regulate the practice and stipulate custodial decisions.[34]

Halpin was not the only New York State legislator to respond to surrogate motherhood before it became a prominent social issue and nationally recognized social problem. Other members of the New York State legislature were also made aware of the practice of surrogate parenting just prior to the onslaught of publicity surrounding Baby M. In July 1986, in the case of Baby Girl L. J., Judge Raymond Radigan of Nassau County's Surrogate Court was faced with an uncontested adoption application that arose out of a commercial surrogacy agreement. Although uneasy about the commercial component of the arrangement, Judge Radigan approved the adoption, maintaining that New York State's laws against baby selling did not specifically outlaw payments to a surrogate mother.[35] Because he was unhappy over having to make a decision in what he considered a legal vacuum, the judge asked the legislature to fill this void. He forwarded his request for legislation to Senator John Dunne (R), who was then chair of the Senate Judiciary Committee. Dunne looked into the issue.[36] Early in 1987, he and fellow Senator Mary Goodhue co-sponsored S 1429, a bill that regulated the practice of surrogacy. At the same time, Assemblyman Oliver Koppell (D), who later played a key role in slowing the progress of antisurrogacy legislation, introduced an identical companion bill, A 4748, in the Assembly. Assemblyman Halpin also submitted a version of his earlier regulatory bill again in 1987. These bills, like the first few introduced in California, were designed to allow the practice of surrogate parenting to continue under specified guidelines. By this time, however, the media had introduced the public to surrogacy via the Baby M case. (See the graph of newspaper coverage in figure 1.) The Whitehead-Stern custody battle shifted the terms of the debate. Now many more legislators started to have an opinion on surrogate motherhood, and many were far more favorably disposed toward an outright ban on the practice. The next section chronicles the institutional response to the rise of surrogacy as a nationally and politically recognized social problem in the years immediately following the Baby M controversy.

The Immediate Legislative Aftermath to Baby M: 1986–88

New York State legislators responded to the Baby M case with a flurry of bills, hearings, and reports. Between 1984 and 1992, twenty-one bills pertaining to surrogate motherhood were introduced by ten different legislators.[37] Of these bills, nineteen were introduced post–Baby M. Meanwhile, starting in October 1986, four public hearings on surrogacy were held in New York. The first was jointly sponsored by the New York State Assembly and Senate Judiciary Committees. Its purpose was "to determine if legislation is appropriate to address the current phenomena of surrogate parenting and the new reproductive technologies which made such events increasingly practical."[38] The hearing had been organized by Senator Dunne after Judge Radigan's ruling on the uncontested surrogacy adoption, but by the time the hearing was held, news stories about the Baby M case had started to break. (See chapter 4 for details.) The first article in the *New York Times* regarding the Baby M case appeared on August 22, 1986. Between that date and the start of New York's first legislative hearing on surrogacy in October, seven more articles and one editorial appeared in the *New York Times.*

On the basis of the testimony provided at this first hearing, the staff of the Senate Judiciary Committee issued a report at the end of 1986. This report, *Surrogate Parenting in New York: A Proposal for Legislative Reform,* recommended regulating surrogate practices, reasoning that the enforcement of contracts would best protect the welfare of children. (See chapter 5 for details.)[39] This report was the basis for S 1429, the regulatory bill Senators Dunne and Goodhue introduced in 1987. The report also turned out to be the only official endorsement of surrogate parenting ever made by a New York State government agency or task force.[40] By the beginning of 1987, the public was being inundated with news about the Whitehead-Stern surrogate custody battle. This led to further scrutiny of and changing opinions about surrogacy. Additional public hearings were held to survey lay and professional responses to the practice. In April 1987, the New York State Senate Committee on Child Care held a meeting to discuss the merits of S 1429. Senator Goodhue was chair of this committee. A month later, the Senate Child Care Committee held another public meeting to discuss the same bill. Over thirty people testified at these two hearings, mostly proponents of the practice, from surrogate mothers and infertile women to judges, attorneys, and those involved in arranging surrogate parenting transactions.[41]

Despite the mostly positive testimony at two hearings, the Dunne-Goodhue bill never got out of committee. Instead, the pendulum started to swing in the other direction. Legislators who did not support the practice began to introduce their own proposals. In the 1987–88 legislative session alone, nine bills were introduced in the Assembly. Of the four introduced in 1987, Halpin's bill and the Dunne-Goodhue bill regulated surrogacy, while the other two either prohibited payment or declared surrogacy contracts void and unenforceable. Of the five bills introduced in 1988, four declared surrogacy contracts void and unenforceable. The number of bills and the number of legislators who became involved with the issue indicate the level of legislative concern. While there was no consensus on how the state should proceed, the immediate response to Baby M from New York legislators was largely negative. Most sought to ban the practice.

Then-Governor Mario Cuomo (D) also became involved in defining and resolving the problem of surrogate motherhood. In 1987, he asked the New York Task Force on Life and the Law to consider the issue. Cuomo had established the task force in 1985, directing its appointed members (leaders from fields such as medicine, law, and philosophy, as well as patient advocates and representatives of religious organizations) to develop recommendations on policy issues dealing with biomedical issues connected to new developments in medical technology. Despite its mixed membership, when the task force finished its investigation into surrogate motherhood in 1988 it issued a unanimous report, *Surrogate Parenting: Analysis and Recommendations for Public Policy.* (See chapter 5 for a discussion of the wide-ranging impact of this report.) The task force recommended that "society should discourage the practice of surrogate parenting. This policy goal should be achieved by legislation that declares the contracts void as against public policy and prohibits the payments of fees to surrogates. Legislation should also bar surrogate brokers from operating in New York State."[42] Governor Cuomo adopted these recommendations as a Governor's Program Bill. A Program Bill typically addresses an issue the governor considers especially important or urgent. By law, New York governors may not directly introduce bills into the legislature, except for those pertaining to the budget. Thus Program Bills are introduced on the governor's behalf, generally by members of the majority party.[43] Senator John Marchi (R) and Assemblywoman Helene Weinstein (D) sponsored Governor Cuomo's Program Bill on surrogacy three times. The first version was introduced in 1988.

Despite the task force's detailed report and the solicitation of public opinion at three public hearings, in December 1988 the Assembly Judiciary Committee and the Assembly Task Force on Women's Issues co-sponsored a fourth public hearing on the issue of surrogate motherhood. This hearing was set "specifically to consider comments on Assembly Bill 10851-A, which was introduced at the request of Assemblywoman Weinstein and a number of other members, and was proposed by the Governor's Task Force on Life and the Law."[44] Thirty-nine people testified at the seven-hour event. The numerous hearings on surrogacy are an indication of its contentious nature in New York. That none of the nine bills introduced in 1987 and 1988, including the Governor's Program Bill, made it out of committee also confirms the deep and ongoing nature of the conflict over the appropriate policy response. At the same time, the sheer amount of legislative attention given to an issue with practically no direct constituency also demonstrates the successful and symbolic emergence of surrogate motherhood as a social problem.

In California, as in New York, the Baby M case prompted increased legislative attention to the issue of surrogate motherhood. In the 1987 and 1988 legislative sessions, lawmakers introduced six bills on surrogate parenting, representing over half of all bills on the subject introduced in the eleven-year period from 1981 to 1992. In response to this surge of legislative interest, the Senate Committee on Health and Human Services held public hearings on surrogate motherhood in December 1987. The hearings were scheduled not to discuss any particular piece of legislation but rather to "determine our policy assessment of surrogacy. Fundamentally, we will ask should we permit this practice? Should we regulate it? Should we prohibit it?"[45]

Much as in New York, and consistent with trends nationally, the scope of the bills introduced into the California legislature diverged before and after the publicity surrounding the Baby M court battle. Legislation introduced before the trial permitted surrogacy; legislation introduced after discouraged it.[46] For instance, all three bills introduced in California before 1987 allowed for and regulated the practice of surrogacy. In the 1987 and 1988 legislative sessions, two bills outlawed surrogacy and one permitted it under a regulatory framework. Two other bills did not directly mention surrogacy contracts, but one declared the birth mother as the legally recognized mother regardless of genetics, and the other declared void and unenforceable contracts that stipulated a woman's medical treatment during pregnancy. In sum, most of the bills introduced in California during the 1987 and 1988 legislative sessions sought to discourage and/or prohibit the practice of surrogacy, an almost complete turnaround from the legislative response prior to the Baby M case. But, as in New York, these bills did not get very far in the legislative process.

This slow progress toward resolving the problem of surrogacy prompted Assembly member Sunny Mojonnier (R) to introduce a resolution (ACR 171) in 1988 that established a joint legislative committee on surrogate parenting.[47] The resolution stated, in part, that "[t]his measure would create the Joint Committee on Surrogate Parenting, and direct and authorize the joint committee to ascertain, study and critically analyze facts relating to commercial and noncommercial parenting. . . . The measure would authorize the joint committee, among other things, to appoint advisory committees." Once established, the joint committee appointed a panel of experts. The panel issued its report in 1990. (See chapter 5 for a discussion of the impact of this report.) In that document, entitled *Commercial and Noncommercial Surrogate Parenting,* the majority of panel members concluded that (1) it is illegal to pay for surrogate arrangements; (2) in a surrogate agreement, the sperm donor is considered the legal father; (3) the birth mother is considered the natural mother; and (4) surrogacy contracts are void.[48] Unlike the recommendations issued by New York's Task Force on Life and the Law, these conclusions were not endorsed by all members of the panel. Six dissenting members advocated a regulatory approach to surrogate parenting. In their minority report, these panelists recommended that "legislation relating to surrogate parenting activities would be useful as a matter of public policy. Rather than proposing legislation which involves criminal sanctions for the purpose of restricting and punishing those involved in surrogate parenting, the Minority recommends that statutes be enacted which clarify the legal nature of surrogate parenting agreements and provide that, in the rare cases of dispute, decisions shall be made in the best interests of children."[49] The Joint Committee on Surrogate Parenting declined to adopt its own panel's recommendations. It took no action on the views expressed by either the majority or the minority.[50]

At this point, significant differences between California's and New York's responses to surrogacy started to take shape. California lawmakers' increased attention to surrogate motherhood in the immediate aftermath of Baby M was not sustained either quantitatively or qualitatively. Compared to New York, the overall response by the California legislature was less dramatic. Between 1981 and 1992, a total of eleven bills that pertained to surrogate parenting were introduced—nearly half the number introduced in New York. Of this total, eight bills were directly related to surrogate contracts, two had implications for surrogacy, and one set up the Joint Committee on Surrogate Parenting to study the issue. Six legislators account for all eleven bills. Furthermore, two legislators, Senator Diane Watson (D) and Assemblywoman Mojonnier, sponsored or co-sponsored five of these eleven bills, and four of the eight bills introduced post–Baby M. Therefore, not only did the California legislature respond to a lesser extent than the New York State legislature (as measured by the number of bills introduced), but California's response also was less diffuse—fewer legislators were responsible for the total number of bills. Moreover, as the next section explains, after 1988, legislative interest in surrogate motherhood remained strong in New York, while concern seemed to wane in California. Finally, sentiment about surrogacy remained largely negative in New York, whereas the limited response in California returned to being more open toward the practice.

Post–Baby M Legislative Interest: 1989 and Beyond

In New York, legislative interest in surrogate motherhood did not die down after the torrent of Baby M–stimulated bills introduced in the 1987–88 session. The task force's report, published in 1988, seems to have supplied legislators—particularly those who were against surrogate parenting—with new momentum. In the 1989–90 legislative session, five Assembly members introduced legislation on surrogate parenting. All five bills declared surrogacy contracts void and unenforceable, including the Governor's Program Bill sponsored by Assemblywoman Weinstein and Senator Marchi, in their respective legislative houses. This version of their bill added a provision for criminal sanctions to be imposed on third-party intermediaries who arranged surrogacy contracts.

Another five bills were introduced in the Assembly in the 1991–92 legislative session. Four of the five were against surrogate parenting, and three of these four were identical versions of bills submitted earlier by the same legislators. The Governor's Program Bill was again introduced, but this version eliminated the criminal sanctions that many had found troublesome. This revised bill, A 7367/S 1906, eventually passed both houses—unanimously in the Senate and with cross-party support in the Assembly—and was approved by Governor Cuomo. The one bill that tried to regulate rather than ban surrogacy appeared at the end of the session, two weeks before the Weinstein/Marchi bill passed through both houses. This bill was the work of Assemblymen J. Oliver Koppell (D) and Michael Balboni (R), two of the strongest advocates for surrogacy in the New York legislature. It seems to have been these legislators' last-minute attempt to prevent antisurrogacy legislation from being passed in New York. Koppell and Balboni proposed an identical version of this regulatory bill once again, in 1993, after the Governor's Program Bill against commercial surrogacy had been signed into law. Like most of its predecessors, the Koppell-Balboni regulatory bill died in the Assembly Judiciary Committee.

The Governor's Program Bill had been introduced by Weinstein and Marchi three times, in three different versions, before it finally passed through the legislative process successfully. Assemblyman Koppell was probably partly responsible for the bill's slow progress into law. In addition to being a vocal and adamant supporter of surrogate parenting, Koppell was chair of the Assembly Judiciary Committee, the body responsible for weighing the merits of Weinstein's anti–commercial surrogacy bill. Koppell's powerful position as chair probably resulted in the additional hearings and reports that were deemed necessary before the bill was allowed to pass out of committee. Scholars of New York State politics have noted the effect of who holds leadership positions in the New York State legislature on the fate of bills: "[T]he individual volition of one man in a key position within the existing legislative setup can delay, over several years, the consideration and enactment of legislation desired by millions."[51]

Continuing legislative interest and the persistent efforts of Weinstein, Marchi, and others kept surrogate motherhood on the political agenda in New York, spurring various state bodies to prepare documents on the issue. (See chapter 5 for a detailed discussion of these and other government reports.) One, *Contract Motherhood: Ethical and Legislative Considerations,* produced by the Legislative Commission on Science and Technology in 1991, did not endorse specific legislation, but its closing section implied opposition to laws that would make surrogate contracts enforceable.[52] Another report, published a year later by the New York State Department of Health, much more clearly backed a ban on surrogacy and also drew considerably more public attention. That study, *The Business of Surrogate Parenting,* according to the foreword, was an investigation "triggered by a desire to increase public awareness and scrutiny of surrogate parenting and, ultimately, to avoid the personal tragedies that have attended several instances of surrogate parenting." The report avoided endorsing specific legislation, but it did favorably review the recommendations of the Task Force on Life and the Law that called for legislation that would make surrogate contracts void and unenforceable.[53] Significantly, *The Business of Surrogate Parenting* came out just before the New York legislature considered the third version of the Governor's Program Bill sponsored by Weinstein and Marchi, and the New York press gave the document wide coverage.[54] In June, just over a month after the publication of the Department of Health's report, the Weinstein/Marchi bill passed unanimously in the Senate and by a nonpartisan 104–39 vote in the Assembly. Less than a month later, Governor Cuomo signed the bill, validating a law that declared surrogate contracts void and unenforceable, prohibited the receipt of payment in connection with a surrogate parenting contract, and instructed the courts that a birth mother's participation in a surrogacy contract would not affect her parental rights in a custody dispute.[55]

Meanwhile, on the other side of the country, legislators in California were developing a different reaction to the newly discovered social problem of surrogate motherhood. After the initial surge of bills in the 1987 and 1988 sessions, only two more were introduced into the California legislature in the four-year period between 1989 and 1992. Of these two, only one, AB 2100, opposed surrogate parenting. Introduced by Assemblywoman Mojonnier, this bill was similar to AB 3200, which she had introduced a year earlier. AB 3200 prohibited and criminalized the practice of surrogacy and was drafted by attorney Sharon Huddle, a founding member of the National Coalition against Surrogacy.[56] In 1988 AB 3200 did not make it through the Assembly Judiciary Committee initially. However, Mojonnier and Willie Brown (D), the former leader of the California Assembly, were political allies. Brown's political maneuvering helped ensure that the bill passed when it was put on the Assembly floor as an emergency measure.[57] Brown's influence did not extend to the Senate, however. Mojonnier's bill died there, in the Judiciary Committee. In 1989 Mojonnier's bill did not even pass in the Assembly.

The California legislature's generally unsuccessful efforts to formulate a policy approach to surrogacy left another branch of the government—the judiciary—without legislative guidance regarding this new social issue. When surrogacy disputes ended up in the California state courts, judges had little recourse other than to apply existing laws, despite their poor fit. One case, *Johnson v. Calvert,* garnered a considerable amount of media attention in 1990. (See chapter 4 for a discussion of the media coverage of this case.) Anna Johnson, a black woman, was the gestational surrogate for a baby that was the genetic product of the sperm of Mark Calvert (a white male) and the egg of Crispina Calvert (a Filipina female). After a custodial dispute arose, the Calverts litigated for enforcement of contract. The Superior Court trial judge awarded custody to them and denied visitation to Johnson. Judge Richard Parslow's written opinion compared Johnson to a foster mother, whose role is to provide "care, protection and nurture" to the child while its "natural mother" is unavailable.[58] He ruled the contract legal and not contrary to public policy. A court of appeal declined to rule on the contract, but it did address custody, ruling that Johnson had no parental rights because she was not the natural (i.e., genetic) mother.[59] In 1993, the state's supreme court upheld the lower court's decision, although using a standard of intentionality to break what they saw as equal legal claims—gestational and genetic motherhood.[60] The high court's ruling marked the first time in U.S. history that surrogacy had been declared enforceable and not contrary to public policy.

As the Johnson-Calvert dispute wended its way through the California court system, the judges involved implored the state legislature to fill the legal vacuum. For instance, Judge Parslow urged the state legislature to pass a law permitting surrogate parenting but to regulate the practice so that all parties would be protected.[61] He believed the legislature "better equipped to deal with this sort of problem . . . than the courts."[62] His opinion was seconded by Fourth District Court of Appeal Judge David Sills, who wrote, "We join our colleague on the trial bench who, in delivering his decision, underscored the urgent need for legislative action. . . . To the extent these issues present questions of law they are matters for legislative resolution subject to constitutional restraint. They should not be settled by the judiciary applying its own ideas of what is good 'public policy.'"[63] In *Johnson v. Calvert,* the California Court of Appeal conceded it was acting in "unchartered *[sic]* territory" and urged the legislature to take action on the issue "so that both parents and children can face the future with certainty over their legal status."[64]

The Johnson case renewed Senator Diane Watson's interest in regulating surrogate motherhood. (See also chapter 5's discussion of Watson's role in championing prosurrogacy legislation.)[65] Watson had been chair of the Health and Human Services Committee that sponsored hearings on surrogacy in 1987; in 1988 she had introduced her own bill to regulate surrogate motherhood arrangements (she was the only legislator to do so that year), but the legislation did not make it out of the Judiciary Committee. In 1991, Senator Watson introduced SB 937, another regulatory bill. SB 937 resembled Watson's 1988 bill, as well as the legislation Assemblyman Roos had introduced in the early 1980s, prior to Baby M.

Watson's bill, known as the Alternative Reproduction Act of 1992, was one of the most extensive regulatory bills on surrogacy introduced in any state at the time.[66] It provided for the legality and enforceability of surrogacy contracts, as well as medical evaluations, separate legal counsel, reasonable monetary compensation, limitations on advertisements for surrogates or ovum donors, inheritance rights, maintenance of records, custodial rights and responsibilities, and psychological counseling.[67] This was a very different policy approach from the one that was being pursued simultaneously in New York. Whereas New York legislators continued to push for a ban on commercial surrogacy, the response that emerged in California in the early 1990s indicated a willingness to accept the practice as long as it was properly regulated.

Watson's bill was passed by both the Assembly and the Senate, by 49–19 and 22–12 margins, respectively. Both votes crossed party lines. SB 937 was sent to then-Governor Pete Wilson (R), who later vetoed it. According to people closely involved with the bill, Wilson was responding to pressure from Catholic campaign contributors and prolife groups when he vetoed SB 937. (See chapter 5.)[68] There was not enough support in the legislature to override the veto. In 1993, Senator Watson again introduced a regulatory surrogacy bill, SB 1160. This bill never got out of the Senate Judiciary Committee, partly because of differences between it and SB 937 and partly because the governor's veto undercut the earlier legislative momentum.[69]

These events have left California with no specific legislation on surrogacy. Despite their many pleas, California judges must continue to make decisions about surrogate parenting arrangements without legislative guidance. In the California Fourth District Court of Appeal's decision, *In re the Adoption of Matthew B.* (1991), the court noted pointedly, "It is, of course, for the Legislature to consider these important questions and provide answers through legislative action."[70] In the meantime, California judges rely on the legal precedent established by the 1993 California Supreme Court decision in the Johnson case, which recognized surrogacy contracts as valid and used the intention of the parties as a key determinant.[71] Reliance on this legal precedent has created a more positive environment for those who arrange surrogacy contracts in California, as the intention of the parties favors the enforcement of the original contract, at least in the case of gestational surrogacy.[72] California's lack of legislated social policy on surrogate parenting and its growing acceptance of the practice thus seem to reflect the trends nationally with regard to legislative responses (or lack thereof) to the problem of surrogacy.

Nevertheless, the courts continue to call for legislation. For instance, using nearly identical language, in the decisions handed down in *In re the Marriage of Moschetta* (1994) and *In re Jaycee B. v. The Superior Court of Orange County* (1996), California Court of Appeal justices wrote, respectively, "Once again the need for legislative guidance regarding the difficult problems from surrogacy arrangements is apparent," and "Once again, the need for legislation in the surrogacy area is important. We reiterate our previous call for legislative action."[73] As of 2005, only one additional bill had been introduced in the California legislature since Watson's last attempt in 1993. This legislation, introduced in 2001, used intent as the legal standard to establish parent-child relationships, and, like most similar bills in state legislatures across the country, it died in committee.

This chapter has provided a descriptive account of the legal responses to and opinions about surrogate motherhood. In brief, while most other nations have responded to surrogacy by quickly enacting laws prohibiting the practice, the response in the United States has been less quick and more ambivalent and varied. Hesitancy regarding surrogate parenting is apparent in the lack of national legislation, in the inability of the majority of states to pass laws on the issue, and in the history of legislation in the minority of states that have enacted laws specifically on surrogacy. In these last two groups, which include New York and California, further evidence of the lack of consensus about surrogate motherhood is provided by the diversity of laws that have been proposed and enacted on the issue. By exposing the degree and types of legislative reaction to surrogacy, this chapter has shown how this problem was defined and responded to in the institutional setting of legislative politics. As with other social problems, the emergence of surrogacy as a publicly perceived social problem was connected to other social issues and controversies of the time. Subsequent chapters will turn to these cultural debates in order to understand why surrogate motherhood emerged as a social problem, what explains the United States' seemingly unique response to the issue, and how this case of reproductive politics sheds an important light on the interests and issues that are at stake in the twenty-first century.

Chapter 2 | "CHOICE" AND THE "BEST INTERESTS OF CHILDREN"

Claiming the Problem of Surrogate Motherhood

Reproductive politics and debates about families and children at the end of the twentieth century shaped how social actors, from politicians and political activists to feminists and infertile women, chose to frame the problem of surrogacy. Legislative debates over surrogate motherhood prominently featured the rhetoric of reproductive choice, and all parties claimed the problem as a women's (rights) issue. Supporters of surrogate motherhood *and* its opponents cast their arguments in terms of a "woman's right to choose." "[T]he right of procreative choice encompasses all forms of procreation," surrogacy supporter Michael Balboni argued in 1987, in his capacity as counsel to the New York State Senate Judiciary Committee.[1] In the aftermath of the Baby M case, Bill Handel, director of the Center for Surrogate Parenting in Los Angeles, publicly defended surrogate arrangements. "A woman has the right to do with her body as she chooses," he emphasized.[2] But among those who sought to ban surrogacy, choice had a very different meaning. Opponents worried about the *loss* of choice a surrogate might face. They argued that women who enter into surrogacy contracts risk a profound erosion of autonomy over their own bodies and over their rights as a genetic parent. New York Family Court Judge Karen Peters, for example, was of the opinion "that by entering into this contract and having the court approve it, [a woman] has to some extent waived the right to control her own reproductive capacity."[3] In backing

New York's ban on surrogacy, Assemblyman Frank Barbaro (D) insisted that women must have freedom of choice, meaning that the state can not and must not allow surrogacy contracts, as they would necessarily lead to infringements on that freedom. "[I]t is up to [each woman] to decide what to do with her body," Barbaro maintained, "Nobody else should have the right to interfere."[4]

At the same time, a second discourse, one that emphasized "the best interests of children," also played an important role in the debates over surrogate motherhood. This rhetoric allowed surrogacy to be viewed primarily as a children's rights issue rather than one chiefly about women's rights. Here, too, both sides laid claim to the same discourse and put identical rhetoric to use in support of very different resolutions to the problem of surrogacy. Thus, when New York Assemblyman Anthony Genovesi (D) voiced his support of the antisurrogacy bill, he stressed his belief that "[i]t is really the child here that this legislation surrounds. All of this legislation is designed to protect the interests of the child."[5] During the same legislative debate, however, Assemblyman Richard Brodsky (D) referenced the same imperative when he urged New York legislators to back surrogacy: "I share the view that the ultimate question of custody and location of surrogacy should be the best interest of that child." He explained that he opposed the proposed 1992 bill that applied existing adoption law to surrogacy transactions because "I do not share the view that current law allows that [children's best interests] to be adequately considered without creating enormous tragedy."[6] In some cases, children's rights and women's rights were cast as complementary rather than competing. In opposing surrogacy, certain organizations and individuals who regularly advocated on behalf of women deliberately linked the rights of women and children, arguing, for instance, that surrogate arrangements jeopardized the welfare of children and undermined the dignity of women.

In the long debate over the appropriate policy response to the challenge of surrogacy, neither the use of reproductive choice rhetoric nor the emphasis on the best interests of children was a random or serendipitous choice for defining what was at stake. The political climate and prevailing cultural trends in the closing decades of the twentieth century made these two discourses especially visible and uniquely appealing. This chapter draws on letters to politicians, transcripts of hearings and debates, interviews with key activists, and position papers to show that both opponents and supporters of surrogate parenting framed their arguments similarly, even as they strongly disagreed over which policy approach—banning surrogacy or regulating it—best represented the issue of "choice" and/or "the best interests of children."

The next section sketches the political and cultural climate from which surrogate motherhood emerged as a social problem. It provides an overview of what reproductive politics looked like as the twentieth century came to an end—from the erosion of abortion rights to the rise of fetal rights—and notes the associated cultural shifts that gradually assigned higher priority to the rights and welfare of children and fetuses than to the rights and welfare of women and mothers.

REPRODUCTIVE POLITICS AND CULTURAL TRENDS IN THE LATE TWENTIETH CENTURY

What did reproductive politics look like as the twentieth century came to an end, and how did this shape the discursive politics of reproduction with regard to legislative debates over surrogacy? Despite the Roe decision, abortion rights, particularly for poor women, have been circumscribed since 1976 with the passage of the Hyde Amendment, which prohibited Medicaid-funded abortions. During the late 1980s and early 1990s, further assaults were made on a woman's right to abortion, most dramatically with the 1989 *Webster v. Reproductive Health Services* Supreme Court decision.[7] This decision and subsequent ones upheld state restrictions on abortion, from waiting periods to parental consent.[8] In the aftermath of the Webster decision, state legislatures nationwide began a feverish effort to follow the high court's lead, introducing, "[b]etween 1989 and 1992, more than seven hundred anti-choice bills."[9] Abortion rights advocates saw both the court decisions and the legislative activity as seriously threatening women's autonomy over reproductive choices.

The imposition of judicial and political restrictions on abortion rights was accompanied by a surge in antiabortion activists' use of overtly aggressive tactics. Activities from picketing and blockades to clinic bombing physically endangered women as well as symbolically threatening their reproductive rights.[10] Over the approximately two years between 1983 and March 1985, the number of violent incidents reported by clinics increased almost threefold compared to the five-year period between 1977 and 1982.[11]

The late 1980s also saw a rise in antiabortion activism aimed at disrupting the provision of abortion services. Randall Terry led his first clinic blockade in 1987. By the spring of 1988, he had formally established the organization known as Operation Rescue.[12] That group gained national media attention during the 1988 Democratic National Convention in Atlanta, when over 1,300 antiabortion demonstrators were jailed for trespassing at clinics. Prochoice groups estimated that over the next year Operation Rescue sponsored at least one clinic blockade every weekend. By 1990, over thirty-five thousand people had been arrested in such actions.[13]

As fear grew among choice advocates that *Roe v. Wade* itself would be overturned, abortion rights activism increased.[14] In spring 1989, after the *Webster* decision, and again in 1992, in anticipation of the Supreme Court's decision in *Planned Parenthood v. Casey,* hundreds of thousands of people converged on Washington, D.C., to protest the Court's rulings and to show their support for abortion rights and the original Roe decision.[15] Proponents of choice also organized on the local level, launching a prochoice movement of "clinic defenses" to ensure that clinics remained open to serve women.[16]

Direct threats to abortion access were not the only development to characterize this period. Fetal rights discourse emerged as well. Reproductive and women's rights activists were alarmed by this new trend, since advocates frequently pitted the rights of fetuses against those of women and mothers. Fetal rights gained prominence from the mid-1980s through the mid-1990s. During the heyday of the war on drugs, public, medical, and political attention turned to crack babies, thus merging racial anxieties with gendered and reproductive concerns. Between 1985 and 1990, eighty articles on prenatal cocaine exposure appeared in medical journals. By 1993, the general public was saturated with information on cocaine addiction and pregnancy: nine well-regarded national newspapers had published more than 197 stories on the topic by then. Congress took up the cause as well (most likely in response to the growing media and public concern). There were fourteen separate congressional committee hearings on prenatal drug exposure between 1987 and 1991. State legislatures also addressed fetal rights issues. In California, for instance, between 1986 and 1996, legislators introduced fifty-seven bills pertaining to prenatal drug exposure; half of these were introduced in the 1989–90 legislative session.[17] Nationally, in the early 1990s, several states considered bills to broaden the definition of child neglect to include prenatal drug or alcohol use, seven states also sought to subject women to criminal penalties if they took drugs while pregnant, and at least one state introduced a bill to mandate the use of Norplant (a contraceptive surgically implanted in a woman's arm) for women who were convicted of "fetal abuse."

Attempts to prosecute women for fetal neglect began in the late 1970s, but wide media attention arrived in 1987 with the prosecution in San Diego of Pamela Rae Stewart, an alleged amphetamine user whose baby, born with severe brain damage, died at two months. Media attention surged again in 1989, when Jennifer Johnson of Florida became the first woman in the United States to be convicted of delivering drugs to a minor after both she and her newborn had tested positive for cocaine exposure. Although most fetal abuse cases (including Stewart's and Johnson's) eventually were dismissed, from 1985 to the early 1990s at least 167 women were criminally prosecuted in the United States for using drugs or alcohol during pregnancy. That the vast majority of defendants in such cases were poor women of color is further evidence of the racialized nature of reproductive politics in the United States.[18]

Increased regulation of pregnant women symbolized the decreasing reproductive autonomy of pregnant and yet-to-be pregnant women. Perhaps most troubling to reproductive activists and others who advocated on behalf of women were instances in which women were forced by court order to undergo medical procedures against their will. One of the most dramatic—and tragic—cases of unwanted medical intervention occurred in 1987 when Angela Carder received a court-ordered cesarean section during her sixth month of pregnancy. Carder was dying of cancer. Since the surgical procedure would probably hasten her death, both she and her family members strongly objected. The court prevailed. The newborn baby died two hours after the surgery, and Carder herself died two days later.[19]

The late 1980s also saw rising concern over workplace restrictions against women. In one of the most famous cases, *UAW v. Johnson Controls,* all women under the age of seventy were excluded from working certain jobs in which there might be a high exposure to lead unless they could medically certify that they could not bear children.[20] This case was not unusual.[21] Women were excluded from over one hundred thousand jobs between the early 1980s and the mid-1990s because of potential reproductive hazards.[22] Overall, reproductive and women's rights activists saw a dangerous trend toward ever-greater legislative control of pregnant women—from court-ordered cesareans, to the criminalization of "crack mothers," to workplace sterilization laws.

This troubling shift in the political and legal arenas was linked to an equally unsettling cultural change in the 1980s in which the rights of children and fetuses gained saliency. Because the rights of women and mothers were often pitted against those of children and fetuses, the increasing cultural interest in children's/fetal rights was accompanied by a demonization of mothers/women. Increasingly, women became seen as vectors of risk rather than as victims themselves.[23] For instance, with the 1989 publication of Michael Dorris's book *The Broken Cord,* fetal alcohol syndrome (FAS), a group of irreversible birth defects caused by alcohol consumption during pregnancy, became widely known. The book triggered media response to FAS, including national television programs and print coverage. As the scholars Maureen McNeil and Jacquelyn Litt note, the debate about FAS often was connected to concerns about how children were affected by broad changes in women's roles, alterations signified by the increase in the number of working mothers and the climb in divorce rates.[24]

Other highly visible campaigns targeting pregnant women that emerged during the 1980s included efforts to discourage smoking during pregnancy, a "breast is best" campaign for breast-feeding (mainly focused on the benefit to children, with little attention to mothers' health needs), and the development of fetal surgery (the first in utero surgery occurred in 1981). Occurring at the same time as these events was the seemingly innocuous rise in the number of techniques for prenatal genetic and medical monitoring and in the number of pregnancy advice manuals, as well as a greater emphasis on an appropriate diet during pregnancy.[25] These developments and practices, in combination with the visual emergence of fetuses via the images produced by ultrasound technology, shaped the political and cultural climate.[26] Speaking about and advocating on behalf of "fetal rights" and interests—and thus diminishing the role and rights of women—gained ascendancy. At the same time, race and class affected which women's pregnancies were most likely to be medicalized and/or were most likely to benefit from advances in biotechnology.

The rise in fetal rights discourse is important in as much as it parallels increased attention to the rights of children, particularly in the last decades of the twentieth century. The emerging prominence of the "best interests of the child" discourse is perhaps most visible in changes in child custody determinations. Starting in the 1970s, the "tender years" doctrine for determining child custody, which assumed that young children would naturally be better cared for by their mothers, began to be replaced by the "best interest" standard, which placed children's well-being and interests at the center of custody decisions. By the 1990s, the child's-best-interest standard was the norm.[27] Similarly, other developments, such as the "discovery" of child abuse in the 1960s, the renewed attention to childhood poverty in the last few decades, and the increasing legal tendency to grant minor children rights in family law, indicate that a focus on children's interests was recognized and seen as legitimate and important within the political and legal arenas.[28]

These aspects of reproductive politics at the end of the twentieth century created a setting in which surrogate motherhood became a key issue that was represented by political and social actors as another possible infringement on women's bodily autonomy. There was no consensus on which policy approach to surrogate parenting truly supported women's reproductive rights, however. As the next section shows, participants on both sides of the surrogacy debate claimed surrogate parenting as a reproductive rights issue by employing the political rhetoric of choice. At the same time, proponents and opponents of surrogacy both also frequently utilized the best-interests-of-the-child discourse to promote their respective points of view. That rhetorical strategy is discussed separately, later in the chapter. The implications of these two strategies for women's rights and feminist activism are weighed in the chapter's last section.

A MATTER OF CHOICE: DEFINING SURROGACY AS A REPRODUCTIVE RIGHTS ISSUE

The cultural recognition of choice rhetoric as a legitimate, successful, and institutionalized political discourse encouraged political actors on both sides to strategically frame their position as representing "choice." The influence of the post–*Roe v. Wade* abortion rhetoric in the legislative debates over surrogate motherhood is indisputable. During the five-plus-hour floor debate in the New York State Assembly, for instance, the issue of supporting a prochoice position and women's rights emerged repeatedly. Of the thirty-seven legislators who gave comments on the floor, many mentioned choice, bodily rights, women's rights, and/or reproductive freedom.[29] Some political actors argued that the only appropriate "prochoice" response would be to allow women to choose to be surrogates if they so desired. During the Assembly floor debate Assemblyman Stephen Kaufman (D), who opposed New York's 1992 anti–commercial surrogacy bill, described the choice position regarding bodily rights and autonomy this way: "I believe—again, I'm in favor of surrogate parenting. I believe if you're pro-choice, that you should be against this bill. If you declare time immemorial that a woman has a right to choose what she wants to do with her body, how can you be for this bill, because this bill takes away the right for a woman to decide what she wants to do with her body."[30] At other times, as in the comments of Kaufman's colleague Assemblyman William Parment (D), the use of choice rhetoric was tied to constitutional and reproductive rights, particularly those connected with pivotal Supreme Court decisions such as *Roe:*

> Well, it goes back to the Founding Fathers' documents of this country and basically the First Amendment, and perhaps even to the Declaration of Independence citation by Jefferson of inalienable rights. In Griswald *[sic]* v. Connecticut, the decision, as I understand it, Justice Douglas indicated there were a number of rights created by the First Amendment and among them was the right of privacy. Based on that, Mr. Blackman, I believe, who was the justice in Roe v. Wade, indicated that a number of rights also extended to *reproductive rights and rights of a woman* to make a determination in the case before him for abortion. I really believe that to indicate here that we bar contracts between consenting adults for surrogate parenting in a situation where the pregnancy is the result of an in-vitro fertilized embryo being implanted into the womb, we transgress the principle and deny the right of an individual the privacy of *reproductive choice.*"[31]

Not surprisingly, women's and civil rights organizations also used choice rhetoric as a strategy to promote particular—and sometimes dissimilar—policy responses to surrogacy. For instance, the opposition of the California chapter of the National Organization for Women (NOW) to legislation that would have prohibited and criminalized surrogacy arrangements was framed around protecting women's reproductive rights. NOW executive committee member Marsha Elliot, speaking at a California Senate committee hearing in the late 1980s, explicitly defined the issue as one involving choice: "We affirm our commitment to the *right of every woman to control her body* which includes among other things the right to have and not to have children as a single parent, as part of a couple *and as a surrogate. . . .* Our bottom line on this issue is that *women have the right to control their own bodies*—not you, not me, not the legislature, but each individual woman."[32] Kathleen Peratis, president of the New York Civil Liberties Union, expressed similar concerns about the state's interference with women's reproductive choice when testifying about an earlier version of the 1992 anti–commercial surrogacy legislation. "We believe that the State may not prohibit, much less criminalize, surrogacy arrangements," she asserted, "because the participants in such an arrangement are *exercising their rights to procreative choice* and intimate association with future offspring, forms of protected activity under the Constitution."[33]

The strategic integration of choice rhetoric was also visible in the lobbying efforts of the infertile community and surrogacy advocates. In a letter to California State Senator Diane Watson, supporting her 1992 regulatory bill, Fay Johnson, director of the Organization of Parenting Through Surrogacy (OPTS), deliberately linked the issue of choice in its abortion rights context to the area of surrogacy, expanding on the meaning of *choice* to encompass this new realm: "I have spoken to The Greater Los Angeles Coalition For Reproductive Rights to hopefully have them understand that the 'other side' of the right to 'choose' is the right to 'choose to HAVE'. I have spoken about [your] bill and our absolute support of it. Hopefully, I will be able to educate some of the other members of the Coalition that surrogacy IS a choice issue, just like abortion."[34] Much like New York Assemblyman Parment, some surrogacy advocates were even more explicit in their belief that legislation that banned the practice would turn back the clock with regard to reproductive rights. Thus Joan Einwohner, psychologist and consultant to the Infertility Center of New York,[35] in her testimony against Assemblywoman Helene Weinstein's anti–commercial surrogacy bill, observed pointedly, "It is a return to an era before Roe v. Wade to legislate only one choice for all women."[36]

It was not only public officials and interest groups who used the rhetoric of choice to defend the practice of surrogate parenting. Women who had been surrogates were important witnesses at the many public hearings held on surrogacy. These speakers drew heavily on the notions of choice and bodily rights to defend the practice of surrogacy. In a public hearing before the New York State Senate Standing Committee on Child Care, Judy Tannebaum, who had served as a surrogate mother, used a popular refrain from the abortion rights movement to defend her right to be a surrogate. Referring specifically to the issue that even her husband should not be allowed to prevent her from being a surrogate, she succinctly stated, "It is my body, my choice."[37] Echoing that sentiment at a different public hearing, the potential surrogate mother Dawna Krengulec testified that "surrogacy should be a woman's choice. . . . A woman should be able to do with her body as she sees fit."[38] Similarly, regarding her two experiences as a surrogate mother, Donna Regan stated, "I made a choice . . . it was my choice."[39] The use of choice discourse among surrogates is also illustrated in Hilary Hanafin's testimony at a California hearing. Reporting on her study of women who served as surrogates, she said, "All of them reported that they feel they should have the right to bring a child into the world and a right to relinquish the child. They feel, as do the infertile couples, that is a matter of *freedom of choice.*"[40] This choice rhetoric is particularly significant, since ethnographic studies of surrogates find that these women tend to have traditional views on women and families and, in fact, are often opposed to abortion.[41]

Prochoice rhetoric was not claimed and employed solely by those who supported surrogate parenting. Indeed, legislative debates over surrogate motherhood entailed a conflict over what policy response to this new issue truly reflected a choice position. For instance, just as the opponents of the 1992 anti–commercial surrogacy bill did, Assemblyman Frank Barbaro (D), who supported the legislation, argued in its defense by employing choice rhetoric. During the lengthy floor debate in the New York State Assembly, he claimed that a prochoice position was anti–commercial surrogacy (and thus required supporting the New York bill) because surrogate parenting contracts infringe on a woman's choice of whether to keep or relinquish her traditional parental rights and her autonomy during pregnancy, since they entail giving up custody rights prior to giving birth:

> If you're for freedom of choice, the basis for your freedom of choice, it seems to me, is the woman is carrying this baby or will not carry this baby, and *it's up to her to decide what to do with her body.* Nobody else should have the right to interfere. So, *if you're for freedom of choice, then you have to be for this bill* because this bill says that if the woman does enter into such an

arrangement, she is the one to decide what happens with that baby. If you're right-to-life, then you have another [different] problem.[42]

Democratic Assemblywoman Susan John, another supporter of New York's anti–commercial surrogacy bill, also used choice rhetoric to legitimize her position. She began by providing her own prochoice credentials and then linked the choice issues that surrogacy transactions involved to the possibly serious encroachment on pregnant women's rights that legally enforceable pregnancy contracts could instigate:

> I feel that *I am as strongly pro-choice as any member of this Legislature.* I've worked very hard to advocate for the rights of women to always be able to make that choice of when and whether to have a child, and I would ask all of my colleagues who feel that way to think very carefully before they join any stampede to another type of regulation of this activity because if we move down the path of saying we can put these provisions in a contract or we can regulate the activity this way, *you are opening the door wide open to say that there can be restrictions on a woman's choice of whether or not to carry a pregnancy to term.*[43]

In the context of heated debates over reproductive politics, it is not surprising that many women's rights organizations and activists described surrogacy as a slippery slope that could threaten women's reproductive and parental rights more generally. For instance, a representative of New York State NOW testified against a regulatory bill in 1987, framing the group's opposition to surrogate motherhood around concerns about reproductive freedom and the proposed legislation's impact on women: "We are concerned as women's rights advocates about the potential emergence of an exploited baby breeding industry in this state and *the potential erosion of parental and reproductive and privacy rights of women.*"[44] Similar worries over the threats that surrogacy posed to women's reproductive freedom and rights were also expressed by several prominent feminists, including Betty Friedan, Gloria Steinem, Phyllis Chesler, Gena Corea, and Janice Raymond, all of whom were co-signers to an amicus brief written in response to the Baby M case. Subsequently, parts of that document were adapted into a statement, "Feminists on Commercializing Childbearing," that was sent to Senator Watson's Sacramento office. In expressing their opposition to surrogacy, these feminists too framed the practice of surrogate motherhood as one that simultaneously threatened to abuse women's reproductive capacity and to strip women of their parental rights:

> The enforcement of surrogacy contracts *victimizes women* physically, emotionally, and economically. The surrogacy contract represents a *unique form of exploitation of women's bodies* and will lead to the full scale commercialization of women's reproductive organs and genetic makeup. In the future, surrogate mothers may come to be viewed more as "alternative reproductive vehicles"—uteruses for hire in the commercial reproductive marketplace—than as individually important persons with the right to the integrity of their own relationships with husbands and children, and to the privacy and independence of their reproductive capabilities. Indeed, the very word "surrogate" is a euphemism used to diminish the *rights of the natural mother.*[45]

While such concerns about the erosion of choice and potential threats were often framed in a general way around the denigration of women's reproductive bodies, the employment of choice rhetoric and a discourse of a slippery slope were often connected to specific concerns arising from the state's involvement in women's reproductive decision making. For instance, at a California state hearing in the 1980s, Susan Nash, testifying on behalf of the Women's Lawyers' Association of Los Angeles, linked any potential infringement of choice by the state as an abandonment of the rights secured under *Roe:* "[W]e believe that, once the Legislature involves itself in deciding which uses of *women's bodies* are and are not sound social policy, women will lose the *right to make voluntary choices* of this and other types. . . . It is very possible, or at least one could make the argument, that a woman, by entering into this contract, is waiving her constitutional rights under *Roe v. Wade.*"[46] At the same hearing, a California NOW representative expressed concerns about the state's involvement in pregnancy and the threats this posed to women's reproductive autonomy if contracts controlled prenatal medical decision making: "A major concern of ours is the provision requiring court monitoring of the contract and the pregnancy. We fear this could establish a dangerous precedent whereby the court monitors reproductive functions."[47]

This awareness of a potential for the further erosion of abortion rights and concern over the rise of the medico-legal monitoring of pregnancy led some opponents of surrogacy to link the two issues when they argued against legislation that would permit surrogate arrangements. Indeed, social and political actors often advocated for women's reproductive autonomy and employed a discourse of choice with explicit reference to the rise of fetal politics. A member of the New York Task Force on Life and the Law that crafted the New York State anti–commercial surrogacy bill, and a prominent activist who lobbied on behalf of many interest groups when the legislation was introduced, reviewed the multifaceted role of choice in framing a response to the challenges presented by surrogacy:

> [O]n all sides of the issue . . . there were people who were arguing that *there's a choice issue underlying this.* And the choice issue is complicated, but it means that if the state authorizes and permits these contracts and acknowledges there's a contract . . . then . . . it is a concern that the state might have an interest in the fetus, and what interest is that, and is there a contractual interest in the fetus. For instance, if the birth mother is. . . . drinking, or taking drugs, or not taking appropriate medical care. . . . could the contracting parents try to assert the contractual rights, and how does that come out. So, *embedded in the whole debate is an underlying reproductive rights issue or women's issue* . . . and that's an area that the choice movement is always worried about. . . . [T]here's been a big ongoing concern, and *there have been those on the other side who have said that the fetus has interests,* especially late in pregnancy, and especially in their third trimester.[48]

WILL THE REAL FEMINISTS PLEASE STAND UP? CLAIMING THE RIGHT TO SPEAK FOR WOMEN

When proponents and opponents of surrogate parenting made prominent use of choice rhetoric during the debates over what type of problem surrogacy represented, they also necessarily relied on rhetoric about women's rights and/or gender equality. As a result, in articulating their positions, debate participants frequently alluded to sex discrimination and sexism, as well as women's rights and gender equality. For instance, at a public hearing, the radical feminist Janice Raymond, acting as a representative of the Institute of Women and Technology, made the grounds for her organization's interest clear: "[M]y testimony is specifically directed to the issue of women's rights."[49] In particular, surrogacy should be opposed because it undermined basic principles of gender equality. "Many of us [feminists] see surrogate contracts as a practice of sex discrimination," she explained.[50] However, as with the debate over which approach to surrogate parenting represented a true choice perspective, there was no consensus on what social policy approach to surrogate motherhood best reflected women's interests. Those who supported surrogate parenting often made an effort to discredit the many prominent feminist activists who opposed the practice. From advocates' perspective, no feminist could legitimately claim a monopoly on representing women's rights. Assemblyman Alan Hevesi's (D) comments during the New York State Assembly floor debate on the 1992 anti–commercial surrogacy bill highlight the tension over determining the policy position that best reflected women's interests: "Well, I still remained convinced, even if some of my friends in the women's movement or in the civil rights movement are not convinced in this case that a woman should have those rights to decide for herself what is right for her life, when to have a baby, when not to have a baby, even to have a baby as an act of love for another couple, I believe that should be her right. I believe this bill destroys that right, and I'm going to vote against it."[51]

Other proponents of surrogate parenting framed their support of the practice around particular women's issues. Former Senator Mary Goodhue (R), one of the first sponsors of regulatory surrogacy legislation in New York, cited the issue of gender equality when she explained what initially led her to her policy position:

> I looked up in the New York law about sperm banks. In other words, females whose husbands were unable to impregnate them had easy access to a sperm bank. As I recall, there is a separate section of the law that says that those children, and obviously the husband is not the [genetic] father of the child, but the law says that the husband is the father of the child. . . . And the woman has no idea who the true father of the child is because the sperm in the sperm bank is just sperm for sale. So it seemed to me that there ought to be some corresponding advantage for the female who was unable to carry to term. And that definitely ran through my thinking as *an equal rights thing.*[52]

In a similar vein, when infertility consultant Joan Einwohner defended the position that women should be allowed to be paid for their role as surrogates, she referenced classic feminist insights. Einwohner argued that those who do not want women to be paid for surrogacy arrangements lend their support to an overall process that oppresses women. Her analysis made use of well-known feminist critiques of women's unpaid labor, the false dichotomy between the so-called public and private spheres, and the danger of exalting pregnancy: "I personally do not understand why certain segments of our society expect women to receive no material compensation for their services. It would seem to me a new way of devaluing women's work. It should rank with the unpaid status of homemaker. It is rationalized by saying women must fulfill the role of spiritual guardian of our society. Pregnancy is given a special status that should not be 'debased' by being concretely rewarded."[53] Additionally, Einwohner maintained that those who question the enforceability of contracts regarding parental rights are part of a larger, historical trend of using female hormones as the basis for discrediting women's ability to be rational decision makers. "I believe that women are fully capable of entering into agreements in this area and of fulfilling the obligations of a contract," she asserted. "Women's hormonal changes have been utilized too frequently over the centuries to enable male dominated society to make decisions for them."[54] Einwohner's statements were meant to make clear that a women's rights position was a prosurrogacy position.

Because women's rights and choice discourse figured prominently in the legislative debates over surrogacy, establishing solid feminist credentials was important. As California NOW's representative put it in 1982, "[W]e feel surrogating is an area where *the feminist perspective* is needed."[55] But what was the feminist position on this choice/women's rights issue? Once again, women's rights advocates found themselves split.[56] Evidence of this conflict can be found in a memorandum to NOW's national board written by board member Priscilla Alexander. The California-based Center for Surrogate Parenting's program coordinator subsequently sent the memorandum to Senator Watson. Alexander reviewed the challenges surrogacy posed for feminists this way:

> Surrogate or contract birth mothering is a difficult issue for feminists for a variety of reasons. Because of the Baby M case, it is not only difficult, it is controversial, and feminists are lined up on all sides of the issue. In the name of feminism, Phyllis Chesler wants to prohibit birth mother contracts, and *in the name of feminism,* I think women must have the right to make that decision for themselves on the same basis that they have the right to decide

who to have sex with, or whether to bear a child or have an abortion, or whether they want to engage in sex in exchange for money. For me, it all comes back to the question of *who controls women's bodies:* the state, other women, or themselves?[57]

At the same time, feminists opposed to surrogate motherhood emphasized that surrogacy did *not* facilitate women's rights and that supporting it did not represent a feminist position. Janice Raymond, for example, pointed out that "there are many feminists who do not subscribe to the view that surrogacy upholds a woman's right to control her own body." She also was openly skeptical about the use of women's rights rhetoric to defend the practice of surrogacy: "[I]t is curious that women's rights become increasingly defended in the most abstract context, either where they do not really benefit most women or where there is substantial benefit that accrues to men from selective defenses of women's rights."[58] Raymond hoped to lay claim to the antisurrogacy position as *the* feminist position, since doing so successfully would discredit supporters of surrogate parenting arrangements who used the rhetoric of women's rights to defend their policy position.

For their part, prosurrogacy individuals and groups used a similar strategy. They tried to undermine the feminist credentials of those who opposed the practice. Betsy Aigen, an adoptive mother and director of a surrogate parenting program in New York City, refuted hormonal accounts of women's inability to waive parental rights prior to the birth of the child by labeling this contention as sexist, regardless of who championed it: "To say that women are incapable of being held to their commitments because of hormonal changes reeks of the worst male chauvinist attitudes even when it is espoused by some feminists."[59] Additionally, attacks against antisurrogacy feminists often focused on feminism's goal of gender equality. Terry, an adoptive mother who testified at a New York hearing, expressed her frustration at the feminist antisurrogacy stance: "I think I must have misunderstood what feminism was all about when I embraced as tenets equality between the sexes, particularly regarding men's and women's roles as parents."[60] Likewise, in testimony at a 1987 public hearing sponsored by the California Health and Human Services Committee, Jan Sutton, spokesperson for the National Association of Surrogate Mothers (NASM), directed her closing statement at feminists who opposed surrogacy. "Finally, in response to the feminists who have spoken out against surrogate parenting, we in the NASM are appalled. We view ourselves as progressive and wonder why these women think they have the right to tell us what we can do with our own bodies. We are disappointed in the assumption that we cannot make voluntary and intelligent choices about pregnancy. We thought that feminism was about breaking down the barriers between the sexes."[61] Interestingly, even the California Right to Life organization described its antisurrogacy view as in line with a feminist position. A letter to then-Governor Pete Wilson expressing the organization's opposition to Senator Watson's bill noted that "it [Watson's bill] should be offensive to and aggressively opposed by every feminist and supporter of feminist principles since it would possibly create a stable of broodmares—women who might be reduced to renting their wombs."[62]

These quotes from both supporters and opponents of surrogacy demonstrate that debate participants viewed associating their position on surrogate parenting with feminism as politically strategic. The Right to Life organization's employment of the same rhetorical strategy, however, is an important reminder that political labels and discourses can be co-opted. In fact, such co-optation may be viewed as further evidence of the institutionalization of feminist ideas in defining social issues that are successfully associated with women. The discursive battles over surrogate motherhood in states like California and New York show how a new social problem became defined and constructed as a women's issue. Allusions to the abortion debate, choice rhetoric, procreative rights, bodily rights, and women's rights figured largely in defenses of both positions on surrogate parenting. But claims to protecting choice, and concomitantly, women's rights, were not the only ways the problem of surrogacy came to be represented by both its supporters and detractors.

IN THE BEST INTERESTS OF CHILDREN: FRAMING SURROGACY AS A CHILDREN'S RIGHTS ISSUE

Debates about family and paternity necessarily include and affect the lives of children as well as those of women and men. It is not surprising, then, that social and political actors frequently used the rhetoric of the best interests of children as they struggled to construct the appropriate policy response to surrogate motherhood. For example, Assemblywoman Weinstein recognized the importance of promoting her legislative proposal as concerned with protecting children's rights. A memo from her office entitled *Important Principles Underlying the Surrogate Parenting Bill—A. 7367* listed concern over "baby selling" and "risks to children" first, just prior to "risks to women."[63] Similarly, Assemblyman Halpin (D), one of the first to introduce legislation regulating surrogate parenting, testified in a 1986 New York hearing that his proposed bill prioritized children's interests: "The ultimate goal of my legislation is to ensure that the child is protected."[64] At another hearing, held two years later, the attorney Aaron Britvan, a representative from the Bar Association of Nassau County, framed his testimony using best-interests-of-the-child rhetoric. "I think the most important issue is, number one, the best interests of the child," he stated, and then continued, "[T]aking everyone's other factors into account, be it the birth mother's or genetic parents' factors into account, but the ultimate decision has to be based upon the best interests of the child."[65] Speaking at the same hearing, Sally Shank, the adoptive mother of a surrogate-born child, connected the traumas of infertility and the option of surrogate parenting with promoting children's interests. "*In focusing on the children,* I think one of the great ironies of this debate is there is so much hostility and rage about the children and the baby selling and the terrible things," she told lawmakers at a legislative hearing, "*whereas after ten years of infertility,* my main reason for selecting surrogate mothering as an alternative for creating a family was that I thought it would be so *much more positive for the children.*"[66] Californians, too, emphasized the overriding need to protect children. The *Los Angeles Times,* for example, made clear that children's interests were central to the issue of surrogate parenting by headlining an editorial response to the *Johnson v. Calvert* case, "Child's Interest Is Paramount."[67]

The primacy accorded to protecting children was also visible in reports produced by task forces in both New York and California. The New York Task Force on Life and the Law emphasized that "[t]he interests of children are at the center of the debate about surrogate parenting."[68] Likewise, the majority report from the panel of experts established by the California Joint Legislative Committee on Surrogate Parenting argued:

"Through its review of the issues that arise in the adoption context and the ways in which society has responded to those issues, the Panel was able to conclude that surrogacy could have sufficiently adverse effects to warrant legislative attention by the State in order to protect the interests of the persons involved—*especially the children,* who are involuntary parties to arrangements made by adults."[69]

Like the issue of choice, the issue of children's interests was one of the most frequently mentioned and widely agreed-upon topics during the 1992 antisurrogacy bill debate in the New York State Assembly. Over 25 percent of the speakers specifically raised the issue of children's rights and interests. The centrality of this concern was articulated by Assemblyman Roger Green (D): "I stand to articulate my support for this bill [the 1992 anti–commercial surrogacy bill] and primarily around the principles that again I think we have a moral imperative, indeed, a moral *obligation to first protect children,* and I say not just the child in this particular case, but all children."[70] Assemblyman Michael Balboni (R), on the other hand, voted against the anti–commercial surrogacy bill, also citing the need to protect children as his primary motivation: "[A]s far as I'm concerned, *infertility is a very serious problem,* but the people we have to give a rat's pitutti about are the children of this state. *It's the children.*"[71]

Legislators in California, like their colleagues in New York, claimed children's rights as a central concern. Thus a similar use of discursive frames, particularly a discourse of the best interests of children, occurred in floor debates and hearings held there. For instance, in a statement to the Senate Judiciary Committee in support of her regulatory bill, Senator Watson defended regulatory legislation as a policy that respected children's best interests, noting, "Our measure makes the best interests of the child the guiding principal *[sic]* in any dispute."[72] Opponents of the regulatory bill, such as the Child Welfare League of America, also cited children as their central concern. A 1989 memorandum sent to the league's member agencies (and to Senator Watson) stated, "The Child Welfare League opposes the practice of surrogacy as a means of creating families. Our commitment is the welfare of children; surrogacy is not in their best interests."[73] In his opening remarks at a 1987 California hearing, a vocal opponent of surrogacy similarly described his main argument and the purpose of his comments: "to convince you that surrogate mother arrangements are both unethical and inimical to the interests of children."[74]

Clearly, framing a policy position as in the best interests of children was viewed as strategically important by actors on both sides of the policy debate about surrogate motherhood. However, even as both groups framed their positions using the same best-interests rhetoric, each had a different understanding of what constituted children's best interests. Among those who opposed commercial surrogacy, a key concern was the intrusion of commercial interests into the private realm of families. For many, surrogacy threatened children at a very basic level by transforming them into commodities. Tracy Miller, executive director of the New York State Task Force on Life and the Law, summed up this argument at a legislative hearing in 1988. Explaining why the Task Force opposed commercial surrogacy, she said, "Of all the individuals affected by surrogacy, children are the most vulnerable. Focusing first on their interests and society's obligation to them, the Task Force concluded that commercial surrogacy cannot be distinguished from the sale of children. As such, it violates the dignity of children and deep-rooted prohibitions against the purchase and sale of human beings."[75] Similarly, when testifying at the same New York hearing, Mary Beth Whitehead-Gould provided the following explanation for her current opposition to surrogate parenting: "Surrogate agreements violate nature's laws, and they *violate the basic rights of children* they create. Women should not be breeders to bear children for wealthy couples, and babies should not become part of anyone's profit-making scheme."[76]

Letters written in support of the 1992 bill banning surrogacy in New York provide additional indications that a discourse framed around protecting children's rights and avoiding the possibility of baby selling figured prominently. In a letter to Governor Cuomo, the Council of Children and Families clearly opposed the intrusion of pecuniary transactions in the determination of children's custody: "[I]nfants should not become the subject of commercial transaction and the guardianship and custody of an infant should be determined according to child welfare law rather than contract law."[77] The New York Civil Liberties Union also tied its support of the bill to protecting the interests of children. The organization's legislative memorandum asserted that "the bill properly vindicates the child's constitutional rights, including the right not to be sold as chattel."[78] In California, those opposing Senator Watson's regulatory bill also alluded to concerns over children's rights and the commodification of children. For instance, in a letter expressing opposition to the pending legislation, the California Right to Life organization addressed the effect of surrogate parenting on children's rights, arguing that the practice "definitely treats the child as a commodity accessible to the highest bidder."[79]

Another way in which surrogacy opponents framed their best-interests-of-children position was by focusing on the complications of potential custody disputes. The publicity surrounding the Baby M case was often used as empirical evidence to support this contention. As the task force head, Tracy Miller, put it, "[A]ll one needed to do was look at the *Baby M case played out day after day* to appreciate what the *risks are to children,* and that we ought not to conceive children in circumstances that place them at risk."[80] Assemblyman Richard Gottfried (D) delineated the emotional risks associated with custody disputes and the need to put children's interests first as well. On the Assembly floor, speaking in support of the 1992 anti–commercial surrogacy bill, he said:

> I've been concerned about how much of the focus of today's debate has been on the wants and desires and yearnings and what-not of the adults involved and what the adults in this topic should be entitled to do, because for me what is paramount in this discussion is not what the adults want, but what happens once one of those adults gives birth to a child and the subject of this bill is not what adults want and don't want, *the subject of this bill is the future and the lives of the children who are born* and how their future is to be determined.[81]

At the same time, those who supported surrogacy (and who thus opposed New York's proposed ban) also framed their best-interests-of-children position in terms of preventing custody disputes. Supporters of commercial surrogacy reasoned that children's interests would be best met by codifying the parental rights of the relevant parties rather than by outlawing the practice. Law professor Lori Andrews urged a comprehensive regulatory approach when she testified at a 1986 New York hearing in support of Senator Dunne's prosurrogacy bill. In her view, regulating surrogacy practices would "prevent a lengthy custody battle which may interfere with the bonding process of the child to whatever parents are going to raise them, so I would be more in favor of a few disappointed surrogates, a few upset surrogates, and protecting the children with certainty."[82] Assemblyman Balboni, too, understood the goal of protecting children as one best met by regulating—not banning—surrogacy. He had worked for Senator Dunne as a general legal counsel and then, when he gained office himself, had become a strong advocate for surrogacy. At a 1988 legislative hearing, he argued passionately that protecting children meant *not* banning surrogate arrangements: "What you have done here is you have considered the rights of the surrogate mother, and with great sensitivity, but *the person who you've left out is the child,* because what you are doing here is if you have a bill that says surrogate parenting is against public policy in the State of New York, yet if you do it [pursue surrogacy anyway], you have got to go by the Social Services Law, then what you're doing is you're buying that child a custody battle upon birth. How does that help the child?"[83] Other supporters of surrogate parenting, such as Beth Bacon, founder of a surrogacy agency, concurred that state regulation of the practice would be in children's custodial interests: "So why should the legislature get involved? Number one, the welfare of children is involved. The law should clarify who is responsible for these children and no child should be born to abandonment or into a court battle."[84] Surrogacy center director Betsy Aigen even argued that the work she and others did was aimed precisely at securing children's interests: "The involvement of a third party agency is directly related to the best interests of the child."[85]

In addition to stressing how outlawing commercial surrogacy would not prevent custody disputes, and thus was not in children's best interests, those who supported surrogate parenting transactions noted the irony inherent in their opponents' efforts to advocate on behalf of the interests of children who would not be born if commercial surrogacy were banned. Lori Andrews made this point at a 1987 New York hearing: "Now there's much concern that surrogate motherhood is not in the best interest of the resulting children. I think it is. These children would never have been conceived in the first place were it not for the desire of the biological father and his wife to have children. Is being the child of a surrogate so horrible that we would want to prevent these children from being born? I don't think it is."[86] Assemblyman Hevesi, who opposed the 1992 New York anti–commercial surrogacy bill, took a similar position during the floor debate on the bill. When he assessed the testimony of fellow legislator Richard Gottfried, and others who claimed to speak on behalf of children's interests, Hevesi commented, "The theme of your [Gottfried's] statement is *the best interests of the child,* that's been a theme of the proponents of this bill, and I accept that as a very significant issue. My question for you is if we pass this bill and because of two or three provisions that we have already outlined, no woman will enter into a surrogate contract because she would be crazy to do it, *then there will be no child and therefore, no issue of the best interests,* isn't that correct?"[87]

Similarly, the minority report issued by members of the panel appointed by the California Joint Legislative Committee on Surrogate Parenting clearly utilized a children's-best-interest discourse in arguing that it is in the best interests of children to be born: "As far as the *'best interests of the child'* are concerned, we can distinguish between two separate processes. First, there is conceiving and gestating children. Second there is the process of raising children. . . . As to the first, and as emphasized, existing at all would seem fundamental to the best interests of the child. Any possible concerns relating to conception and gestation by means of surrogate parenting arrangements are overwhelmed by the fact that *the child's best interests are served by his [sic] existence rather than his nonexistence!*"[88]

Of particular significance, a key moment in the California Senate Judiciary Committee's consideration of the regulatory bill was perceived to be tied specifically to the portrayal of the bill as putting children's interests first. According to a member of Watson's staff, a senior Republican on the committee (whose opinion was known to be influential with his fellow Republicans) threw his support to Watson's bill after he became convinced that her proposed regulatory surrogacy legislation would indeed ensure children's rights:

> I had this [chuckle] victory. . . . On the Senate Judiciary Committee was a very thoughtful man, a Republican patriarch kind of . . . Ed Davis. He was a former sheriff down in Riverside County. And, um, I always liked him, he's bright, but real kind of country . . . country boy kind of thing; "I'm just an old sheriff," but . . . well-respected Republican legislator. . . . In the course of the Senate hearing the opposition argued that this [surrogacy] is an abomination, that the children . . . are injured and that they come out flawed and not only is the mother destroyed by this experience . . . the birth mother is destroyed by this experience, but the child is terribly injured, and grows up not knowing why his real mother abandoned him and so forth. And they

> brought in psychologists and stuff who all testified that "yes, these kids are all damaged goods," and stuff like that. . . . And this one guy came in, and I had known him, Krim, from down south, he's a law professor. . . . He got up and said that these people are, these people are criminals and ought to be ashamed of themselves, these people that purchased these babies and stuff like that. . . . And I had anticipated that and had selected from the surrogacy centers this really nice family, really nice young couple who couldn't have children, and they had this little cooing, gurgling, eighteen month-old child. And I had them come to the committee. And without prompting, on his own, the father did the perfect thing. Right after this Krim had called them animals, and said these children were, that they were criminals, he got up, and he holds up this darling little baby and he says that "you tell me that I'm a criminal for creating this life. You tell me I ought to be punished and that my doctor should go to jail for bringing together this family." And his wife stands beside him. It was flawless. And then, with prompting, I had him go up and hand the baby to Ed Davis [chuckles]. Right in the hearing room. . . . And Ed is "oooh oooh." You know. And then they voted, and I got Ed's vote.[89]

Conflating Children's Rights with Women's Interests

There can be no doubt that the rhetoric of the best interests of children and the rhetoric of choice were key strategic tools in the debates over surrogate parenting, deployed by *both* supporters and opponents of the practice to make claims for their policy approach to the practice. Also of significance was the strategy of linking these two—that is, of arguing for the need to protect both the rights of women and the rights of children. Many organizations in support of the anti–commercial surrogacy bill couched their position in those terms. For instance, in the New York State Department of Health's letter of support for the 1992 bill, their counsel wrote, "The practice [of surrogate parenting] . . . violates the dignity of children and the societal prohibition against the purchase and sale of human beings. By transforming gestation into a commodity, surrogacy also undermines the dignity of women."[90] Likewise, Professor Vicki Michel, associate director of the Pacific Center for Health Policy and Ethics at the University of California, in her testimony at a California Senate Judiciary Committee hearing, advocated simultaneously for women and children: "SB 937 reinforces many of the concerns that those of us who opposed legislative endorsement of surrogacy have had over the years. It subordinates the *interests of children* to those of adults and *undercuts the dignity of women* who carry a fetus to term."[91]

Of note, this strategic linking of children's with women's interests was often undertaken by those who were known for advocating on behalf of women. For instance, while touting the rights of women, Assemblywoman Weinstein—a known women's rights advocate—also conceded during her statements on the Assembly floor that "the purpose of the bill is to protect children."[92] Indeed, in a memo, her associate counsel instructed Weinstein to "continue to stress the effects of this practice on children, families, and women."[93] Likewise, in a position statement, the Division for Women from the state of New York described the negative repercussions of surrogate motherhood for women and then added that "surrogate parenting places children at risk."[94]

Other women's advocates also aligned their surrogacy position with children's interests. Testifying against surrogate parenting at a New York State hearing, feminist sociologist Barbara Katz Rothman clearly positioned children's interests as carrying at least as much import as women's: "It is precisely to avoid such nightmare visions . . . to protect the interests of children we can create, and to protect the interests of women who bear children, that I ask you not to legalize surrogacy contracts."[95] A position statement entitled "Women and Children Used in Systems of Surrogacy," issued by the Institute of Women and Technology and sent to Senator Watson, also illustrates the defense of children's rights while advocating for women: "Surrogacy is a practice of *sex-discrimination.* It threatens the health, welfare, and *equality of women* and the *welfare of those children* who may be born from surrogate arrangements. . . . Rather than granting control over her body, these arrangements transfer control of a woman's body to brokers and clients. *They deprive women of the right to control their bodies.* To defend surrogacy as consistent with reproductive liberty, is to equate freedom with slavery."[96]

Yet an important question remains. Are the interests of children necessarily aligned with those of women?

The discursive alignment of women's and children's rights is troubling in as much as historically the concern for children's interests, from the development (or lack thereof) of child care to the recent medicalization of pregnancy, has been positioned against concern for the interests of women, or at least in contrast to women's rights.[97] These instances illuminate how calls for children's rights are often entwined with normative constructions of full-time mothering—for those women with race/class privilege—and appropriate gendered behavior for women. Indeed, this cultural interest in and concern for children existed alongside the rise of an ideology of intensive mothering that held that children were sacred[98] and an ideology that saw children as "priceless."[99] According to journalist Susan Faludi, the 1980s was a decade of "backlash" against the women's movement, a period in which maternalism and babies were the focus of much media attention.[100] At the same time, a culture of "blaming mothers" flourished. Women, particularly poor mothers, were blamed for social problems from childhood poverty to drugs and violence, while (white) working women were blamed for creating "latchkey kids" and prompting the rise in divorce rates.[101] Thus, while the increased legitimation of and focus on children's interests and rights often is associated with attention to women's issues, it is important to remember that the rise in claims to children's rights just as frequently has been coupled with the demonization of women as mothers.

This chapter has shown that the association of women's and children's rights, and the simultaneous use of rhetoric on behalf of both, was an important discursive strategy in the political debates over surrogate motherhood legislation. That actors on both sides of the debate drew on choice rhetoric indicates that this type of frame not only was institutionalized into political discourse by the late 1980s but also was a viable and perhaps necessary way of understanding the problem of surrogacy. This in turn suggests that by the last decades of the twentieth century certain women's and reproductive rights claims on the state had gained recognition and legitimacy. On the other hand, the prevalence of choice discourse also indicates a possible co-optation and dilution of women's rights issues. Furthermore, the concept of choice has been criticized as too narrow in the claims it makes on the state for women's social rights,[102] its failure to consider the race/class inequalities that shape the lives and options of differently situated women, and its tendency to be manipulated by neoliberal ideology into a rallying call for unabashed consumerism and against social regulations of any sort.

The discursive battles over surrogate parenting also show that both women's and children's rights rhetoric were prevalent and frequently linked. The case of surrogate motherhood illustrates the political effectiveness of aligning the rights of women with those of children, but at the same time it suggests the possible dangers of this linkage. In the end, the social ambivalence and conflict over surrogate motherhood captured in the rhetoric of women's choice and children's interests reflected general cultural anxieties over reproduction, motherhood, children, and families at the end of the twentieth century. These broader concerns provided the larger framework within which worries and conflicts over how best to support couples'/women's "natural" desire to have a family (i.e., have a child) and widespread distaste for the "unnatural" commodification of parent-child relations took form. The next chapter turns to these tensions over and agreements about the private versus public nature of the family and examines how they shaped the battles over surrogate parenting legislation.

Chapter 3 | "MORAL CONUNDRUMS AND MENACING AMBIGUITIES"

Framing the Problem of Surrogate Motherhood

I would assume that the future of our country hangs in the balance because the future of marriage hangs in the balance. . . . Isn't that the ultimate homeland security, standing up and defending marriage?

Senator Rick Santorum, R-PA, quoted in "Senate Scuttles Gay Marriage Amendment," *New York Times,* July 7, 2004

It is society's basic institution for raising children. . . . Like private property and the rule of law, marriage is one of a few institutions that hold up democracy.

Lisa Schiffern, Republican speechwriter, Op-ed, *New York Times,* January 29, 2004

Traditional marriage is about children and must be protected by the Constitution.

Senator John Cornyn, R-TX, quoted in *New York Times,* March 30, 2004, A:16

It seems to me that the sound social policy ought to protect and give legislative emphasis to support the basic and fundamental unit of society, the family.

Testimony of Monsignor William Levada, California Assembly Committee on Judiciary, *Hearings on Surrogate Parenting Contracts,* Los Angeles, November 19, 1982

The debate about surrogacy . . . touches upon values and beliefs about the interests of children, marriage, the family, women and human reproduction. All members of society may therefore feel some stake in society's response to the practice.

New York State Task Force on Life and the Law, *Surrogate Parenting: Analysis and Recommendations for Public Policy* (1988)

In the late 1980s and early 1990s, when public debate about surrogacy peaked, the concept of "family values" was prominent in political discourse. It is not surprising, then, that the rhetoric surrounding surrogate motherhood and its construction as a social problem was tied to concerns over and debates about the future of the family (its form, its members' obligations, and even its existence) and to the state's role in protecting families. For some surrogacy opponents, such as the hierarchy of the American Roman Catholic Church and the orthodox Jewish organization Agudath Israel of America, the practice represented one more threat to the stability and continuance of the family.[1] For others, surrogate motherhood signaled worrisome changes in the value placed on family relationships. Commercial surrogate parenting, the attorney Cathleen Holka told New York State lawmakers, "demeans the dignity of men, women and children, and traditional family notions."[2] Questions about what defines the family and who can be counted as family members were also part of the public debate about the problem of surrogate motherhood. For instance, in the early 1980s, conservative commentator George Will noted the seemingly endless "attempts to 'broaden' or 'transcend' the traditional role of the family" and warned that "there is no end to the moral conundrums and menacing ambiguities that arise when people improvise changes in the family's functions regarding procreation and child-rearing."[3]

Surrogacy supporters vigorously challenged these attempts to label the practice as a threat to the family. Those who championed surrogate parenting insisted that the practice was strongly profamily. For instance, during their testimony at a Los Angeles hearing, a couple who had had a child with a surrogate dismissed the notion that surrogacy "breaks up families" as "a lie." Surrogate parenthood, they asserted, arises "out of a couple's desire to create a family."[4] A year earlier, Betsy Aigen, head of a surrogacy agency (and an adoptive mother), had advanced a similar view at a New York hearing: "Infertile couples themselves who choose this option have been through the mill. Their marriages have stood the test of fire and they are strongly committed to each other and to raising a family together. . . . There's no more wanted child than the child born to an infertile couple."[5]

One point surrogacy proponents and opponents did agree upon was that the practice challenged traditional notions of kinship and parenthood. In fact, these very transformations were accepted—even advocated—by those defending surrogate parenthood. For example, at a California hearing in support of regulatory legislation and against a ban on surrogate parenting, Center for Surrogate Parenting Director Bill Handel argued that the state's policy response should "recognize that traditional notions of family and motherhood are indeed changing."[6] Similarly, in explaining her organization's objection to a regulatory bill that would have limited surrogate parenting transactions to married infertile women and their husbands, Judith Breidbart of New York City NOW noted the important role reproduction and parenting can play in all people's lives, regardless of sexuality and marital status. "Today, other forms of families exist widely," she reminded listeners, "and it is too narrow an approach to confine legislation only to the traditional form of nuclear family." Equality in reproductive rights is essential, since "the desire to be parents, or the need to enter into such special parenting arrangements, may be as strong for single men and women, homosexual or not, and for heterosexual couples who live together without marriage, as it is for the traditional husband and wife."[7] Five years later, however, New York City NOW, as well as other feminist individuals and groups, supported New York's 1992 ban on commercial surrogacy. While this change seemed to contradict the earlier support of nontraditional families, it did reflect these groups' concerns about equality of treatment. The proposed complete ban would prevent all parties—heterosexual, homosexual, single, or married—from pursuing commercial surrogate parenting transactions. Thus those who were reluctant to curtail options for nontraditional families, such as Debra Glick (D), an openly lesbian New York State Assembly member, had to break with long-standing feminist allies in the legislature in order to vote against the 1992 ban.

Tensions such as these were central to the political debates over how the state should respond to the newly emerging social problem of surrogacy. The New York State Task Force on Life and the Law described the impact of competing visions of families and of the future of the family this way: "Practices to assist reproduction, with surrogate parenting as a vivid example, pose the possibility of entirely new relationships and a different blueprint for the family unit. For some, the technologies present the opportunities for new relationships that must be assessed in light of the already eroded traditional framework for family life. Others view the technologies to assist reproduction as a powerful new source of instability for the already beleaguered family."[8] As this chapter will make clear, however, social policies created in response to the problem of surrogate motherhood were shaped by ideological agreements as well as disagreements. The discursive politics over surrogacy legislation did not represent a culture war of mutually exclusive, opposing viewpoints. Rather, the debate was marked by a mixture of consensus and conflict regarding both the status and value of children and mothers and the norms defining appropriate family relationships.

BABY SELLING VERSUS THE PLIGHT OF INFERTILE COUPLES: COMPETING FRAMES ABOUT SURROGATE MOTHERHOOD

From a social constructionist perspective, policy development is a struggle over what a social problem represents.[9] The different policy responses to surrogacy and how a given policy was framed were linked to different causal stories about surrogate parenting.[10] An analysis of textual documents, including newspaper articles, transcripts of legislative debates, position statements, and government reports, reveals two main competing frames and two associated types of policy approaches. While some groups expressed discomfort at the infiltration of marketplace and consumer values into the private realm of the family, other groups expressed sympathy for infertile couples and their "natural" desires to reproduce and have a family without state interference. I label the frames associated with these two sides of the surrogacy debate "baby selling" and the "plight of infertile couples" (see table 5).

Media presentations of surrogacy frequently noted these alternative framings and the tensions between them, probably as an attempt to provide "balanced" coverage of the topic. The three examples below, drawn from the *Los Angeles Times,* the *New York Times,* and the *Washington Post,* respectively, are typical:

> Opponents said the practice amounts to baby selling and exploits women, while supporters say surrogacy offers childless couples the opportunity to have children.[11]

> [S]urrogate parenthood is viewed by proponents as a humane and ethical way to allow infertile people to reproduce and by opponents as a perversion of science that equates life with a product.[12]

TABLE 5. Discursive Frames of Surrogacy

	Commodified Reproduction	*Reproductive Freedom*
Frame	"Baby selling"	"Plight of infertile couples"
Problem	Economic intrusion	State intrusion
Solution	Discourage/ban	Permit/regulate

> One group sees the dilemma as too intense and too close to the social taboo against child-selling for society to solve. Another group believes the benefits of enabling infertile couples to have children far outweigh the considerable risks involved in surrogate parenting.[13]

The aspect of surrogacy each frame emphasized made certain kinds of policy solutions desirable and ruled out others. Those who framed surrogate motherhood as a form of baby selling viewed an outright ban on the practice as the only morally and socially acceptable policy solution. Those who framed surrogate arrangements as a compassionate response to infertility that would safeguard the right of the individual to procreate saw legalizing and regulating the practice as the only equitable and just solution. To promote these alternative frames and their associated policy responses, each side of the surrogacy debate used specific rhetorical strategies. A *Los Angeles Times* reporter summed up the two strategies commonly evoked this way: "If you say the contracts are unenforceable, you're seen as rejecting the desire of infertile couples to have children of their own, a deep and enduring human desire. If you make them legal, you can be seen to have possibly participated in the exploitation of women [and] cheapened the family."[14]

The remainder of this chapter examines these and other rhetorical strategies, as well as the accompanying cultural metaphors and ideologies each side drew on to advance its position. The analysis shows how the debates over surrogacy reflected fundamental differences about the nature of—and thus the solution to—the "problems" of surrogate parenting transactions. Equally important, however, the analysis also shows how those advocating both for and against commercial surrogacy shared many fundamental assumptions about the nature of the family and were similarly blind to the significant disparities between racial/ethnic groups' real access to procreative rights.

Rhetorical Strategies Used to Portray Surrogacy as Baby Selling

The framing of surrogacy as a problem of baby selling was explicit, and often dominant, in newspaper stories about surrogacy, particularly when its opponents' views were presented. For example, reporting on California State Senator Diane Watson's (D) regulatory bill in 1991, the *Los Angeles Times* noted, "The proposal drew immediate fire from the National Coalition Against Surrogacy and others who believe contracts to produce children degrade women and amount to baby-selling."[15] In an article on the Catholic response to surrogacy, the *Washington Post* reported that "[s]urrogate motherhood is the moral equivalent of selling a child, New Jersey's Roman Catholic bishops told the state Supreme Court."[16] Connie Binsfield, a Michigan state senator sponsoring a legislative ban on surrogacy, was quoted as referring to the practice as "baby-selling pure and simple," while critics of a newly opened surrogacy center were described as "blast[ing] the practice as tantamount to baby-selling."[17]

These examples reveal the literal equating of commercial surrogacy with "baby selling." Opponents of the practice also used several discursive tropes and metaphors to rhetorically and dramatically construct surrogacy as essentially about baby selling. Perhaps because of the growing cultural acceptance of the importance of children's rights (see chapter 2), a common rhetorical strategy involved comparing children to everyday commodities—surrogacy made children "goods for sale." Andrew Kimbrell, attorney for the National Coalition Against Surrogacy, used this strategy when he insisted that "you cannot have a commercial contract for the sale of a baby. You cannot have people turning over their children like they were televisions or tennis rackets."[18] A state senator from Nebraska charged that infants conceived by surrogates "become commodities like corn or wheat, things which can be purchased on the futures market."[19] Active opponents of surrogacy were not the only ones to make use of the child-as-commodity metaphor. In one of the first editorials to consider the implications of surrogate parenting, the editors of the *New York Times* compared the first publicly known surrogate-born child to a made-to-order product: "[H]e himself, being custom-tailored, is the human equivalent of a bespoke suit." Taking this commodity metaphor to its logical conclusion, the same editorial later queried facetiously, "Is the baby then subject to the sales tax?"[20]

A second dominant discursive strategy used in the rhetorical framing of surrogacy as baby selling was to compare women's bodies and reproductive capacity to factories. This analogy cast the practice as yet another aspect of out-of-control industrializing processes. In the early 1980s, a *Washington Post* columnist criticized the public's misplaced acceptance of the emerging practice in these terms: "[I]f some woman wants to act like a brood mare and turn her body into a baby factory, well, we reason tolerantly, that's her business."[21] Andrew Kimbrell charged that owing to the infiltration of consumerist values into women's reproductive processes, "women are treated as anonymous baby factories."[22] Louisiana Representative Arthur Morrell (D) suggested an equally disturbing picture when, during his testimony at a U.S. congressional hearing, he denounced the practice as creating a "surrogate mother mill."[23] Sometimes surrogate mothers were not described as the actual factory or mill but instead likened to factory or mill workers—that is, people who produce goods for sale. This type of discursive strategy is evident in feminist sociologist Barbara Katz Rothman's testimony at a New York State hearing: "The baby becomes a commodity, something a woman can produce and sell much as a factory worker produces a car."[24] In much the same vein, David Zweibel, another opponent of commercial surrogacy testifying at the same hearing, argued that legalizing surrogate motherhood would amount to equating reproduction to any other service-for-hire. It "would tell society that a woman's reproductive capacity is something that can be sold in the open market like a sack of potatoes, like tax advice, like any other commodity or service."[25] And, at a U.S. congressional hearing, Representative Henry Hyde (R) of Illinois warned against the dangers of formulating a policy response to surrogate motherhood that would result in "discard[ing] long-held principles of human worth, reducing childbearing into an occupation, making children into commodities and transforming maternity wards into showrooms."[26]

Framing surrogacy as being about baby selling also led some opponents to focus on the exploitative aspects of the employer-employee relations embedded in surrogacy. From this perspective, surrogacy arrangements were viewed as casting the infertile couple in the role of employer and the surrogate in the role of employee. Using labor market imagery made it possible to draw on a discourse of inequality and disadvantage, with a particular emphasis on the economic vulnerability of potential surrogates. New York Assemblywoman Weinstein relied on this kind of discourse when she defended her anti–commercial surrogacy bill during the floor debate in 1992. She argued that "[c]ontract surrogacy . . . poses a grave potential for the exploitation of poor women who may be coerced by the need for money into this practice."[27] During this same debate, Assemblyman Edward Sullivan (D), also a critic of surrogate parenting, drew a sharp distinction between jobs that were acceptable for the disadvantaged and those that were not: "We are talking about the rich and poor here. There is no escaping it. . . . This is where the rich hire the poor. I don't mind the rich hiring the poor to mow the lawn. I used to be one of the hirees of that situation. I don't mind the rich hiring the poor to clean their house, but I think it is immoral for the rich to hire the poor to have their children."[28] Barbara Katz Rothman spelled out the harsh realities of the U.S. labor market when she testified at a New York State hearing, explaining why class, as well as race and immigration status, made some women workers especially vulnerable: "The same women who are pushing white babies in strollers, white old folks in wheelchairs, can be carrying white babies in their bellies. Poor, uneducated, third-world women and women of color from the United States and elsewhere, with fewer economic alternatives, can be hired more cheaply. They can also be controlled more tightly."[29]

Another dominant rhetorical strategy employed in the promotion of a "baby-selling" frame involved emphasizing the mercenary and exploitative role that surrogacy brokers played in the process. In the early 1980s, one columnist dismissed surrogacy with the cynical observation that "the whole business has been a boon to lawyers who found yet another way of making money."[30] Six years later, the practice still struck some as too closely tied to moneymaking. News coverage of the New York legislative debate over surrogacy reported the opinion of Laurie Yates, a surrogate mother who sued for custody of her twins. She felt that "the only people who benefit from such arrangements . . . are the 'baby brokers' who bring the two sides together and make 'sizable profits.'"[31] When the Family Section of the American Bar Association tackled the issue, a news story noted that surrogacy opponents believed that "babies are becoming 'products' of entrepreneurships run by attorneys and gynecologists for profit."[32]

The "baby-selling" frame was so pervasive and powerful that surrogacy advocates could not afford to ignore it. Most supporters of the practice deliberately avoided expressing any viewpoints that might be interpreted as endorsing baby selling.[33] In fact, many went out of their way to reject the charge that surrogacy involved baby selling. One early news story in the *Washington Post* illustrates an alternative framing of commercial surrogacy favored by its supporters: "Philadelphia attorney Burton Satzberg contends that 'baby-selling' statutes would not affect surrogate parenting arrangements, 'because we're not selling babies. We're selling a service.'"[34] Similarly, an even earlier news story in the *New York Times* reported, "[A]dvocates deny that the surrogate mother is selling her baby. 'There's not a baby there when we start the process,' said Mr. Keane. 'I think the surrogate is being paid for the use of her body, she's not selling her baby.'"[35] During the initial attempts in the 1980s to pass regulatory legislation in California, another *New York Times* article pointed out that supporters of the legislation explicitly distanced their position from one of baby selling and from the child-as-product metaphor. Instead, they focused on the appropriate compensation for women who served as surrogate mothers: "In an attempt to quell charges of baby selling, the [California] bill would have declared money given to a surrogate 'compensation for her services' and not payment for the child."[36] Supporters' emphasis on women's right to control their bodies was a potentially very effective rhetorical strategy because it simultaneously highlighted women's reproductive/privacy rights and downplayed and rejected the "exploitative" frame proposed by surrogacy opponents.

Another important way in which surrogacy supporters refuted their opponents' efforts to cast the practice as an essentially mercenary transaction was to stress the "gift"-giving role of the surrogate.[37] Metaphors invoking the notions of "gift," "love," and "nurturance" were strategically employed to shift the rhetoric around surrogacy to emphasize the emotionally satisfying aspects of family life. For instance, Jan Sutton, spokesperson for the National Association of Surrogate Mothers, tried to bring about this kind of refocusing in her testimony at a hearing in Los Angeles. To move the discussion away from one centered on baby selling to one encompassing more culturally accepted views of family relations, she asserted that "the child born of this process is not 'bought,' 'rejected,' 'abandoned' or 'sold,' but is 'planned,' 'desired,' 'loved,' 'given' and 'nurtured' by the adults involved."[38]

Clearly, supporters of surrogate parenting had to contend with entrenched opposition to practices or behaviors that might result in the buying and selling of children.[39] The framing of surrogacy as baby selling was much too culturally powerful to simply ignore or dismiss as unimportant. At the same time, though, they had recourse to an equally powerful alternative frame. To advance their own position, supporters of commercial surrogacy arrangements drew on a "plight of infertile couples" frame.

Rhetorical Strategies to Portray Surrogacy as a Solution to the Plight of Infertile Couples

Surrogate parenting advocates, like their opponents, used several rhetorical schemes to promote their "plight of infertile couples" framing. One dominant discursive strategy involved providing poignant vignettes from those who suffered from infertility. These personal and moving stories were used to garner sympathy for those who might want access to surrogacy services. A *Los Angeles Times* article entitled "The Pain of Infertility" includes examples of this strategy. The article profiled three different couples' difficulties in having a child. The story's opening paragraph reported one husband's stark description of his and his wife's despair: "'Every month, when she had her period, it was like having a death in the family.'" The association between infertility and trauma was reinforced later in the article, when readers were told that "[w]hat people seem to forget in the controversy over surrogate mothers . . . is the pain they [infertile couples] suffer."[40]

Infertile couples who attended public hearings often presented this type of personal story of tragedy. Nellie Bright, for instance, told panel members at a New York State hearing that learning of her own infertility at age seventeen was so crushing, "I thought I would never get over it."[41] Diane Baker also advanced this "plight of infertile couples" frame in a letter she wrote to California Governor Pete Wilson in support of the state's 1992 regulatory bill: "I suffered nine miscarriages. Although willing to adopt, I knew how perilous the road to adoption frequently is. . . . I was ready to proceed with surrogacy when the miracle happened to us and I bore two healthy girls, but even as I write this letter from my enviable position, my eyes flow with tears from the gulf of misery where I lived with my infertility."[42] Emotional testaments like these often were reported in media accounts of hearings on surrogacy. A *Los Angeles Times* article, for example, described committee members at a U.S. congressional hearing as being "moved by the testimony of Mark and Joyce Stevens. . . . Joyce Stevens cradled the baby in a blanket as she testified. Her voice broke as she told the congressmen that the special arrangement 'was our only hope. . . . It's the only hope for thousands of other parents who cannot have children. Please don't take this right away from them.'"[43]

The pain of infertility and the plight of those who suffered from it were recounted not only by the infertile but also by the people who stood ready to help them. Women who wanted to be or who had already acted as surrogates used the "plight of infertile couples" frame to explain their willingness to fill this role. In one of the first news articles on surrogacy, a woman accounted for her decision to act as a surrogate this way: "I had a close friend who couldn't have a baby, and I know how badly she wanted one. . . . It's just something I wanted to do."[44] Another surrogate mother provided a similarly compassionate explanation during her testimony at a New York hearing: "Can those of us who are fortunate in being able to conceive a child naturally ever understand the heart rendering *[sic]* agony of infertility. Most young girls grow up dreaming of getting married and eventually being a mother."[45]

The framing of surrogate motherhood as about the plight of infertile couples required not only making the pain and suffering of those unable to have children more widely known but also drawing public attention to the extent of the problem of infertility. This was done by presenting data that suggested that a worrisomely high absolute number or proportion of the population were infertile. Some examples of this type of storytelling, drawn from newspaper articles on surrogacy, include "The National Center for Health Statistics says there are 3.5 million American married couples who have not been able to have a baby";[46] "About one American couple in six is unable to have children of their own";[47] and "Proponents said that surrogate parenthood is a boon to the 15 percent of married couples that are infertile . . . and have been unable to adopt a baby."[48]

The apparently large numbers of infertile couples was troublesome, but what was presented as particularly alarming was the increase in infertility rates. Two separate *New York Times* editorials informed readers that there was a "marked increase in infertility among younger couples"[49] and that "more and more American women are knowing that pain."[50] Surrogacy supporters relied on these kinds of infertility statistics and trend data as rhetorical tools. New York Assemblyman Michael Balboni (R), arguing against the anti–commercial surrogacy bill on the Assembly floor, attempted to sway his colleagues by alerting them to the "startling" data on infertility. "Now you know what's going on with infertility in the United States? . . . In 1988, about 4.9 million women. . . . in the United States, 8.4 percent of the total population of women, were deemed to have been infertile or had impaired fecundity. Think about that number; that is startling. And it is increasing."[51]

The effectiveness of infertility statistics as a rhetorical strategy turned, in part, on the fact that public discourse and debate about surrogacy was conducted within a broader context of social concern over perceived threats to the family function of raising children. Specifically, the combination of increasing infertility rates and a decline in "adoptable" babies suggested the need for some sort of intervention. Two *New York Times* editorials on surrogate motherhood placed the emergence of surrogate parenting transactions squarely within this context. The first noted that "fewer and fewer children are available for adoption and more and more couples report fertility problems,"[52] and the second concluded, "Given the small number of adoptable babies, surrogate mothers were perhaps inevitable once the medical technology became available."[53] Joan Einwohner, a consulting psychologist with the Infertility Center of New York, placed both the demand and the need for surrogate parenting within the "infertility epidemic" and the "adoption crisis" when she testified against an anti–commercial surrogacy bill at a New York State hearing in the late 1980s. "I would also like to mention," Einwohner said, "that in an era when one out of six couples desiring children are infertile, and with the lack of adoptable children, and in a society that is very accepting of procreation being planned at the convenience of the parties involved, there may be no way to withhold this option from infertile couples."[54]

It is important to note, however, that in this context the rhetorical use of an "adoption crisis" referred to the problems of reproducing white families and babies.[55] Indeed, the public discourses on the twin "crises" of infertility and adoption were always implicitly—and frequently explicitly—about race. A news story on surrogacy made this racial subtext especially clear: "The increasing popularity of artificial techniques of reproduction grows out of an increase in infertility in the United States. While more couples are seeking to adopt children, the available number of the most often desired babies, those that are healthy and white, has been dropping, and aspiring parents have been turning to medicine for alternatives to adoption."[56] Similarly, a news article about a study on surrogate mothers' motivations reported that the researcher who conducted the study "speculates that its growing popularity is a result of an increased demand for newborn white babies for adoption along with a decreasing supply."[57] This focus on finding a solution to the problem of (re)producing white babies reveals the extent to which the debates over surrogacy reflected and reinforced taken-for-granted racially stratified notions of reproduction. In the United States, health and "normality" are routinely linked with racial identity. As one father-to-be remarked, "And I want a healthy baby. And there just aren't any available. They're either retarded or they're minorities, black, Hispanic.'"[58]

The desirability of and need for surrogate parenting were also discursively constructed around the culturally valued relationship between genes and kinship.[59] For instance, one newspaper article about a couple who had turned to surrogacy explained, "She and her husband had ruled out adoption, in part because of the shortage of available infants, but more important because they wished to have some genetic link to their child."[60] Another story, profiling several infertile couples, quoted a prospective father as listing among surrogacy's advantages the fact that "[t]he child would be '50% genetically ours.'"[61] Finally, the widespread belief in what one adoptive mother referred to as the "basic human drive to have your own biological child"[62] was cited as a reason to choose surrogate arrangements. These three factors—the "natural" human desire for a genetic link to one's child, the perceived increase in infertility, and the adoption "crisis"—led prospective parents and other surrogacy advocates to consider it imperative that the state facilitate the practice. A *New York Times* columnist, summing up the appeal of surrogacy, noted the importance of these same three elements: "With one in every 10 American couples unable to have children of their own, and very few infants available for adoption in the United States, surrogate parenting offers an alternative to couples hoping to have a child with a biological link."[63]

In the political arena, similar expressions concerning the desirability, if not the need, for biologically related offspring were aired by those fighting legislative bans on commercial surrogacy. At a 1987 U.S. congressional hearing on surrogate parenting, Kansas Representative Bob Whittaker (R), after noting the "very limited opportunity for adoption," concluded that "surrogacy may offer the last opportunity for a child, and it is an opportunity that may be appealing since it allows for at least one spouse, if not both, to be genetically related to the child."[64] In 1992, before the legislature passed the anti–commercial surrogacy bill, New York Assemblyman Oliver Koppell offered the following impassioned defense of the overriding importance of genetic ties:

> Obviously, for everybody in the House, having a genetic child, if they had them or if they want to, is the most important thing they can do in life. I know it is for me. I cannot imagine anything more important than that, and we want to deny people that right. . . . It is the wrong thing to do. It is wrong from the point of view of those many couples . . . who need this arrangement to have the greatest gift of life, the gift of a child that is, indeed their own.[65]

During the same floor debate, Assemblyman Arthur Eve (D) used similarly personalized and dramatic language to compare the shortcomings of adoption to the advantages of surrogate parenting, asking, rhetorically, "Why deny that couple the right to have a genetic child? That's crazy. It doesn't make sense. . . . [If s]omebody said to me, 'Art, you can go and adopt.' Well, I would rather have a genetic child that my wife and I contributed to. That's better than adopting a child. I would rather have that experience."[66]

Given the racially stratified nature of U.S. society, the emphasis given to biology and genes can be viewed as a coded reference to race. For instance, at the congressional hearing on surrogate parenting held in 1987, Dr. Richard Levin addressed the twin "need" for racial and genetic similarity to solidify kinship ties, observing that "[t]he hopes and desires of infertile couples are the same as those of us who have been fortunate enough to bear children without any assistance. They would like a healthy infant who is not only racially the same as they are, but genetically related to their marital unit."[67] These concerns for a biological link between parents and children can be linked to the rising "geneticism" of the late twentieth century,[68] as well as to normative views of biological determinism and racial classification. In the context of socially constructed notions of racial purity, genetic connections were seen as a way to ensure racial similarity. At the same time, the assumption that humans are endowed with a "natural" need for genetic kinship rendered the alternative family constructions (e.g., fictive kin and other-mothers) found in racial-ethnic minority communities invisible.[69]

Furthermore, as noted by legal scholar Dorothy Roberts, in the United States, reproductive politics cannot be disentangled from racial politics.[70] For instance, she finds that the cultural preoccupation with the so-called infertility epidemic, including media accounts of infertility, focused almost exclusively on white couples. Nearly all of the "miracle babies" produced by new fertility technologies and featured in various media accounts were white; meanwhile problems of infertility in the black community were dismissed by the medical establishment as insignificant and were ignored by the public at large. In the end, then, the "plight of the infertile" frame succeeded in evoking significant concern because of the assumption of what a normative (white) family should look like. In other words, those who used a rhetoric that focused on the shortage of adoptable babies and the crisis of infertility had in mind only the babies and bodies of those with race privilege.

DEFENDING THE FAMILY: THE RHETORICAL USE OF A PUBLIC/PRIVATE DIVIDE

The debate over whether to permit or ban surrogacy captured larger societal conflicts over and concerns about the meaning of motherhood, parenting, and family. However, the way the social problem of surrogate parenting was framed also reveals important *similarities* in both sides' views about families and in the dominant cultural beliefs they chose to use when advocating for their respective positions. In particular, both surrogacy supporters and opponents drew on the dominant ideology of a public/private divide, in which the family was understood to occupy the private realm. As a result, both frames reinforced the idea that relationships pursued and formed in families should not be interfered with by the outside world. At the same time, in evoking privacy rights, both sides often ignored how such individually based rights historically have upheld racial and class privilege. These underlying similarities are significant for more than their influence on the policy debates over the problem of surrogate motherhood. They reveal the fundamental and quintessentially American notions of privacy that are intrinsic to the politics of reproduction as a whole.

The remaining sections of this chapter identify and analyze the shared assumptions behind each policy framing of surrogate motherhood. Arguably, it was this commonality in belief, rather than intransigent differences, that slowed the legislative response to this new social problem.

"The Money Changers Have Entered the Temple of Our Most Sacred Human Relationship": Keeping the Marketplace out of the Family

Those opposed to commercial surrogacy framed concern around the threat of capitalist marketplace forces infiltrating the market-free realm of the family. Theirs was a fight against commodified reproduction. "Surrogacy is part of the industrialization of human reproduction. A reproductive supermarket is in the making," Sharon Huddle DeAngelo, attorney and founder of the National Coalition Against Surrogacy, warned at a California hearing.[71] Similarly, Robert Arenstein, attorney for Mary Beth Whitehead, the surrogate mother of Baby M, questioned the economic and utilitarian takeover of the private sphere and intimate relations in his testimony at a U.S. congressional hearing: "As a society, do we want to industrialize reproduction? Is absolutely everything grist for the capitalist mill? Are there any limits to what can be bought and sold?"[72] For Representative Thomas Luken (D) of Ohio, commercial surrogacy was an intrusion of economic relations into the private and even "sacred" realm of the family. At the 1987 congressional hearing on surrogacy, he cast surrogate motherhood as a problem of national import in need of legislative attention: "[C]ommercial surrogacy threatens to make a sordid business out of family relationships that we consider most sacred, and therefore we must consider the desirability of removing the profit motive from these otherwise sacrosanct areas of human activity. . . . The money changers have entered the temple of our most sacred human relationship. . . . [W]e have responsibility not to sit idly by."[73]

New York State legislators opposed to surrogacy shared Representative Luken's deep distaste for what they viewed as surrogacy's economic intrusion into the family. "[T]here is something wrong with the very notion that people would enter into a financial arrangement for the bearing of a child. I find it to be repugnant. I find it to be not something which we should be supporting as a purpose of social policy in our state," Assemblyman John Faso (R) told his fellow legislators during the 1992 debate on the state's proposed ban on commercial surrogacy.[74] Similarly, during the same Assembly debate, Assemblyman Richard Gottfried (D) argued that the commercialization of parent-child relations was contrary to dominant cultural beliefs: "[N]one of those arguments [for surrogacy] can counteract the fact the notion of buying and selling children . . . is still something profoundly and inherently abhorrent to what we all stand for."[75]

When the problem of surrogacy was framed as being about baby selling, the concern evoked often focused not only on the intrusion of the marketplace but also on the threat posed to parent-child relations. This is clear, for instance, in the report on surrogate parenting issued by the New York State Task Force on Life and the Law: "Many Task Force members also believe that commercial surrogate parenting arrangements will erode the integrity of the family unit and values fundamental to the bond between parents and children. The Task Force concluded that state enforcement of the contracts and the commercial aspects of surrogate parenting pose the greatest potential harm to individuals and to social attitudes and practices."[76] Assemblywoman Helene Weinstein (D), who co-sponsored the New York anti–commercial surrogacy bill, alluded to these same concerns during the floor debate on her bill. She cautioned that "by commercializing gestation, fees for surrogacy threaten . . . long-standing assumptions about human reproduction and the parent-child relationship."[77] California legislators heard a similar message from Ruben Pannor of the California Association of Adoption Agencies, who testified at a legislative hearing that "[s]urrogacy is the greatest threat of our time to the dignity of humankind. . . . Surrogate parenting condones mercenary considerations in the creation of the parent/child relationship and consequently strikes at the very foundation of human society."[78]

As these examples show, framing surrogacy as baby selling emphasized those aspects of the practice that seemed destined to bring the outside commercial world into the private realm of the family. The central story of the "baby-selling" frame, that surrogacy amounted to the buying and selling of family relations, was not one that would permit compromise. Everyone—children, women, families, and society at large—was jeopardized when pecuniary concerns invaded the affective world of the family. A *Washington Post* columnist, addressing these limits of market forces, noted, "A market economy allows for all kinds of commercialization. But contracts that involve the buying and selling of human beings are not permitted."[79]

This way of understanding the problem of surrogate motherhood—that it involved fundamentally taboo activities—also dictated what solutions would and would not be permissible. Since the "baby-selling" frame told a story about commercial interests gone amok, the only reasonable legislative response to this social problem would be the banning of commercial surrogacy by the state. Therefore, the power of the state was viewed as being appropriately used to protect the family from commodifying influences. Assemblywoman Weinstein made this point when she argued on behalf of her anti–commercial surrogacy bill: "Government . . . has a legitimate interest in protecting these basic values and relationships from commercial activity."[80] These sentiments were also reflected in the Advisory Panel Majority Report to California's Joint Committee on Surrogate Parenting. Panel members recognized the legitimacy and depth of reproductive desires but prioritized the larger goal of protecting family relationships from market forces. "The law should tread lightly when it intrudes on people's dreams," the report cautioned, "but intrude it must when important interests are in need of protection. . . . [S]ociety . . . has an interest in preserving human dignity by keeping people from being treated as commodities, subject to sale by commercial contract."[81]

"What Role Should the Government Play in Our Cribs?": Protecting Reproductive and Privacy Rights from State Interference

Those who opposed surrogacy framed their position as one against economic intrusions into family life and relationships. Surrogacy advocates *also* framed their position as one against the infiltration of outside forces into this private and personal realm. The interference surrogacy supporters opposed, however, was the burdensome involvement of the state in citizens' private lives. From their perspective, attempts by the state to ban commercial surrogacy violated individuals' and families' basic rights of privacy and reproductive freedom. Voicing this view at a New York hearing in the mid-1980s, David Scharf, a social worker and adoptive parent, said, "I believe that New York State should not promote or discourage surrogate parenting. We live in a free society and as we have learned in the past, government is not in the business to promote nor discourage what is essentially, I believe, a private issue."[82] The same commitment to the protection of privacy rights seems to have guided the recommendations provided in *Surrogate Parenting in New York State: A Proposal for Legislative Reform,* a report written by the New York State Senate Judiciary Committee just as national attention was starting to focus on the issue. "[S]urrogate parenting is a logical extension of the right to procreate, and accordingly, a part of the constitutional right of privacy," the report concluded.[83]

The use of a reproductive privacy rights framing to endorse a regulatory approach to surrogacy was common, particularly when supporters were voicing their opposition to legislation that would ban the practice. Assemblyman Balboni, for example, countered an early iteration of Assemblywoman Weinstein's anti–commercial surrogacy bill with the succinct comment, "It's the right of an individual to decide to have a family."[84] In 1992, Assemblyman Richard Brodsky (D) cited the loss of this right when he summed up his own and others' disappointment over the likely passage of a revised version of Weinstein's bill. "It is a sad day," he lamented during the floor debate, "when those of us who have valued the private rights of citizens to reproduce without interference of the state have come to the point of passing such a law."[85]

The protection of procreative decisions from government interference was framed as so fundamental that surrogacy supporters often wove references to the U.S. Constitution into their statements. Assemblyman William Parment (D), in comments made during the New York Assembly debate in 1992, traced the history of privacy rights to the Declaration of Independence and the Supreme Court decisions in *Griswold v. Connecticut* and *Roe v. Wade.*[86] In 1988, when the first version of Weinstein's bill was introduced, Assemblyman Balboni used this rhetorical strategy as well. He referenced Supreme Court decisions upholding reproductive rights to frame the issue as one concerning state interference in the private realm of the family, arguing that "just as the landmark case of Griswold v. Connecticut asked the question, what role should government play in our bedrooms, surrogate parenting will ask the question, what role should the government play in our cribs?"[87] Four years later, he again relied on this strategy, citing four high court decisions to bolster his opposition to the proposed legislative ban: "I think the United States Constitution considers reproduction, procreation to be a fundamental constitutional right.

The cases of Skinner v. Oklahoma, Carey v. Population Services, Griswold v. Connecticut, Danforth v. Missouri, all these cases talk about one of the fundamental rights being procreation."[88]

Legislators were not alone in using the cultural script of keeping the government out of family and procreative decisions as a way to challenge particular pieces of legislation. Robert Walmsley, an attorney involved with the three surrogacy cases under way in California courts when the state legislature was considering the surrogacy regulatory bill SB 937, pursued this approach in a letter to Governor Pete Wilson. In Walmsley's opinion, "[A] prohibition on surrogacy—and thus on infertile couples from resorting to the use of surrogacy, is seriously questionable, on constitutional grounds, as constituting *State action unjustifiably* interfering with the right of procreation."[89] This kind of support for protecting reproductive freedom from state interference was endorsed even by those who were ambivalent about the choices individuals might make. For instance, feminist lawyer Nadine Taub, referencing choice and women's rights, maintained that it was improper and even dangerous for the state to intrude into the personal realm of reproductive decision making: "I wonder, too, if respecting woman's autonomy isn't at least as important as respecting her reproductive freedom in according her dignity. Thus, even though as individuals we might want to persuade her not to undertake contract parenthood, I'm not at all sure that the State should determine in every case what that woman may do and require her to conform to the State's determination."[90] As these examples demonstrate, in the end, those who took up the "plight of infertile couples" frame of surrogacy drew on dominant notions of family privacy and the belief in a "natural" human desire to reproduce as the bases for asserting the existence of a fundamental right to have children without excessive state restrictions.[91]

As with the "baby-selling" frame, this way of understanding the problem of surrogacy—that it was an essential right for couples who otherwise would never be able to have children who shared their biological makeup—defined the available solutions. When surrogacy was framed as involving the plight of infertile couples, the rights to privacy and reproduction were paramount. At the same time, though, supporters of the practice readily recognized that couples, as well as the surrogate and child, could be misused and exploited. As a result, surrogacy advocates endorsed state regulation that was carefully crafted to ensure that these transactions could occur with as few problems as possible. The plight of infertile couples was thus a story about the inability of (certain) couples to reproduce and about the lack of sufficient laws to protect their rights to do so, including the right of all parties not to be exploited by unscrupulous brokers.

This need for limited state protection as part of the solution to the problem of surrogacy when framed as the plight of infertile couples is clear in a letter sent to Governor Wilson. In endorsing California's proposed regulatory bill, the letter's authors, Novelle and Rob Myerhoff, recounted their own experiences as proof that regulation was necessary: "Our first attempt with surrogacy was a fiasco. The problems was not surrogacy as an institution, but with the fact that surrogacy is unregulated. . . . [T]here were very few surrogacy programs to choose from. . . . We chose the one that seemed the best, but they did not properly screen the surrogate. . . . [S]he turned out to be running a scam on us. . . . Had there been a bill such as SB 937, it is unlikely this would have happened."[92] Holiday Jackson, a woman who was in the process of using a gestational surrogate, also alluded to the need for protection from possible economic exploitation. In her letter to Governor Wilson in support of SB 937, she wrote, "We are very concerned about the passage of this bill to protect our own rights as well as to protect surrogates from being taken advantage of."[93] Women who acted as surrogates also embraced the position that the problem of surrogate parenting was its inadequate regulation. This is clear, for instance, in the closing remarks made by Jan Sutton of the National Association of Surrogate Mothers at a California hearing: "We are telling you we want certain protections, but you must afford us dignity of participating in alternative forms of reproduction [that are properly regulated] if we see fit to do so."[94]

Opponents of surrogate motherhood, however, rejected state regulation, deeming it an inappropriate policy solution for what they saw as a problem involving baby selling. They charged that such permissive regulatory social policy would give the state exactly the kind of intrusive control over reproductive decision-making that surrogacy advocates found so repellent. Assemblywoman Weinstein's defense of her anti–commercial surrogacy bill stated this argument explicitly:

> Banning fees for women and barring brokering activity will discourage commercial surrogacy, even if the practice is not eliminated. In contrast,

> a regulatory approach would explicitly endorse the practice, lending the authority of both the courts and the legislature to uphold the arrangements. Moreover, as revealed by an examination of bills embodying a regulatory approach, this response enmeshes both branches of the government in details, procedure and substance of the agreements. Far from ensuring government neutrality or nonintervention, it guarantees that government will be intimately involved with the practice and the decisions encompassed by the agreements.[95]

Here too, then, both sides of the debate over surrogacy shared an important belief. Both saw the state as responsible for shielding reproductive processes and family relations from coercive and/or corruptive influences.

In summary, the "baby-selling" frame emphasized the birth mother's relation to the child, the monetary compensation she would receive for surrendering her parental claims, and the possibility of a future custody battle between two genetic parents whose only ties to one another were those specified in a broker-supplied contractual agreement. According to this frame, surrogate motherhood was a no-win situation in which commercial relations—the acts of baby buying and baby selling—necessarily distorted the private realm of the family, as would state regulation of the practice. Therefore, the only acceptable policy solution to the problem of surrogate motherhood was to ban the practice. The "plight of infertile couples" frame, on the other hand, emphasized a couple's legitimate and natural desire for a child of their own and the current inability of the law to secure their rights to a child who would not exist if it were not for their use of surrogacy. In this frame, the problem to be solved was inadequate laws that impeded reproduction within a family unit. Consequently, this framing told a story that emphasized the need for laws that would specify and protect the rights of those involved in surrogate practices. Underlying both frames was a shared ideological belief in the private nature of family relations and reproductive processes. This common belief in turn led also to a shared blindness to racial privilege embedded in each framing of surrogacy.

In most modern societies, the family is considered a bedrock institution—a social arrangement that provides for the ongoing reproduction and socialization of new members of the group and thus helps ensure social stability and continuity. In the United States, the family has, in addition, been viewed as a "haven in a heartless world," a sanctuary from the depersonalization and rationalization of a capitalist economy and a refuge from the complex and sometimes dangerous world of politics.[96] Viviana Zelizer's study of the twentieth-century cultural transformation of childhood shows that children were placed outside the world of fiscal concerns when the cultural belief in their sentimental value replaced the previously dominant view of them as economically valuable. Zelizer argues that, with this shift toward perceiving children as "sacred," practices interpreted as "baby selling" become defined as social problems.[97] Similarly, Sharon Hays argues that the ideological distinction between home and world is manifested in the belief that children are to be protected from the ruthless logic of the market and that this in turn leads to an ideology of intensive mothering. More specifically, she maintains that motherhood is frequently the arena in which our society's general ambivalence about market rationality and competitive self-interest is played out.[98]

Other research, such as Mitchell Stevens's study of home-schoolers, confirms the existence of social ambivalence about the overarching reach of economic forces and values. Stevens's work also demonstrates that this uncertainty is not limited to one political perspective. Both the liberal and conservative branches of the home-schooling movement agree on the sanctity of children and the need to protect them, as well as the family generally, from the competitive self-interest of the outside world.[99] Historian Eileen Boris's work is relevant as well. Her investigation of the rhetorical debate over American mothers' employment in paid labor (e.g., garment making) done in their private homes in the mid–twentieth century documents the entrenched belief in the importance of keeping motherhood unsullied and thus separate from the commercial world. Boris found that culturally idealized views of motherhood as a privatized, personal, and affective practice that should not be interfered with shaped the views of those on both sides of the debate. Responses to working at home varied precisely because each side defined the threat of outside forces differently. On the one hand, supporters of industrial homework opposed state regulation because it symbolized the invasion of the state into the private realm of the family, an arena that should be immune to social policy interference. On the other hand, opponents of industrial homework saw the factory and office, symbols of the economic world of the capitalist marketplace, as the unwanted intruders into the private and sacrosanct space of the family.[100]

The debate over surrogate motherhood, as we have seen, also drew on culturally dominant notions of the family as a private sphere that should not be interfered with by outside forces. Thus, much as with the question of industrial homework, those on both sides of the surrogacy debate shared the goal of protecting family relations from outside intrusions. Therefore, *both* supporters and opponents of surrogacy used rhetoric that drew on and reproduced the dominant ideology of a public/private divide. Within this ideological framework, commercial transactions and family relations occupy separate spheres, children are deemed precious, motherhood is defined more as a calling than as a biologically determined status—and class- and race-based privilege goes unacknowledged and unexamined. Although some participants, particularly several antisurrogacy feminists, were aware of the class and racial dimensions of the issue, the "baby-selling" and "plight of infertile couples" frames generally drew uncritically on narrow notions of procreative rights and the privacy of families. Few on either side questioned whether these rights existed equally for all members of American society or whether the legalization of private reproduction options would promote some groups' reproduction while thwarting the reproduction of others.

These shared understandings regarding rights and privilege help explain why the emergence of surrogate motherhood was viewed as a social problem by those on each side of the debate. The extent to which supporters and opponents of surrogacy embraced the same cultural assumptions suggests that conflict in late-twentieth-century reproductive politics did not necessarily represent a clash of mutually exclusive worldviews. Instead, overlap between and contradictions within the two frames of surrogacy may be responsible for the difficulty U.S. legislators had in formulating and passing legislation to address this social problem. Because they respected reproductive freedom and privacy, most proponents of the "baby-selling" frame had no objection to surrogacy arrangements that were altruistic (i.e., noncommercial). Moreover, they, as well as proponents of commercial surrogacy, sought to minimize state regulation of and control over reproductive arrangements. This overlapping interest probably contributed to the difficulty in developing consensus over the exact nature of state involvement in regulating surrogacy arrangements. In the end, the emphasis on either economic or state intrusions into the realm of the family shaped the framings of and policy responses to surrogate motherhood. Why and when does one frame prevail over the other? The next two chapters provide answers to this question by comparing the very different legislative responses that took shape in New York and California.

Chapter 4 | COMPETING FRAMES OF SURROGACY

Comparing Newspapers' Coverage of "Horror Stories"

Over sixty years ago, sociologist Robert Park argued that the news constitutes an important source of our knowledge about the world.[1] More recent studies note both the media's influence in bringing public and political attention to a particular social problem and its "agenda-setting role."[2] Print and broadcast media tell us not so much how to think as what to think about. For instance, in their pioneering work on the power of the media, Maxwell McCombs and Donald Shaw found a positive relationship between media coverage of issues and salience of topics to voters.[3] Others have identified similarly significant influences on the perceptions of government elites.[4] The media, then, are important claims makers because they choose what events to report and the extent of coverage given to any specific issue.[5] Moreover, by publishing accounts of "horror stories" and "dramatic events," the media not only bring attention to an issue "assumed to be pregnant with meaning for the general public"[6] but also evoke strong emotional reactions to it.[7] Focusing news coverage on these kinds of events has important consequences. These stories come to define what is at stake: "Our attitudes toward social problems often reflect our reactions to such 'typical' cases; the example comes to represent the larger problem."[8]

The practice of surrogate parenting, as previous chapters have explained, touches on issues that have great meaning for both lawmakers and the general public—ideas, beliefs, and conflicts about family (e.g., Who are a child's mother and father? To what lengths should a couple go to have a child?). In this transitional period, the number and type of stories covered and the interpretations of events provided by the media significantly shaped individuals' understanding of surrogacy as a social problem. This chapter clarifies the role of the media by comparing the coverage and content of stories about surrogate motherhood in major newspapers on both coasts.[9] The analysis shows how happenstance and the contingent nature of local incidents, personalities, and controversies helped determine which definition of the problem emerged as dominant. Newspapers might only tell us what to think about, but particular news stories (i.e., horror stories) may influence the way we think about a certain issue.

Why focus on horror stories? In part, this is an analytical decision. Dramatic events are ones that are most likely to rivet the public's imagination and create strong reactions to a given social problem. Media coverage of surrogate parenting, particularly the horror stories that focus on custodial disputes over surrogate-born children, reflected and reinforced anxieties over the future of motherhood and the family in an era of rapidly changing beliefs about women's roles and the decline of the normative nuclear family.[10] In addition, surrogacy stories involving biological and racial themes seemed to captivate the public. A second important reason to focus on horror stories is empirical. The great majority of the coverage that appeared in the *New York Times, Los Angeles Times,* and *Washington Post* focused on stories of this sort. Between 1986 and 1992, the period of peak newspaper coverage on surrogate motherhood, horror stories constituted 71 percent of the articles about surrogacy in both the *New York Times* and the *Los Angeles Times* and 62 percent of the stories covered in the *Washington Post.*

In comparing print media coverage of surrogacy, this chapter focuses on two prominent disputes—the Baby M case, tried in New Jersey, and *Johnson v. Calvert,* tried in California. Regionally based quantitative and qualitative differences in the newspaper coverage of these two surrogate parenting custody battles influenced how the problem of surrogacy was perceived in each state. Both court cases were local dramatic events and critical discourse moments[11] that shaped the dominant framing of surrogate parenting in different ways in New York and California. At the same, it is clear that despite differences in the horrors and the frames, underlying the telling of each news story about surrogacy were traditional constructions of family, kinship ties, motherhood, gender, and race.

SURROGACY AND THE STORY OF BABY M: "BABY SELLING"

Media accounts of the Baby M custody dispute in 1987 were what introduced most Americans to the world of surrogate parenting, but newspaper coverage of surrogacy dates back to the late 1970s and early 1980s. The *New York Times* and *Los Angeles Times* briefly covered the case of Elizabeth Kane in the early 1980s, when Kane was being touted as the first known surrogate. Although the arrangement was novel, there was little controversy over Kane, who at the time was an enthusiastic supporter of surrogacy.[12] Stories about her and about surrogate motherhood created interest but not an onslaught of media attention. In 1981 and 1982, respectively, only seven articles each year appeared in the *Los Angeles Times;* meanwhile, the *New York Times* ran eight stories on surrogacy in 1981 and one in 1982. During the rest of the decade, neither these two newspapers nor the *Washington Post* ran more than a handful of articles yearly. This all changed with the Baby M case. During the custody trial in 1987, newspaper coverage of surrogate parenting peaked, with 69 articles on the topic appearing in the *Los Angeles Times,* 70 in the *Washington Post,* and 131 in the *New York Times.* As a result, the struggle between Mary Beth Whitehead and William and Elizabeth Stern over the custody of Baby M (see the introduction for a description of the case) can be viewed as instrumental in making surrogate motherhood a permanent fixture in the American vocabulary and consciousness. The Baby M case served as a critical discourse moment in the public understanding of surrogacy as a social problem, and this horror story affected how the problem came to be framed.

When the press first reported the Baby M case, competing views toward surrogate motherhood were presented. One definition focused on the commercial aspects of the transaction and considered surrogacy to be baby selling; another definition focused on the desire of infertile couples to have children and on surrogates' altruism in helping these couples. For instance, near the start of the Baby M trial, the *New York Times* ran an editorial with the headline "Giving Love, or Selling Life?" The editors questioned, rhetorically, "Is bearing a child for someone unable to do so a 'gift of love' as its enthusiasts suggest? Or is it simply baby-selling?"[13] Two weeks later, the editorial page of the *Los Angeles Times* queried, "Is it proper for women to rent out their wombs in this way? Or should this be viewed as a good way for a childless couple to have a baby?"[14] These editorials reflect the unresolved nature of the definition of surrogate parenting and the uncertainty over what its potential problems might be. Both newspapers hint at possible conflict over different constructs of family, motherhood, and paternity. On the one hand, surrogate motherhood represented an infertile couple's "natural" desire to complete their family with a child; on the other hand, commercial surrogacy represented the purchase of a baby, since the birth mother sold her maternal rights to the child once it had been born.

These competing frames—baby selling versus the plight of infertile couples—that were evident in news coverage of surrogate motherhood were prevalent during coverage of the Baby M custody trial. For instance, during the Baby M trial, an article in the *New York Times* "Week in Review" section discussed the lack of consensus on the issue and identified the tension between the contrasting approaches and alternative frames: "Most people agree that new means of helping infertile couples procreate should be pursued, while almost everybody is against measures that would devalue life by making babies into commodities."[15] A second "Week in Review" piece appeared in the wake of the New Jersey Superior Court's decision validating the surrogacy contract, severing Whitehead's claims to Baby M, and awarding full custody to the Sterns. That article included excerpts from interviews a *New York Times* reporter had conducted with people who held differing views about surrogacy. Barbara Katz Rothman, feminist and sociologist, for example, expressed concern over "baby selling." She was quoted as saying, "It's terribly sad and terribly frightening to see a state in the business of upholding these contracts. It's sad enough that we've constructed for ourselves a world in which motherhood is up for sale." The quote from prosurrogacy law professor Lori Andrews emphasized the "plight of the infertile." "I think it was a very brave decision," Andrews asserted, " . . . It is important to remember that the only reason that the child is on earth is because of the Sterns' desire for the child. They wanted the child as part of their family."[16]

In the early coverage of surrogate motherhood, the gravest concern expressed in the media regarded the lack of legislation. Reports on surrogate parenting, particularly those around the Baby M trial, blamed the conflict on this legal vacuum. For instance, in reports two days apart, both on the Baby M case, *New York Times* readers were told, "The tangle over the agreement stems from the absence of laws on surrogacy here and in all other states,"[17] and "The case has prompted intense debate on the legal and moral implications of new reproductive technology. It has also prompted calls for swift legislative action that would prevent other children from being caught in similar tug-of-wars."[18] Using more dramatic language, a *Washington Post* columnist depicted the chaos fomented by the lack of laws:

> The ultimate tragedy is that this case should never have happened. The Sterns and the Whiteheads are in court not because of some unavoidable dispute over a child, but because the New Jersey Legislature, like others throughout the country, has failed to come to grips with the phenomenon of surrogate motherhood. Despite the birth of more than 500 children in this manner and despite every indication that the procedure is here to stay, there simply is no law on the subject. In most states, it is more legally complicated to open a hot dog stand than to produce a child by surrogate motherhood.[19]

In writing about the Baby M case, news reporters often constructed the problem of surrogacy as one shaped not simply by the absence of laws but by the combination of swift advances in medical science and slow changes in legal regulation. Two clear examples from the *Washington Post* and the *New York Times* are, respectively, "[The Baby M case] vividly illustrates the difficulty faced by a judge acting in a legal void, when scientific progress has outpaced legislative response,"[20] and "[N]ew issues such as surrogate motherhood dramatized by the Baby M trial have shown how changes in technology and social practice have outrun jurisprudence and legislation."[21]

Despite this emphasis on the lack of laws specifically dealing with surrogate motherhood, in covering the Baby M case the news media did not necessarily endorse prohibiting surrogacy as the best solution. In fact, most coverage addressed the importance of properly regulating the process, not banning it per se. For example, near the beginning of the Baby M case, a *New York Times* reporter wrote, "Legal experts say the Stern-Whitehead dispute is one bound to arise when surrogates are used, and that it points out the need for legislation. They say there is a specific need for laws regulating the enforceability of surrogate contracts, the legal obligation of the parties involved and the legality of payment to surrogates."[22] Indeed, at the time of this sensational case, many hoped that the publicity created by the Baby M trial would prompt policy makers to act to end the existing legislative vacuum. A front-page story in the *Los Angeles Times* took just this position: "Modern surrogate mothers . . . as well as legislators and litigators, want a more certain structure of law to protect the rights of the parents, the children and the public. Virtually none exists. . . . [T]he greater hope is that the Baby M case will prod action by legislatures that have wrestled reluctantly with surrogacy proposals for half a dozen years."[23]

Clearly, media coverage of surrogate motherhood in the 1980s, and of Baby M in particular, captured competing visions of the practice. At this point, though, the press did not strongly suggest that the solution to this newly discovered social problem was to ban commercial surrogacy. Yet, as chapter 1 documented, a surge of legislative bills accompanied the unfolding story of the Baby M battle, and the tenor of these bills changed direction from acceptance of to hostility toward the practice. The question, then, is, Why did sentiment on surrogacy shift toward a position that predominantly viewed the practice within a "baby-selling" frame? One very important factor, most likely, was the Baby M case itself. This custody battle was a dramatic event that aided in the telling of a particular story about surrogacy, one that lent support to those defining surrogacy as a type of "crass commerce" that needed to be banned, and thus influenced a dominant framing of "baby selling." At the same time, this case reveals dominant discourses and assumptions about children, maternity, kinship, genetics, race, and class that continue to shape reproductive politics in the twenty-first century.

Several aspects of the telling of the Baby M horror story are especially important. Two of these aspects are closely related. First, the case depicted a woman who seemed willing to exchange a child she gave birth to for a sum of money. As described in the New Jersey Supreme Court decision, "The contract provided that through artificial insemination using Mr. Stern's sperm, Mrs. Whitehead would become pregnant, carry the child to term, bear it, deliver it to the Sterns, and thereafter do whatever was necessary to terminate her maternal rights."[24] Mary Beth Whitehead was to receive $10,000 for conceiving and gestating the baby. Second, the Baby

M case told a story about the Sterns and baby buying. William and Elizabeth Stern were seen as an upper-middle-class couple who purchased a child. "Mr. Stern, on his part, agreed to attempt the artificial insemination and to pay Mrs. Whitehead $10,000 after the child's birth, on its delivery to him. In a separate contract, Mr. Stern agreed to pay $7,500 to the Infertility Center of New York."[25]

These two characteristics of surrogate parenting transactions were thoroughly covered by the media. A *New York Times* editorial titled "On Bearing Someone Else's Baby" began, "Elizabeth Stern, a 40-year old New Jersey pediatrician, cannot bear a child. Mary Beth Whitehead, a 30-year old housewife, can. So, with the Infertility Center of New York acting as agent, Mr. and Mrs. Stern leased Mrs. Whitehead's reproductive potential for $10,000. She was to be artificially inseminated with Mr. Stern's sperm, bear the baby and then give it to the Sterns."[26] Similarly, a *Los Angeles Times* editorial on the case summarized, "William and Elizabeth Stern wanted a child but couldn't have one because of Mrs. Stern's health. Instead, they agreed to pay $10,000 to Mary Beth Whitehead to be artificially inseminated by Mr. Stern, to carry and bear the child and then turn it over to the Sterns."[27] Excerpts from the New Jersey Supreme Court decision reported in the newspapers also emphasized that the transaction entailed "baby selling": "Mr. Stern knew he was paying for the adoption of a child; Mrs. Whitehead knew she was accepting money so that child might be adopted; the Infertility Center knew that it was being paid for assisting in the adoption of a child."[28]

These were not the only aspects of the story of Baby M that were reported, however. During the trial, a key part of the story line revolved around the Sterns', particularly William Stern's, desire to have a child, and specifically one to whom he was biologically related. This "need" for genetic kinship and progeny, a potential basis for the framing of surrogacy as being about the plight of infertile couples, also was reported by the press. Coverage of his testimony at the custody trial and subsequent descriptions of William Stern noted his "natural" desire to biologically reproduce. In particular, newspaper accounts of the trial reported that given the impact of World War II on his family, Stern's "infertility plight" was particularly compelling: "William Stern had a particular reason for wishing a child with his genes. Most of his family was wiped out in Nazi death camps";[29] "it was compelling for him to have a child because he has no blood relatives 'anywhere in the world.' Stern was born in Berlin shortly after World War II, the only child of two survivors of the Holocaust in Nazi Germany";[30] and "he wanted a child biologically related to him so that his family would not die out."[31] Stern's narrative resonated with culturally dominant notions of genetic kinship and the "natural" desire to biologically reproduce. These claims were also implicitly gendered—the only way for men to claim biological kinship is through genetic ties. That his background included the horrors of the Holocaust and the attempted genocide of Jews meant that Stern's version of the story also drew on a particular racial-ethnic narrative likely to evoke much sympathy.[32]

Still, William Stern was not the only actor in the story of Baby M with a compelling narrative rooted in "natural" needs and gender-based biological ties. The strength of Mary Beth Whitehead's biological maternal instinct over the crassness of commercial and contractually formed parental relations was a very prominent story line as well. Newspaper accounts of Whitehead's testimony frequently focused on the primacy of maternal bonding, as this excerpt shows: "'At the end, something took over,' the New Jersey housewife testified today. 'I guess it was just being a mother. . . . It overpowered me. . . . I just cried and cried. I didn't want the $10,000. I just wanted my child.'"[33] For some, Whitehead was "a symbol of maternal instinct."[34] Indeed, several columnists commenting on the case drew on this naturalized discourse of maternal-infant bonding to account for their sympathies toward Whitehead and their critical views toward commercial surrogacy: "The mother must not be deprived of her baby, to which she is now bonded in the natural way,"[35] one argued; another wrote, "Also on trial, however, is the validity and worth of the bond between a mother and child, the most fundamental bond in the perpetuation of the human species. . . . That this is being questioned in this case is truly extraordinary, but it serves to underscore the fact that surrogate motherhood violates the most fundamental instinctual drives of women";[36] and a third explained, "I believe Mary Beth Whitehead, a surrogate mother, when she says she really did intend to surrender her child until after it was born. . . . [I]nstinct overruled commerce, and she changed her mind."[37]

In the end, although competing discourses were present in media accounts from the beginning of the coverage of the Baby M case, by the time the trial was over, the "baby-selling" frame and associated concerns about commodified reproduction dominated. Public reaction toward surrogacy that took shape around the Baby M case eventually tilted toward an endorsement of the views that parental relationships are supposed to be free of commercial transactions; that a price tag had been put on a human life; that Whitehead had agreed to sell her child for a sum of money; that the Sterns had sought to purchase a child with their money; and that enforcement of such a contract would signal the triumph of commercial relations over the "natural" and sacrosanct maternal-child bond. Surrogate parenting thus became a story about an arrangement that seemed morally unredeemable—it was baby selling.

Another factor that encouraged the predominant use of the "baby-selling" frame to tell the story of the Baby M case was the commercial basis of the original arrangement. The Whitehead-Stern transaction had been brokered by the Infertility Center of New York (ICNY), a professional surrogate parenting agency owned and operated by attorney Noel Keane: "The Center's advertising campaigns solicit surrogate mothers and encourage infertile couples to consider surrogacy. ICNY arranged for the surrogacy contract by bringing the parties together, explaining the process to them, furnishing the contractual form, and providing legal counsel."[38] As the case unfolded, it was revealed that Whitehead had expressed doubts about her ability to relinquish a child even before she had entered into a surrogacy relationship with the Sterns. A psychological report on Whitehead, commissioned by ICNY, stated that she "expects to have strong feelings about giving up the baby at the end."[39] Despite this evaluation, ICNY accepted Whitehead as a surrogate. The Sterns did not question their surrogate's credentials. As William Stern put it, "They [ICNY] said she was approved. We assumed the expertise on their part."[40] Consequently, as reported in the press, surrogacy became a story of commercial interests run amok. Given the evidence that those responsible for screening potential surrogates were more interested in profits than in taking proper precautions, surrogate parenting was a problem that could be fixed only by discouraging such arrangements in the first place. Banning commercial surrogacy would eliminate agencies and brokers whose only interests were pecuniary—thereby severely curtailing the practice and any possible problems (i.e., custody disputes).

The involvement of ICNY—and especially of Noel Keane—in this highly publicized case cast a negative light on the role of surrogacy brokers and surrogacy practices in general. Keane's notoriety did not stem from this case alone, however. As early as 1981, his name had surfaced in a case where the surrogate changed her mind while still pregnant and the couple petitioned for custody. According to the *Los Angeles Times,* this case "was the first of its kind in the United States." The husband involved withdrew his paternity suit just before the ruling was to be made, when it was revealed that his wife was a transsexual.[41] Keane's name continued to be connected with controversial surrogate parenting arrangements. Two years later, a second case (briefly described in chapter 1) arose. That one involved a dispute over a congenitally deformed baby that initially all parties refused to claim.[42] Another surrogacy transaction arranged by Keane was contested in 1988, just after the infamous Baby M trial. In this third dispute, a surrogate mother, Patty Nowakowski, successfully fought for the custody of the fraternal twins she gave birth to after the adoptive couple, who already had three sons, took home only the girl and sent the boy to foster care.[43] A *Washington Post* column entitled "Nature Too Chancy for Contracts" made the association of Keane with this horror story as well as the Baby M case clear: "We can now add another sad story to the growing lists of reasons that surrogate motherhood is a bad answer to infertility problems. . . . The baby broker involved in this situation was Noel Keane, the Dearborn, Mich., lawyer who arranged the 'Baby M' case that backfired when the birth mother decided she could not give up the baby."[44]

Keane's direct association with multiple surrogate parenting transactions that went awry did more than generate negative press for surrogate motherhood. His poor record also helped spur legislators to take an antisurrogacy stance. For instance, when Michigan became the first state to declare involvement in surrogate parenting arrangements a felony, a *Los Angeles Times* headline emphasized that this policy response was a direct reaction to Keane's practice in their state: "Michigan Outlaws Surrogate Maternity Contracts; Ban Aimed at 'Baby M' Clinic."[45] The story reported that "[t]he bill's sponsor in the Michigan state Senate admitted Monday that the legislation was aimed specifically at shutting down the Dearborn, Mich., surrogate clinic run by attorney Noel Keane, who arranged the Baby M Surrogate contract." The *Los Angeles Times* also linked Keane's slipshod practices to the brief legislative attention given to commercial surrogacy by the U.S. Congress in the late 1980s: "On Feb. 3, the first anniversary of the Whitehead decision by the New Jersey Supreme Court, a bill was introduced in Congress to ban the practice of paying a woman to conceive. The bill is aimed primarily at baby brokers such as Noel Keane who arranged the Whitehead surrogacy in New York City."[46]

Most of the dozen or so surrogacy disputes that went to court in the 1980s and early 1990s were associated with Keane, and others in the business resented the bad publicity his activities brought to the practice.[47] Several used the media to distance their centers from Keane, his practice, and the publicized cases that had gone awry, hoping to preserve their own programs' reputations and legitimacy. A *Washington Post* story provides an example of this strategy: "Those who support surrogacy say the opposition has sprung up because of a few bad situations. . . . The bad cases might never have occurred if those arranging surrogacy had held to higher standards, said Dr. Betsy Aigen, director of the Surrogate Mother Program in New York City and one of the founders of a new group called the American Organization of Surrogate Parenting Practitioners."[48]

Indeed, much of the hostility directed toward surrogate motherhood, and Keane in particular, was due to the lack of screening that occurred in arrangements he brokered. Wiley Beane, an attorney representing two surrogates filing lawsuits against Keane, one involving a "woman who was accepted into Keane's program even though she had had a long string of pregnancies by the time she was 24," specifically directed his criticism to how ICNY was run: "When Keane allows women to get into his program when they shouldn't, just because they need the money, then there is something wrong."[49] Another article noted that Keane appeared unperturbed by what others considered lax standards: "Noel Keane . . . admits he does minimal pre-sign-up screening of the surrogates—some he never even meets before these Saturday morning matchups."[50] Similarly, a *New York Times* story provided the following perspective from Keane's competitors about the consequences of the "loose" way he ran his surrogate matching: "[E]ven while Keane is coming under mounting criticism for running an operation that his competitors charge is so loosely controlled that he is now the target of at least four lawsuits. . . . some smaller operations in the surrogate parenting field say Keane's high-pressure practice of throwing surrogates and couples together to be matched before the surrogate has been psychologically and medically screened can lead to disasters like the Baby M case."[51]

In sum, the dominant frame of surrogate motherhood that emerged from the Baby M case was a story of "crass commerce"—a process guided solely by financial motivations. Commercial surrogacy was not acceptable because it was contrary to dominant norms regarding reproduction and maternal-child relations. Surrogate parenting was perceived as a problem that needed to be stopped. Consequently, in the political arena, the policy response was a ban on commercial surrogacy. However, another horror story, one that arose from a different surrogate custody dispute, appeared in the media a few years later. This dramatic event provided an alternative framing for surrogate motherhood and thus opened the possibility for other types of policy responses to the problem of surrogate parenting.

SURROGACY AND *JOHNSON V. CALVERT:* THE PLIGHT OF INFERTILE COUPLES

In 1990, after the publicity surrounding Baby M had subsided, a surrogate parenting dispute in California involving Anna Johnson and Crispina and Mark Calvert began to receive media attention. Except for the period of the Baby M trial (spanning the years 1986 through 1988), the most extensive national news coverage of surrogacy occurred during 1990.[52] This spike in media coverage indicates that the dispute between Ms. Johnson and the Calverts can be considered another critical discourse moment in the social construction of surrogate motherhood. *Johnson v. Calvert,* like the Baby M case, was a custodial battle over a surrogate-born child (see chapter 1 for an overview of this lawsuit). Once again, issues of motherhood, paternity, and family were brought to the fore. However, this horror story had a different set of actors and plots, and these became the basis for an alternative framing of surrogate motherhood. This section examines how the specific ingredients of this dramatic event opened up the space for different understandings and reactions to the problem of surrogate parenting.

The most important factor, at least explicitly, that distinguished the Johnson-Calvert case from the Baby M case was that, unlike Mary Beth Whitehead, Anna Johnson, the surrogate, was not genetically related to the baby she gave birth to and sought custody of. The description of the transaction provided in the lower court ruling specifies the parties' intended relations to the surrogate-born child: "During the fall and winter of 1989–1990 Anna Johnson and a married couple, Crispina and Mark Calvert, met and discussed entering into an agreement whereby Anna would serve as a surrogate and carry the *Calverts' fertilized the[sic] embryo to term.* Anna was to be paid $10,000 for doing so, and the child would go to the Calverts and Anna would claim no interest in the child."[53] Newspaper stories drew explicit comparisons between the two types of surrogacy arrangements (gestational vs. traditional surrogacy) and the two court cases (Baby M vs. the Johnson-Calvert battle). In particular, the media contrasted the two different types of claims for motherhood—one founded on genetics and one not—made in the two cases:

> The decision . . . marked the first time in the nation that a judge has had to decide the rights of a surrogate mother who is genetically unrelated to the baby she bears. In most surrogate arrangements, including the famous Baby M case in New Jersey, a woman's own egg is artificially inseminated, so she is the *child's genetic mother.*[54]

> Unlike the Orange County case, previous court rulings, such as the Baby M. decision in New Jersey, have centered on surrogate mothers who provided the ovum and so had a *genetic claim to motherhood.*[55]

> Attorneys in the case said it is unprecedented because Johnson is seeking custody of a child to whom she has no genetic link. In the Baby M case in New Jersey, the surrogate seeking custody was the *baby's genetic mother.*[56]

The clear distinction that media accounts drew between the types of surrogacy arrangements involved, as well as differences in the "horrors" the two stories described, laid the groundwork for the emergence of an understanding of the problem of surrogacy quite different from the one associated with the Baby M case.

Although the two cases centered on a disputed surrogacy arrangement, the plots of the two stories differed in ways that proved to be very important. In the Baby M case, the horror focused on was that an enforcement of the contract between the Whiteheads and the Sterns could signal a commodification and commercialization of kinship relations. In the Johnson-Calvert case, on the other hand, the horror focused on was the possibility of a dramatic change in the criteria used to determine parenthood. As reported by the media, the Johnson-Calvert story was about an unprecedented inability to definitively define parental rights toward children. This definitional chaos was neatly captured in the subheading to a newspaper article describing the trial's opening: "Hearing may lead to redefinition of 'parent.'"[57] At the same time, the possibility that the number of people who could be deemed a child's parents was subject to change added its own aspect of horror to this dramatic event. An editorial in the *Los Angeles Times* expressed the magnitude of the custody decision and its implications for the meaning of *parent* with this allusion to a well-known biblical story: "The custody issue before Solomon was difficult enough. . . . [Judge Parslow] is trying to decide an issue almost as vexing. That is the possibility that a test tube baby could be found to have three parents—its genetic mother and father, and the birth mother who carried the fetus to term."[58]

This media focus did not mean, of course, that there was only one way to frame the Johnson-Calvert horror story, or even that the story constituted a horror. In fact, as noted in chapter 3, some commentators explicitly championed the expansion of the definition of family relations that the case implied. In a *Los Angeles Times* op-ed, Ramona Ripston, executive director of the Southern California American Civil Liberties Union (ACLU), located surrogacy's historical place in changing kinship relations and family transformations over the later half of the twentieth century. At the same time, she also endorsed a radical redefinition of what could be said to constitute a family:

> It's been decades since the American family could be described as one working father, one homemaking mother and several—usually two to four—kids. In recent years, the definition has expanded to include divorced parents, extended step families, gay and lesbian couples and their children, and now in a new twist, adults brought together by virtue of a surrogate parenting contract. What's new about this familial relationship is that it involves three people who can accurately claim to be the actual parents of one baby. . . . The man and woman who provided the sperm and egg clearly are parents. And the woman who provided her womb and physically nurtured and gave birth to the baby, and in the process bonded with it, clearly is a parent. The reality of these three claims challenges our notions about parenthood and families. And it's the confusion generated by this challenge that has led to debates about who the rightful parents are. . . . The answer to that question is clear: All three individuals are parents.[59]

Thus, as with the Baby M custody trial, newspaper accounts captured the divided ways this dramatic event could be told and interpreted—in this case, as either a threat to or an expansion of viable family formations.

Ripston's conclusions notwithstanding, most media accounts of the Johnson-Calvert case did not endorse a "three-parent family." Instead, there were competing claims over whether gestation or genetics should determine parental status. This central definitional debate was elucidated in a *Los Angeles Times* article that reported on the arguments made by the lawyers on each side of the case. The story recounted that Johnson's attorney "argued that it does not matter how a woman becomes pregnant or whose genetic material composes the embryo. The act of giving birth and the inevitable bond a woman makes to the fetus confers the rights of a mother." As a result, much as in the Baby M case, maternal-child bonding was used to naturalize Johnson's relationship to the baby (i.e., her lawyers stressed the intrinsic relationship between a mother and her child that evolves "naturally" as a result of gestation) and to bolster her claim for custody of the newborn. The same article, however, also included a persuasive rebuttal to this position. In fact, the argument supporting the Calverts' "natural" claim for custody and parental status was the more viable of the two: "[T]he Calverts' lawyer. . . . took the opposite view, saying a couple's sperm and egg are 'the most precious thing they have . . . their genetic heritage.' He said Johnson was trying to steal the Calverts' child, and that permitting it would be against public policy."[60]

Given the strong use of maternal-child bonding to criticize surrogate motherhood in the Baby M case (and to legitimate sympathy for Whitehead), what happened to these claims in the Johnson-Calvert dispute? They were minimized and criticized from two separate angles. First, the claim of maternal bonding was acknowledged as important in determining parental status. However, in Johnson's case, it was argued that no such bonding existed. Therefore, not only did she not qualify as a prospective parent, but she might even be a bad mother. This argument was reported as part of the coverage of a psychiatrist's testimony during the custody trial. Explaining why this expert witness considered Johnson's claim to the baby both invalid and suspect, a *Los Angeles Times* reporter wrote:

> Dr. Justin D. Call . . . said he is suspicious of Johnson's claim to a deep bond with the infant because of a statement she made in a newspaper interview and

> a letter she wrote to the baby's genetic parents. . . . Johnson told The Times in early August, when she was seven months pregnant, that she did not feel bonded to the fetus because it was not made from her genetic material. . . . Call . . . said Johnson's statement "very clearly supports the idea that the mother has not made an attachment to the child." Lack of bonding by seven months into the pregnancy would "carry a very bad prognosis for continuing attachment after birth," Call said. . . . "A reasonable person should be very circumspect about giving a woman full responsibility for a child she had not made a normal attachment to during pregnancy."[61]

Second, the legitimacy and the persuasiveness of Johnson's claim were challenged using arguments concerning the primacy of genetics in determining kinship relations. For instance, the Calverts' lawyer charged that taking a child who possessed the couple's DNA amounted to theft. In this telling, the horror story successfully drew on increasingly salient cultural beliefs and assumptions about genetic determinism. Even though Anna Johnson had gestated the fetus for nine months, in the end, her claim to the child was viewed as less valid than the Calverts' because the child was not "biologically" hers. In his decision, Judge Parslow argued that a non-genetic birth mother is not a real or legal parent. He wrote that "a surrogate carrying a genetic child for a couple does not acquire parental rights." In his oral statement to the court, Parslow elaborated on his reasoning: "Anna Johnson is the gestational carrier of the child, a host in a sense, as some writers put it, and . . . she and the child are *genetic hereditary strangers*. . . . I further find that Anna's relationship to the child is analogous to that of a *foster parent* providing care, protection and nurture during the period of time that the *natural mother*, Crispina Calvert, was unable to care for the child."[62] The judge decided the case in favor of the Calverts, severing all of Johnson's claims to the child. Because he was ruling on gestational surrogacy, as opposed to traditional surrogacy, which was involved in the Baby M case, Parslow was able to forge a new way of thinking about parenthood—at least as regards mothers. In particular, for legal purposes, he separated the maternal role of childbearing from that of genetic ties, favoring the latter.

The *Los Angeles Times* immediately picked up this framework for understanding surrogate motherhood, running the headline "Ruling Brightens Aspect of Surrogate Parenting: Judge Says It Isn't Inherently Exploitative for a Couple Who Can't Have Children on Their Own to Rent the Body of a Third Person for Child-Bearing."[63] That Parslow's decision in favor of genetics as the primary tool for determining parental rights was made explicit in newspaper coverage of his lower court decision is illustrated by the following excerpts: "In reaching his decision, Parslow said he relied heavily on the proven genetic link between the Calverts and the child, and he emphasized the importance of heredity";[64] "The judge agreed with Mark and Crispina Calvert . . . that the couple's genetic relationship to the baby makes them the only *true parents*";[65] and "In the debate over nature versus nurture. . . . the judge placed strong emphasis on nature, saying the role of genetics plays a decisive role *[sic]*."[66]

Other newspaper accounts of the custody trial decision also noted Parslow's use of language, particularly his comparison of Anna Johnson to a "foster mother" who was thus inferior to Crispina Calvert, who held the status of "natural mother."[67] By comparing Johnson to a "foster mother, who feeds, nurtures and may grow attached to the baby but may be required to relinquish the child to the natural mother,"[68] Parslow, a different newspaper article observed, put the genie of expanded definitions of family back in the bottle. His ruling reinscribed a normative view of what a family should be by "[d]eclaring that two parents are better than three."[69] Two years later, the "crazy-making" assumption of a three-parent family was again argued by the Calverts when the case was reviewed by the California Supreme Court. According to one newspaper account of the appeal, an additional argument made on the couple's behalf was that such an expansion of family relations would violate the very nature of the "private," two-parent, culturally normative family: "Lawyers for the Calverts replied that Johnson, in effect, was proposing a 'three-parent family' for the child, which would represent 'an intrusion of an outsider into the integrity of the family unit.'"[70]

Thus, since the baby was not "genetically" Johnson's, the transaction became understood as being less about baby selling and more a story about a couple whose surrogacy arrangement had gone tragically wrong, leaving them fighting a biological stranger for custody of "their" child. That a person who was merely a "caretaker" might be able to successfully lay claim to one's own flesh and blood was the horror story that defined this dramatic event. In a social context in which many parents contracted with a variety of caretakers who were "biological strangers"—from nannies to step-parents—this was an especially scary story. This definition of the arrangement, biological parents fighting parental claims from so-called strangers, was first applied by Judge Parslow and then reaffirmed by the California Supreme Court's ruling in the case. Both court decisions defined Johnson's role as that of a provider rather than a mother.[71] The story that dominated in the Johnson-Calvert case, therefore, emphasized surrogacy as a service rather than a baby-selling transaction. As a result, a political response could emerge that sought to protect the interests of infertile couples so they would not be put in heart-wrenching custody disputes, fighting for "their" children. The headline for the first story appearing in the *Los Angeles Times* on this conflict, "Surrogate Mother Sues to Keep *Couple's Child*," implicitly encouraged such a "plight of infertile couples" frame.[72]

An equally important but only obliquely addressed part of this horror story, one that compounds Johnson's solely gestational role and her tenuous claims to the child born of the surrogate parenting arrangements, was the fact that she was black and the Calverts were a mixed white-Filipina couple. Although ideas about race and family typically were not explicitly discussed when evaluating Johnson's maternal claims to the child, they clearly were an implicit element in the telling of this horror story. For instance, the racial differences between the parties involved were depicted visually—four separate articles contained pictures of both the couple and the surrogate.[73] Additionally, three articles showed a picture of Johnson, two included pictures of the Calverts together (one showed Crispina only from the back), and one provided a picture of the baby. Textual descriptions of the parties' races and ethnicities also highlighted the Calverts' biogenetic relationship to the baby. For instance, one newspaper story used physical similarity as a way to construct who the child "belonged" to: "'He looks like us,' said Crispina Calvert, 36, a nurse born in the Philippines. 'He looks like an Oriental baby with my husband's nose.' . . . Her husband, who is of British descent, said, nevertheless, 'He's a Caucasian baby. *There's no doubt looking at him that he's our child.*'"[74] Mark Calvert's comment is particularly interesting, as it contributes to the common construction of the child as being "white," despite his mixed-race genetic heritage. The baby's "whiteness" held firm, seemingly unaffected by physical descriptions genetically linking him to Crispina Calvert, such as "[he] has his genetic mother's dark shiny hair and wide eyes."[75] Genetics, physical similarity, and kinship relations converged into a single, linked construct in the media coverage of this horror story of a couple who could lose "their" child. Designating the baby as white meant that the Johnson-Calvert case reverberated with ideas regarding race as well as genetics.[76] Not only was Johnson not genetically related to the child, but she was a different race; given cultural notions of racial purity, this further weakened her claims to parental rights.[77]

Another significant racialized element in the media's telling of this horror story was that Johnson had been on and off welfare prior to being a surrogate mother. Given contemporary associations of blacks with welfare, this subplot represents another way that race was embedded in the story. One *Los Angeles Times* editorial referred to Johnson as a "welfare mother,"[78] two editorials alluded to accusations of welfare fraud,[79] and one article was headlined, "Surrogate Mother in Custody Fight Accused of Welfare Fraud."[80] The use of what Patricia Hill Collins refers to as a controlling image of black women—that of the welfare mother[81]—was evident in a lengthy Sunday magazine article in the *Los Angeles Times.* The piece provided a detailed history of the court case, the issues in the custody dispute, and a description of the main participants that included the following details: "The woman who gave birth was indisputably Anna Louise Johnson, an unmarried ex-Marine of African-American, Irish and Native-American ancestry raising a 3-year-old daughter in Garden Grove on part-time nursing work and occasional welfare stints."[82] Johnson's association with welfare, and particularly the allegations of welfare fraud, helped to further diminish her claims to the child.[83]

At the same time, while there was much criticism of the class bias apparent in the determination of Mary Beth Whitehead's parental fitness,[84] there was less concern that Whitehead's motives were pecuniary. The story told in the media about Whitehead was that of a woman motivated primarily by her desire to help an infertile couple after witnessing others' struggles with infertility. She never demanded more money from the Sterns, and she immediately tried to give the money back to them when she changed her mind about custody. Media accounts of Johnson's status as a "welfare mother" (and even more damaging, as a "welfare cheat"), as well as her supposed demands for more money from the Calverts, are in sharp contrast. Johnson emerged as a woman motivated primarily by the need for money. Although this story did allow for a criticism of the profit-oriented status of commercial surrogacy transactions and thus could have supported a frame of baby selling, in the end the dominant story told was one in which surrogates should be properly screened so that couples would not be vulnerable to exploitation by women whose concerns were primarily nonaltruistic. In other words, the commercial aspects of surrogate parenting transactions were not troublesome because they entailed commodified reproductive relationships that exploited women's reproductive capacities (the "baby-selling" criticism). Instead, what made commercial surrogacy potentially problematic was the fact that paying surrogate mothers could attract women whose financial situations were precarious. Such women would not seek to be a surrogate from an altruistic desire to help an infertile couple—a motivation viewed as legitimate and gender appropriate—and thus might demand more money or decide to keep the child. According to this story of surrogate motherhood, if women whose interests were primarily financial weren't properly screened and vetted, they would be more likely to change their minds and cause a custody battle with the commissioning couple (the "plight of infertile couples" frame).

Further contributing to a framing of this horror story as less about baby selling and more about the plight of infertile couples was how the transaction originally had been arranged. The Calverts and Ms. Johnson had reached a private agreement; no surrogate agency was involved. Consequently, whereas the Whitehead-Stern dispute told a story of a surrogate improperly and cavalierly screened by an unscrupulous and greedy surrogacy broker, the Johnson case was a story about a woman who was not screened because the parties agreed to the contract without an intermediary.[85] Precisely because a broker was not used to screen the parties and monitor the process, the Johnson-Calvert custodial battle allowed supporters of surrogate motherhood to defend the practice. The story that emerged about surrogacy from the Johnson-Calvert case was one in which surrogate parenting programs played an important function in screening potential surrogates, providing them with counseling, and mediating the arrangement. The *Los Angeles Times* covered this angle immediately when the case was first filed in Orange County Superior Court. "William W. Handel, an attorney whose Beverly Hills–based Center for Surrogate Parenting is the state's leading broker of surrogate agreements, said the Johnson dispute points up the need for extensive screening of potential surrogates."[86] According to news coverage of this dramatic event, then, surrogate motherhood was not a problem to be stopped but a problem that needed regulation to be fixed.

In fact, unlike the media coverage of Noel Keane, whose main center was located in New York, press treatment of Bill Handel (the major surrogacy broker in California) and his Center for Surrogate Parenting (CSP) business was much more favorable. A news magazine story in the *Los Angeles Times* on the *Johnson v. Calvert* case praised Handel and CSP; similarly, one of the paper's columnists endorsed Handel with the report that "none of the center's 141 surrogate births has wound up in court."[87] This generally positive treatment had been true during the Baby M custody trial as well. For instance, when the New Jersey Supreme Court ruled on the Baby M case, the *New York Times* reported Handel's claim that he "had never had a mother challenge her contract and seek to keep her baby as Mary Beth Whitehead Gould did under her agreement with William and Elizabeth Stern of Tenafly, N.J."[88] During this same period, the *Los Angeles Times* also characterized Handel as having a clean record; his center was reported to have arranged sixty-five surrogate births "without a surrogate mother backing out of the arrangement."[89]

As the Baby M case continued to unfold, the *Los Angeles Times* noted that CSP and another California program, the Surrogate Parent Program in West Los Angeles, took careful steps to prevent litigious custody disputes: "The surrogates and couples in both programs go through careful prescreening, meet with each other, get to know one another well. . . . Throughout the process, the surrogates participate in group counseling which continues months, sometimes years after birth."[90] The paper was still giving the two centers' standards favorable coverage a year later, reporting Handel's assertions about meticulous screening of applicants: "The center, one of two surrogate centers in the Los Angeles area, carefully screens potential surrogate mothers for their psychological and medical suitability, he added."[91]

During this same period, a *New York Times* article profiled both Handel's and a Washington center's stringent screening policies, specifically comparing them to those used by Keane and several other custody disputes he had been involved with, including the Baby M case. "Both Mr. Handel and Ms. Blankfeld said they had escaped court fights similar to the Whitehead-Stern dispute because their potential surrogates undergo a four-to-six month series of medical, psychiatric, and psychological screening before being accepted. 'We reject 19 out of 20 who apply,' Mr. Handel said."[92] Media accounts of the different surrogate programs in the United States commonly compared the standards of Noel Keane's and Bill Handel's programs. This excerpt is typical: "One psychiatrist who interviews would-be-surrogate mothers in Detroit . . . rarely rejects any of the candidates, so long as they understand what they are agreeing to. A program in Los Angeles, on the other hand, accepts only one in ten applicants."[93]

This variation in the ways surrogacy transactions were managed was used to show why regulating the practice was a sensible course of action. A *Los Angeles Times* article on the Baby M case reported that "William Handel, attorney and director of Los Angeles' Center for Surrogate Parenting, Inc., . . . added that legislative regulation is 'desperately needed' to prevent abuses by some surrogate brokers."[94] Later, covering the Johnson-Calvert dispute, a *Los Angeles Times* columnist attributed CSP's record of never having been involved with a custodial dispute to the center's careful, professional approach. "Such steps [e.g., counseling] are already taken at the Center for Surrogate Parenting in Beverly Hills. . . . Couples and potential surrogates are both screened in a wide range of areas before the center agrees to match the parties."[95]

The very different and much more positive portrayal of Handel and CSP as compared to Keane and ICNY contributed to the different policy responses to surrogate motherhood in California and New York.[96] Handel's ability, unlike Keane's, to avoid contested arrangements and consequently negative publicity allowed surrogate motherhood to be seen as a redeemable practice.[97] The fact that CSP and other California surrogate programs received favorable press on their screening practices and that they had never been the focal point of a disputed surrogacy arrangement helped make the dominant framing of surrogate motherhood's problem as one of "inadequate laws."

To summarize, media coverage of *Johnson v. Calvert* opened up a legitimate and viable alternative framework for understanding the problem of surrogacy. In particular, because this custody dispute involved gestational surrogacy, meaning that the surrogate and the baby she carried and bore were not genetically related to one another, and just as importantly, because the surrogate and the baby were of different races, the story about surrogate parenting that became dominant was one that emphasized the plight of infertile couples. Because of their own inability to conceive, the Calverts had turned to surrogacy and then found themselves in the tragic position of having to fight to keep "their" child from a biological stranger—a surrogate who held neither a genetic nor a racial tie to the baby. This telling of the story in turn helped shape a policy response that sought to erase the kind of ambiguities and pitfalls that had trapped the Calverts by regulating the process. But why did the Johnson-Calvert and Baby M horror stories have different effects on how legislators in New York and California framed and responded to surrogacy?

CONTRASTING NEWS AND EDITORIAL COVERAGE

Baby M quickly became a national news story. As noted earlier, 1987—the year of the trial—saw the largest amount of news coverage on surrogate motherhood in the *New York Times, Los Angeles Times,* and *Washington Post.* Over its two-year span, the Baby M case garnered media attention on both coasts, and this was associated with a corresponding jump in legislative activity (see chapter 1). However, the long-term effects of the media coverage of this one case differed with regard to the perception and framing of the practice in New York and California, as indicated by the two states' divergent legislative responses in 1992. A further comparison of newspaper coverage sheds some light on the reasons for this divergence.

The *New York Times, Los Angeles Times,* and *Washington Post* have a national readership, but they are also local papers. Research has shown that location (i.e., distance between media outlet and the event) is a strong predictor of what events are likely to be reported in the *New York Times* and *Washington Post.*[98] With respect to surrogacy, an analysis of the three papers' coverage indicates that geography not only influenced what was covered but also affected the *amount* of coverage allotted to a particular event. In 1987, the *New York Times* published almost twice as many stories on surrogacy as did the *Los Angeles Times,* 131 versus 69; and specific coverage of the Baby M case that year also constituted a larger share (76 percent) of the *New York Times*'s overall reporting on the issue than of the *Los Angeles Times*'s coverage (61 percent). This difference hints at the importance of location. The Baby M transaction was arranged at a Manhattan-based agency, and the trial took place just across the Hudson River from New York City—three thousand miles from Los Angeles. The onslaught of Baby M news coverage in the *New York Times* may have shaped the public and political reaction to surrogate motherhood in the state of New York. First, it probably caused the stronger and longer reaction—in terms of number of bills introduced in the legislature. Second, given that the legislation signed into law in 1992 was anti–commercial surrogacy, the media coverage seems to have shaped the dominant framing of surrogacy in New York as a problem of baby selling.[99]

Of course, despite the distance, Californians too were exposed to the Baby M case through reports in both the *Los Angeles Times* and the *New York Times,* and elsewhere. That the Baby M story affected the political response to surrogate parenting in California can be seen in the brief surge of anti–commercial surrogacy bills introduced into the state legislature in the 1987 and 1988 sessions. This response was not sustained, however (see chapter 1). By 1992, the California legislature was prepared to pass a bill that would allow surrogacy, with regulation. The backing for this kind of policy seems to have been shaped by two elements related to media coverage of surrogacy. One factor was the more limited coverage of the Baby M case—in absolute and relative terms. In addition to providing less coverage of Baby M, though, the *Los Angeles Times* provided significantly more coverage of the Southern California–based *Johnson v. Calvert* dispute than did the *New York Times,* and that court battle presented an alternative framing for the problem of surrogate parenting. In 1990, during the *Johnson v. Calvert* trial, the *Los Angeles Times* published nearly 1.5 times more stories on surrogacy than did the *New York Times.* And twenty-three of the twenty-four stories that appeared in the *Los Angeles Times* that year concerned the Johnson-Calvert dispute, while only six of the ten stories about surrogacy in the *New York Times* that year did so. One can also gauge the impact of geography on regional newspaper coverage by looking at the coverage of surrogacy provided by the *Washington Post.* In this national newspaper, the total amount of articles published mimicked the level found in the *nonlocal* newspaper. In 1987, the Baby M case was nonlocal news for the *Los Angeles Times.* That year, the *Washington Post,* like the *Los Angeles Times,* published sixty-nine articles on surrogacy. In 1990, when the Johnson-Calvert case was nonlocal news for the *New York Times,* the *Post* published seven articles on surrogate motherhood, compared to the *Times*'s ten articles.[100]

The structure of news organizations probably accounts for the difference in the degree of coverage of the Baby M and Johnson cases. As other analysts of news media have shown, the placement of beat reporters affects what type of news and which stories get reported.[101] Here, too, location matters. In 1987, of the 102 news stories in the *New York Times* that mentioned the Baby M case, just under 50 percent carried the byline of one reporter, Robert Hanley. In contrast, during this same year, of the forty-three stories that appeared in the *Los Angeles Times* about Baby M, 72 percent had no byline. Similarly, of the six stories the *New York Times* published on *Johnson v. Calvert* in 1990, four had no byline. Of the twenty-three articles about that case that the *Los Angeles Times* published in 1990, almost half were written by a single reporter, Catherine Gewertz.[102] Meanwhile, during 1987 and 1990, no single reporter dominated coverage of either case in the *Washington Post.*

It is also significant that editorial coverage of surrogate parenting varied between the two papers—both in timing and in tone (see table 6). In terms of timing, between 1986 and 1992 the *New York Times* published ten editorials that addressed surrogate parenting; five of these specifically commented on the Baby M case, and a sixth mentioned it. Nine of these editorials appeared between 1986 and 1988, when the Baby M case was making its way through the New Jersey courts, and six of these were published in 1987 alone. In contrast, the *Los Angeles Times* published twelve editorials pertaining to surrogacy between 1986 and 1992. Four of these were published between 1987 and 1988, while the remaining eight were published between 1990 and 1992. Of the twelve editorials, only three pertained to the Baby M case; four focused on *Johnson v. Calvert,* and a fifth mentioned it. Much as their coverage of news showed the effects of geography, so too did the editorial pages of these two major and influential newspapers. Both the *New York Times* and the *Los Angeles Times* allotted local cases significantly more coverage on their respective editorial pages. This probably influenced the amount of attention paid to particular horror stories, which, in turn, probably influenced the timing and spread of editorials on the issue of surrogacy.[103]

Another way the local news media may have affected the divergent legislative responses taken by New York and California involves differences in the tone the editors of the *New York Times* and the *Los Angeles Times* took as they discussed the issue of surrogacy. As the next section explains,

TABLE 6. *New York Times* and *Los Angeles Times* Editorials on Surrogacy, 1980–92

New York Times		*Los Angeles Times*	
Date	Title	Date	Title
11/23/1980	Gestation, Inc.		
2/8/1983	Baby Sales		
6/27/1983	New Bioethics For a New Biology		
8/28/1986	On Bearing Someone Else's Baby		
1/9/1987	Giving Love, or Selling Life?		
		1/25/1987	The Case of Baby M
1/26/1987	The Surrogate's Baby Comes First		
3/9/1987	Nothing Surrogate about the Pain		
3/12/1987	The Future of Test-Tube Life		
		3/13/1987	Technology and the Vatican
4/2/1987	Baby M: Groping for Right and Law		
		4/5/1987	All Questions, No Answers
4/30/1987	Now, What about Babies N, O and P?		
2/4/1988	Justice for All in the Baby M Case	2/4/1988	Babies: No Sale
6/4/1988	It's Baby Selling, and It's Wrong		
		8/20/1990	Surrogate Parenting: The Bioethical Issue
		9/22/1990	Give the Baby to the Genetic Parents
		10/12/1990	Profit Is the Wrong Motive

TABLE 6. (*continued*)

New York Times		*Los Angeles Times*	
Date	Title	Date	Title
		10/23/1990	Child's Interest Is Paramount
		4/22/1991	It's Kramer vs. Kramer vs. Somebody Else
		9/28/1991	The Tangled Web of Surrogacy Issues
		1/27/1992	Stand-In Moms: What's the Law?
		2/28/1992	An Invitation to Further Chaos
6/10/1992	Making Money by Making Babies		

the editorial page in each newspaper promoted a different framing of the problem of surrogate parenting.

New York Times Editorials and the Framing of Surrogacy: From Reluctant Acceptance to "Baby Selling"

An editorial that appeared in the *New York Times* just prior to the Baby M custody trial noting the need for regulatory legislation expressed a sentiment typical of most editorials at the time. The paper's editors held that "[t]he public obligation is obvious. If New York, New Jersey and other states wish to tolerate surrogate parenthood, they need to establish guidelines, just as they do for adoption and other related issues."[104] Grudging tolerance, as opposed to an enthusiastic embrace of surrogacy, thus was central to the editorial page's call for regulation. The *New York Times*'s cautious and ambivalent endorsement of state regulation is seen as well in the paper's editorial comments on the Dunne-Goodhue bill in 1987. At the time, that proposed legislation was being touted as possibly becoming the first state regulatory legislation on surrogacy passed in the United States. The *New York Times* editorial acknowledged opposition to the practice, but it also made a case for why this regulatory bill represented a step in the right direction: "Even those New Yorkers who would like to see that route declared illegal will agree that by focusing on the child, the Dunne-Goodhue bill focuses on the right person."[105] A few months later, another editorial, written after the lower court's decision on Baby M, also supported a regulatory approach to surrogacy. This time, the *New York Times* editors made a plea for legislation and endorsed the Dunne-Goodhue bill because it resolved several issues and concerns, but they continued to acknowledge that such legislation was not "ideal."[106]

An examination of the *New York Times*'s editorial support for some sort of regulatory approach to surrogate parenting reveals that the editors agreed that the "plight of the infertile" represented a real need; however, their support of a regulatory approach seemed to be driven more by a reluctant acceptance of surrogacy practices as inevitable than by an enthusiastic endorsement of these arrangements. This "reluctant acceptance" stance is expressed in the following excerpt from an editorial that appeared during the Baby M trial:

> The surrogate mother business appears to have a bright future, given the marked increase in infertility among the young and the marked drop in the number of adoptions. . . . The public obligation is obvious. States need to evaluate the very idea of surrogate parenthood, decide whether it is a tolerable practice in the first place and, if so, establish guidelines just as they do for adoption and other analogous practices. . . . In any case the business is probably here to stay, which is reason enough for regulations predicated on the child's best interests.[107]

This sense of inevitability about surrogate motherhood is present in three other editorials around the Baby M trial, as the following excerpts show: "Given the small number of adoptable babies, surrogate mothers were perhaps inevitable once the medical technology became available";[108] "[T]he surrogate mother business won't go away";[109] and "The surrogate mother industry isn't going to go away."[110]

On the one hand, then, the *New York Times* editorial page used the Baby M trial as a way to spotlight the need for social policy that would specifically address this newly emerging social problem. At the same time, the paper's editorials also used this case to signal disapproval of the practice. This critical attitude was reflected in an editorial that appeared prior to the lower court ruling. Titled "Nothing Surrogate about the Pain," this editorial stated, "The issue cries out for legislation that would minimize the potential imbroglios like this one. . . . Perhaps this trial should serve as a deterrent."[111] Here, the editors' rejection of a "plight of infertile couples" framing and firmer embrace of a "baby-selling" framing was evident. In characterizing the actions of the two women involved in the Baby M dispute, the editorial naturalized and validated Mary Beth Whitehead's role as Baby M's mother by asserting that "[t]he word mother has many definitions, several of which apply to Mary Beth Whitehead. Among them is the first: 'a woman who has borne a child.'" Meanwhile, scorn was implicit in their description of Elizabeth Stern's choice to use a surrogate to attain the status of mother: "Because Dr. Stern feared that pregnancy might aggravate her mild multiple sclerosis, she and her husband deputized Mrs. Whitehead, by contract, to do what Dr. Stern chose not to do: have his baby. It's that simple."[112]

It is not too surprising, therefore, that when the lower court judge ruled the contract for Baby M valid and awarded custody of the child to the Sterns, the *New York Times* editorial the following day expressed relief that the dispute had been resolved but did not fully endorse the ruling:

> In upholding the contract by which Mary Beth Whitehead agreed to bear a child for William Stern, a New Jersey judge created a family and began to shape law. . . . But does the decision indicate the proper direction for the law? That is now the question for searching national debate. . . . Suffice it to say for now that Judge Sorkow's decision in one case hardly ratifies the practice. Instead it has forced all of us, most for the first time, to stare hard at the vexing issues with an eye to giving judges, not to mention prospective parents, more guidance.[113]

A more explicit emergence of the "baby-selling" frame as dominant is evident in later editorials on Baby M and in subsequent endorsements of anti–commercial surrogate parenting legislation. After the New Jersey Supreme Court decision reversed the lower court's ruling and declared commercial surrogacy illegal, a *New York Times* editorial headline proclaimed, "Justice for All in the Baby M Case," and the text began by stating that "[a]t a stroke, New Jersey's Supreme Court brought clarity and justice to the Baby M case, which so tormented the nation last spring: . . .

Mary Beth Whitehead-Gould retains her rights as a parent. . . . William Stern and his wife retain the right to raise his child. . . . [and] New Jersey acquires a convincing judgment that a 'surrogate parent' contract for money amounts to *an illegal bill of sale for a baby.*" The decision was called "wise," as it "reinforces sound values for all who aspire to parenthood."[114]

Several months later, the *New York Times* published an editorial revealingly titled "It's Baby Selling, and It's Wrong." This editorial unambiguously framed surrogacy as being about baby selling:

> The New York Task Force on Life and the Law offers all states a clear, convincing answer: Such a practice is baby-selling, and it's wrong. . . . Proponents of surrogate-mother contracts are fond of euphemisms like "womb rental" or "the provision of services." But the fancy language, the task force said, seeks to conceal a stark fact: The couple who hires a woman to be artificially inseminated does not purchase the pregnancy but its product, a child. . . . In asking for legislation to bar surrogate parenting for pay, the task force seeks to eliminate an industry "devoted to making money from birth and human reproduction." . . . It is up to state legislatures, in New York and elsewhere, to follow through.[115]

As the New York legislature was about to vote on the anti–commercial surrogacy bill in 1992, the *New York Times* printed yet another editorial, with a headline that clearly embraced a "baby-selling" frame: "Making Money by Making Babies." This editorial expressed quite different, and much stronger, sentiments on the issue of surrogate motherhood than those that had appeared prior to the New Jersey Supreme Court ruling on Baby M. In this last of the *New York Times* editorials on this issue, surrogate parenting was referred to as crass commerce. For the editors, Baby M had by now convincingly demonstrated that surrogacy was a story with no happy endings. The editorial opened by stating, "The State of New York may be eager to attract new business, but there's one kind of inflow it would do well to avoid. . . . New York is fast becoming 'the surrogate parenting capital of the nation.'. . . It is a dubious distinction." The editorial ended, "The case of Baby M proved that 'surrogate' motherhood has a terrible potential for pain. . . . For those who want children, infertility can be a tragedy. Allowing this kind of commerce, however, would be a greater one."[116] Given this untenable situation, the editorial endorsed the proposed ban on commercial surrogacy. Thus, although there were competing claims about surrogate motherhood when the story of Baby M first broke, by 1992, hundreds of news articles later and four years after the New Jersey State Supreme Court decision declared surrogate parenting illegal, the framing of surrogacy as "baby selling" had become dominant on the *New York Times* editorial page.

Los Angeles Times Editorials and the Framing of Surrogacy: From Concerns about Baby Selling to the Dominance of the "Plight of Infertile Couples" Frame

While the tenor of *New York Times* editorials shifted from an ambivalent and reluctant acceptance of surrogacy to a firm embracing of a "baby-selling" frame, the editors of the *Los Angeles Times* started with similar concerns but ended up with very different emphases. In an editorial with the title "All Questions, No Answers," after the lower court ruling on Baby M, the *Los Angeles Times* editorial page expressed ambivalence about the decision and concerns about the baby-selling aspects of the practice, much like those that had appeared on the *New York Times* editorial page: "Are we altogether sure that this arrangement should be condoned? Doesn't this transaction smack of baby-selling, which is illegal in every state? Isn't a woman's renting her womb like selling an organ, which is also barred? Shouldn't we pay more attention to the emotional trauma that the biological mother must feel on giving up her baby?"[117] The "baby-selling" frame shaped the reservations expressed by the *Los Angeles Times* editors here, but this same editorial also supported a "plight of the infertile" frame by acknowledging the "real" needs that surrogacy could meet: "As the number of abortions has risen, the number of unwanted babies has dropped, making adoption very difficult for childless couples. Surrogate pregnancy is a way for them to be parents after all."[118]

In the short run, however, the Baby M case seemed to promote greater support for a "baby-selling" interpretation of the problem of surrogacy. During the lower court trial, the *Los Angeles Times* editorial page stressed the importance of the maternal bond. In (reluctantly) siding with Mary Beth Whitehead's parental claims, the editors affirmed that "society recognizes the special affinity between mother and child, and it is reasonable to apply that recognition to this case."[119] By the time the New Jersey Supreme Court issued its decision, the paper's editorial position clearly emphasized commodified reproduction. The "baby-selling" frame was evident from the title "Babies: No Sale," through the text of the editorial:

> With Solomon-like wisdom, the New Jersey Supreme Court has settled one of the most hotly contested child-custody disputes of the decade and struck a blow against surrogate motherhood. . . . The New Jersey court has emphatically said . . . that surrogate motherhood is just a fancy name for *baby-selling* if any money changes hands. . . . [T]he . . . Court has wisely responded . . . [that women] cannot rent their wombs. This means that in New Jersey, at least, babies cannot be treated as chattels, to be bought and sold in commercial transactions.[120]

Once again highlighting the importance and strength of maternal bonding, this editorial also praised the court for "recogniz[ing] a fact well known to adoption specialists—that many mothers become so emotionally attached to their babies during pregnancy that they change their minds about surrendering them after birth."

Yet three years later, with the emergence of *Johnson v. Calvert,* the *Los Angeles Times* editorial page seemed much less concerned with supporting a birth mother's claims based on maternal bonding. Once genetics were separated from gestation, the latter lost out to the former, and claims to nongenetic motherhood (especially those from a racially dissimilar "stranger") were pronounced "disturbing": "The latest disturbing direction involves Orange County, where a surrogate mother, seven months pregnant, has sued to keep a baby she contracted to bear even though the fetus is entirely the product of the egg and sperm of the sponsoring couple."[121] In a later editorial, genetics were given primary weight in determining parental rights: "The Calverts, assuming they are the true genetic parents, should be given permanent custody as soon as possible."[122]

The shift in the editors' position regarding parental rights was not accompanied by a complete disregard for the pecuniary aspects of surrogacy. Commenting on the Johnson-Calvert case, a *Los Angeles Times* editorial argued that "[s]urrogateship for money can be a legal nightmare" as Johnson "fits a classic profile of a single mother whose poverty influenced her decision to become a surrogate."[123] A different editorial, titled "Profit Is the Wrong Motive: Orange County Case Shows the Miseries of Commercial Surrogateship," made a similar argument, using racially coded language: "The larger lesson is that surrogateship arrangements, for all their good intentions and possibilities, become hopelessly clouded by a profit motive. . . . This troubling case turns out to be no breach-of-contract lawsuit at all, but rather a change-of-heart story about a poor woman whose burden of poverty complicated her initial decision to carry someone else's child. . . . What it [Johnson's wavering] does suggest is a lack of preparation for changes that pregnancy brought about, and its emotional consequences. The profit motive only complicated this unwise choice."[124]

Thus it was because of the problems that profit-oriented surrogacy begot that the *Los Angeles Times* editorial page urged legislation regulating the practice: "It is sad that courts have to play referee while society wrestles with the wizardry of science. It is also sad that more cases are bound to reoccur before the government puts restrictions on surrogateship-for-profit."[125] The editors saw regulation as the best way to prevent the problems that unregulated commercial surrogacy could entail, while still allowing the practice to occur. Recognition of surrogate parenting as helping the "plight of the infertile" was evident in other editorial comments, such as "Medical science now can address the age-old problem of childlessness; with wise choices and proper counseling, surrogate parenthood has the potential to bring satisfaction to couples who in the past would have lived out their lives without children."[126]

This more accepting attitude toward surrogacy is present in an editorial about the lower court ruling in *Johnson v. Calvert,* in which the Calverts were deemed the legal parents of the disputed child. Unlike the paper's position just a couple of years earlier, when maternal bonding was deemed central in determining parental rights, in 1990 the *Los Angeles Times* editorial page described Judge Parslow's ruling as a "wise decision" that "came down squarely on the side of common sense." In the editors' opinion, the judge had chosen the right course because he "upheld the contract and ruled that the surrogate was a 'genetic and hereditary stranger' to the baby. He chose an appropriate model for defining Johnson's role: she was, he said, like a foster parent who may have special feelings for nurturing a child, but *who is not to be mistaken for the real mother.*"[127] In both the 1988 and 1990 editorials, the "real mother" was favored for custody. What changed was the basis the editors used to determine who the "real mother" was in each dispute. In 1990, genes, as well as racial similarity, were asserted as the markers of motherhood.

The *Los Angeles Times* editorial page again praised Parslow's decision when the case was before the California Supreme Court, precisely because his ruling did not allow for the "confusion" of an expanded definition of familial relations: "Orange County Superior Court Judge Richard N. Parslow Jr. put the child's interest first by establishing the biological primacy of his sponsoring parents and by saying that to allow the surrogate into the picture, in effect as a third parent, would only confuse the issue."[128] Later, this editorial clearly disparaged the parental claims of Johnson, who had no genetic relationship to the child, observing that "[i]t would take a profound shift from the lower court's sound reasoning for the high court to discover a parental right for a plaintiff who essentially had let her womb out for rent. . . . [W]e hope it affirms the lower-court ruling." When the California Supreme Court did so, concurring that the Calverts were the parents, the subtitle of the paper's editorial read, "A Good Ruling," and in the commentary the court was described as having "made the correct ruling."[129]

Throughout the editorial coverage of both the Baby M and Johnson-Calvert cases, the *Los Angeles Times* editors indicated their desire for legislation on the issue. Worries over the "baby-selling" aspects of the practice also were evident in their reaction to both cases, but as the Johnson-Calvert case (and others) worked their way through the California court system in the early 1990s the paper's editorials more strongly affirmed the "plight of infertile couples" framing. In particular, and in contrast to the reluctant and limited acceptance of a seemingly inevitable practice expressed by the editors of the *New York Times* in the mid-1980s, the *Los Angeles Times* editors were optimistic about the "promise" of surrogacy, if properly regulated. For instance, around the time the Johnson-Calvert case started to gain media attention, they argued that "[w]riting rules to cover any contingency will be difficult, perhaps impossible. . . . There are no good answers. The best hope may be to find a legislative approach that would remove as much ambiguity and contention from these agreements as possible. . . . Contracts involving a profit motive for the surrogate are full of risk. . . . [A]rrangements among friends can result in unanticipated disagreements. Only with careful provisions, adequate supervision and counseling can the promise of scientific advancement hope to produce satisfactory results in human life."[130] Two years later, using nearly identical wording, the editorial page noted, "While the state generally should be wary of surrogacy contracts for profit, it is possible that with careful provisions, supervision and counseling, reproductive science can fulfill the dream of childless couples."[131]

The Johnson-Calvert case seems to have tipped the balance toward the "plight of the infertile" frame and allowed the *Los Angeles Times* editorial page to focus on genes and biology. At the same time, the implicit use of race as a marker of biological relatedness crept into the paper's editorials regarding other surrogate horror stories. Of particular interest is a custody case that received attention in 1991, in a period between the coverage of the lower and high court rulings on the Johnson-Calvert case. The *Los Angeles Times* reported on the case *In re the Marriage of Moschetta* in seven separate news stories in 1991, and the editorial page addressed the case twice.[132] In this custody dispute, a traditional surrogacy transaction broke down when, several months after bringing home the surrogate child, the biological father, Robert Moschetta, left his wife, Cynthia, and took the baby with him. At first the surrogate, Elvira Jordan, backed Cynthia Moschetta's rights to custody, but when the courts ruled Cynthia Moschetta ineligible to make parental claims, Jordan herself filed custody claims against Robert Moschetta. The trial court judge eventually awarded joint custody to Jordan and Robert Moschetta. What is interesting in this case, in which all the parties were white, is that despite Cynthia Moschetta's lack of a biogenetic connection to the surrogate-born child, the *Los Angeles Times* editorial page expressed sympathy for her, noting in particular that her status as a nongenetic parent stripped Moschetta of a legal right to claim the baby. The paper's first editorial about the case said: "Cynthia Moschetta gets a double whammy. For all of her efforts to overcome the anguish of infertility, she got more pain in the end—disqualification from the playing field in the custody fight that is now shaping up. She was found to have no claim at all because she had no biological tie to the child. Yet she helped arrange and pay for the birth and took maternity leave to care for the child."[133] A second editorial then described the ruling as an "ultimately disappointing outcome" because, among other reasons, the decision gave "no rights for the sponsoring mother."[134] Thus, when there were no racial differences among the parties, the editors of the *Los Angeles Times* seemed to care much less about genetic ties.[135] Likewise, a number of years later, in the case of *Jaycee B. v. The Superior Court of Orange County* (see Introduction), when racial difference again was not a factor (all the parties were white), the *Los Angeles Times* editorial page explicitly backed the argument that biology should not determine parenthood or be considered a criterion for good parenting. "The case affirms the capacity of courts to look beyond biology in the establishment of the rights and obligations of parents," the editors stated, and added, "The ruling also should inspire clearer thinking about the debt that society owes parents, who, without biological ties to a child, establish and maintain good home environments whether together or as single parents."[136]

This difference in news coverage of surrogate horror stories further attests to the importance of recognizing both the implicit and explicit racial assumptions that are deeply embedded in the politics of reproduction in the United States. In particular, and as other scholars of reproduction have noted, determination of maternal fitness and rights, qualities of "good mothers," and the worth and value of babies are tightly interwoven with American racial politics and prejudices.[137]

The considerable and different media attention given to surrogacy cases and horror stories in the *New York Times* and *Los Angeles Times* seems to have allowed alternative definitions of the practice to emerge in New York and California. The editors of the *New York Times* initially encouraged the state to implement regulation of surrogacy, but their acceptance of the practice was less about the "plight of infertile couples" and more about a resigned acceptance that such transactions could probably not be kept from occurring in the future. As the Baby M trial went through the courts, even this limited endorsement of the practice was gradually withdrawn as the editorial page embraced a "baby-selling" frame of surrogacy and began to strongly endorse legislative attempts to ban the practice. In contrast, while the *Los Angeles Times* editorials expressed similar trepidations about surrogate motherhood around the time of the Baby M case, later editorials, written to address *Johnson v. Calvert* and other California-based cases, reveal concern about surrogacy's commercial aspects, but a concern tempered by the growing dominance of a "plight of the infertile" framing.

One informant involved with the surrogacy issue in California explained why the differential impact of these two surrogate custody disputes, each of which constituted a critical discourse moment, was consequential:

> [T]here's a very big difference in the political climate of California versus New York. Remember, Mary Beth Whitehead happened in New Jersey, and I think that tainted the whole [thing]. . . . So when we talk about surrogacy on the East Coast you can imagine Mary Beth Whitehead, even here to some extent it's the same thing. What is surrogacy? It's Mary Beth Whitehead on the courthouse steps of Hackensack, New Jersey, screaming, "They're taking my baby from me, they're taking my baby." That's surrogate parenting.
>
> [By contrast, in California] . . . we still have Mary Beth Whitehead, we still have people who argue that, but we don't have [just that] case. We have, you know, Johnson, you know, this lunatic. . . . I think there's more acceptance of surrogacy, certainly here in California, because of the Calvert case. Because of the fact that we actually do it fairly professionally here.[138]

By comparing the specific coverage and content of local media, this chapter has revealed how regional incidents can shape different policy responses to the same issue in different places. In the case of surrogacy, the location of a dramatic event affected the amount of media coverage it received in regional newspapers. This in turn suggests that the haphazard and contingent nature of local incidents, personalities, and controversies can affect what frame emerges as dominant. Thus, while the media might only tell us what to think about, particular news stories about specific horror stories can influence the way we think about a certain issue by creating different critical discourse moments. At the same time, as the next chapter shows, once the media, serving as an initial claims maker, had established surrogate motherhood as a social problem, the institutional legacies of and political alliances in each state affected how the politics of reproduction over the framing of surrogate motherhood played out in New York and California.

Chapter 5 | UNITY, DIVISIONS, AND STRANGE BEDFELLOWS

Divergent Legislative Responses to Surrogate Motherhood

New York and California are often considered bellwether states since they frequently take the lead in formulating policies and laws in response to changing social needs.[1] Previous chapters have shown that with respect to surrogate parenting, the two states' approaches diverged widely by 1992. One possible explanation is that the California and New York State legislatures were influenced by their respective preexisting political cultures and legislative environments. This chapter's brief comparison of the two states' institutional tendencies suggests, however, that legislative tendencies and political cultures only partially explain the 1992 policy outcomes. A more complex and contingent set of factors seems to have been at work—which is not surprising, given the contradictory and overlapping nature of reproductive politics more generally.

To identify the most significant of these additional influences on the two states' approaches to surrogate motherhood, this chapter examines how the discourses and rhetoric used to frame the problem of surrogacy—from women's interests, reproductive choice, and children's rights to commodified reproduction and the infertility epidemic—were taken up by various political actors and institutions. Unlike chapter 1, which provided a descriptive historical overview of each legislature's pre– and post–Baby M efforts to draft and pass legislation, this chapter takes an analytical approach that emphasizes the intersection of multiple factors. It provides a detailed examination of the varied and often contradictory forces that shaped the political environment and influenced legislators as they debated the pros and cons of commercial surrogacy. The analysis reveals how and when certain claims regarding surrogacy gained greater legitimacy. This, in turn, may shed light more generally on how the "politics of reproduction" may play out in the future as state legislatures continue to contend with advances in reproductive and genetic technologies.

INSTITUTIONAL TENDENCIES OF THE NEW YORK AND CALIFORNIA LEGISLATURES

That distinct institutional tendencies in New York and California might have influenced the disparate surrogate parenting policy approaches each state took in 1992 seems to some people less an interesting possibility and more an indisputable fact. As one informant in California put it, "I don't know that New York is seen as a cutting-edge kind. . . . [I]n California we just are ahead of everybody else. . . . It's the West Coast and we don't accept the status quo."[2] A brief comparison of several family law issues does confirm that California, more than New York, has been a leader in developing legislation that redefines family relations and obligations; this in turn might suggest why in the long run the state has taken a more permissive approach toward surrogate motherhood.

Perhaps one of the most revolutionary changes in family law in the last quarter of the century was the implementation of no-fault divorce. In 1969, California became the first state in the country to embrace this approach and allow individuals to file for divorce on grounds of "irreconcilable differences" or "irretrievable breakdown." New York adopted somewhat similar standards later, but the new statute contains a requirement that the couple undergo one year of separation before similar divorce proceedings can begin, and it is still not possible to dissolve the marriage by mutual consent.[3] Also, unlike New York, California has a community property standard (meaning that except for gifts, any property or assets either the husband or the wife acquires during marriage belong equally to the two parties and thus must be split equally upon divorce).[4] Both aspects of divorce law indicate a different approach to family relations in California than in New York. California's no-fault divorce provisions make it easier to dissolve a marriage, so the state is less involved in regulating marriage, and the rules of community property treat marriage as an arrangement about property rights and possessions. In California, then, family is about contractual and commercial relations, a less traditional view of the institution than is typical elsewhere.

In another area of family law, child custody, California also leads New York with respect to legislative change. Prior to the 1970s, the "tender years" doctrine prevailed nationwide; this standard assumed that young children were best off with their mothers. Starting in the early 1970s, child custody standards began to shift as a new concept of "best interests of child" took hold and the mother was no longer presumed to be the best custodial parent. Furthermore, experts and courts supported joint custody as in the best interests of the child. The Uniform Custody Act, which advocated the joint custody standard, was eventually adopted by all fifty states. California adopted the law in 1973, four years prior to its adoption in New York.[5]

In addition to embracing new approaches to divorce and child custody laws, California has taken a different approach to artificial insemination, an issue closely related to surrogate motherhood. In particular, compared to New York's statute, California's laws with respect to artificial insemination by donor (AID) break more with traditional notions of family. While both states recognize the husband of a woman artificially inseminated by an anonymous donor to be the legal parent of a child born of such an arrangement, they take different approaches to the status of these transactions when the woman is unmarried.[6] New York's AID statute does not protect unmarried women from donors' paternity claims; California's law extends the same protection to both married and unmarried women.[7] California's willingness to allow a child to be born without any particular man having paternal rights implies a possibly greater tendency to recognize the legitimacy of nontraditional family forms—another issue at the heart of surrogate motherhood.

This cursory review of family law in New York and California suggests that preexisting institutional tendencies in each state may have influenced their divergent policy responses to surrogate parenting.[8] If these legislative approaches to surrogate motherhood are viewed as an application of standing adoption law in New York and as a break from traditional adoption laws in California, this finding makes sense. In particular, California seems to take a more trend-setting role when it comes to family law. California has enacted new family policies earlier than New York and has gone further in breaking down traditional notions of parent-child relations based on genetics. These state-specific institutional tendencies may help explain why the same social problem was understood and solved differently in California than in New York.

Yet a focus on differences obscures significant overlap and similarities between the two states on other issues involving family, reproduction, and assisted reproductive technologies, from abortion laws and infertility coverage to domestic partner benefits and adoptions by gays and lesbians. For instance, although California was one of the first states to liberalize its abortion laws (in 1967), New York was the first to legalize abortion (in 1970), paving the way for the landmark *Roe v. Wade* decision in 1973. In this instance, New York can be viewed as taking a more groundbreaking approach, although both states were among the few to provide access to abortion prior to the Roe decision.[9] Today, both states continue to have fairly liberal abortion laws; neither imposes the restrictions of waiting periods, parental consent, and limitations on public funding common in other states.[10]

In terms of a newer reproductive issue, New York and California are two of fifteen states to require health insurance to cover infertility treatments, although they are the only two to exclude coverage of IVF.[11] More recently, in November of 2004, California voters approved earmarking $3 billion in state funds for stem cell research.[12] This could indicate Californians' greater general openness to advances in biotechnology and general belief in the progress of science. At the least, California can be viewed as still on the "cutting edge." Yet only a couple months after the California proposition passed, the New York legislature introduced legislation to fund similar research.[13] With regard to gay rights, both New York and California require that employment benefits be offered to domestic partners.[14] Both states also allow gays to adopt, and both permit step-parent adoptions.[15] Thus a history of and a continuing tendency for supporting nontraditional family formations are common to both California and New York.

In the end, institutional tendencies may have had their most significant effects as factors shaping the terrain of the political battlefields on which the problem of surrogate motherhood took place. Other factors, explored in the remainder of this chapter, also contributed significantly to the 1992 legislative outcomes in New York and California. Interactions among state actors and institutions and the media generally are important elements when it comes to establishing and framing social problems. State agencies establish claims and often do so in interaction with the media. State actors and public and private organizations frequently respond to issues precisely because of the attention given to them by the press. At the same time, the media, in disseminating information regarding policy positions taken by governmental officials, agencies, and organizations, may legitimate (or undermine) these positions.[16] Chapter 4 suggested ways in which the media on each coast acted as claims makers in the framing of surrogate parenting. The next section examines the role state agencies in New York and California played in staking claims regarding this problem (typically by issuing reports and investigative studies) and the interplay among these claims, media coverage, and legislative outcomes. Intersections involving task forces, state legislators, organizations such as NOW and the Roman Catholic Church, and the media are taken up in subsequent sections.

STAKING CLAIMS: THE ROLE OF TASK FORCES AND GOVERNMENT REPORTS

In reaction to surrogacy custody disputes that emerged in the 1980s, and the subsequent media and legislative attention these battles prompted, various governmental agencies and committees in both New York and California studied the issue and then released reports with policy recommendations. These documents, as explained below, seem to have affected the divergent ways in which surrogate motherhood became dominantly framed in the two states. The roles the reports played in the claims-making process differed because of several factors: the composition of the investigative committee, the type of recommendations made, and the media coverage received.

In New York, the first government-produced report on surrogacy was sent to State Senate President Pro Tem Warren M. Anderson on December 31, 1986. The report, *Surrogate Parenting in New York: A Proposal for Legislative Reform,* was prepared by the staff of the Senate Judiciary Committee at the request of Senator John Dunne (R), then head of that committee. The staff reviewed the testimony of nineteen witnesses at a joint legislative hearing in 1986 as well as existing literature and research on surrogate motherhood. Among the report's policy conclusions was the recommendation that "the state recognize surrogate parenting contracts as legal and enforceable."[17] This recommendation was specifically grounded in concerns over children's rights and problems of commodification: "The first and foremost concern of the Legislature must be to ensure that the child, born in the fulfillment of a surrogate parenting agreement, has a secure and permanent home. . . . In addition, legislation should be designed to prevent . . . excessive commercialization of the practice."[18] The rationale for the recommendations endorsed the frame of the "plight of infertile couples" and reflected concerns about reproductive rights frequently articulated in the debates over surrogacy (see, especially, chapter 2): "Any surrogate parenting law must recognize the benefits the practice provides for infertile couples and resolve the present uncertainties regarding the legal status of the child. . . . In addition, the law must attempt to limit the possible abuses of the practices while preserving, to the greatest extent possible, the right of privacy in reproductive matters."[19] A "plight of infertile couples" understanding of surrogacy is evident in the committee's assessment of the growing "need" for the practice: "An examination of the phenomenon of increasing infertility supports the conclusion that, because surrogate parenting meets a perceived need, it will continue to gain in popularity in the foreseeable future."[20]

Senator Dunne used the findings from this committee report to craft S 1429, the regulatory surrogacy legislation that he introduced, with cosponsor Senator Mary B. Goodhue (R), in 1987. (See also chapter 1.) This legislation proposed that the child of a surrogacy transaction was the responsibility of the intended parents from birth, and it provided for judicial approval and enforcement of informed consent agreements.[21] The proposal died in legislative committees in both houses.[22] The committee report fared no better. In the years after its publication, it was not referenced again in any of the political debates over how New York should formulate policy toward surrogacy. Moreover, until two weeks before the legislature approved the 1992 anti–commercial surrogacy legislation, no one again attempted to introduce into the New York legislature another regulatory bill similar to the Dunne-Goodhue proposal.

Meanwhile, also in 1987, then-Governor Mario Cuomo (D) asked the Task Force on Life and the Law to consider the issue of surrogate parenting. This existing committee, whose members represent a wide assortment of opinions and fields of expertise, was established in 1985 to address issues of medical ethics, such as euthanasia, organ transplants, and IVF (see chapter 1 for further details about the task force).[23] At the beginning of the twenty-first century, New York's task force remains the only standing government commission in the United States with a mandate to study emerging biomedical issues in order to recommend public policy solutions. To date, the task force has produced eleven reports, and the state has enacted seven of its policy recommendations. Additionally, the stature and influence of the task force are exceptionally high, as evidenced by its impact on other states' legislation, its frequent referencing in both the media and academic literature, and its citation in Supreme Court decisions.[24]

The task force issued its final report, *Surrogate Parenting: Analysis and Recommendations for Public Policy,* in 1988. Its conclusions—that surrogacy contracts be void and payment to surrogates prohibited—were a strong indictment of commercial surrogacy. In lamenting "the growth of a business community or industry devoted to making money from human reproduction and the birth of children,"[25] the task force promoted a "baby-selling" frame for surrogacy. A few pages earlier, the report explained the rationale behind the proposed policy recommendations with the following criticism of the commodification of reproductive processes and its consequences:

> The gestation of children as a service for others in exchange for a fee is a radical departure from the way in which society understands and values pregnancy. It substitutes commercial values for the web of social, affective and moral meanings associated with human reproduction and gestation. This transformation has profound implications for childbearing, for women, and for the relationship between parents and the children they bring into the world. . . . The Task Force concluded that this assignment of market values should not be celebrated as an exaltation of "rights," but rejected as a derogation of values and meanings associated with human reproduction. . . . Rather than accept this contractual model as a basis for family life and other close personal relationships, society should discourage the commercialization of our private lives.[26]

That the task force's report and policy recommendations had an important impact on the framing of and public response to surrogate motherhood can be gauged by attitudes expressed toward surrogate parenting in the immediate aftermath of the document's release. In the editorial section of the *New York Times,* the headline read, "It's Baby-Selling, and It's Wrong." Extensively quoting the report, the editorial praised the task force for a "clear, convincing answer" to the problem of surrogacy, since "[s]uch a practice is baby-selling, and it's wrong."[27] Other papers in the state, from the *Buffalo News* to *New York Newsday,* also published editorials that praised the task force's report and its recommendations. Moreover, copies of these editorials were included in the materials submitted to Governor Cuomo in 1992.[28] Four years after the report was published, its findings were still being cited by supporters of anti–commercial surrogacy legislation, such as the New York State Catholic Conference.[29]

What accounts for the strength of the effect the task force had on the framing of and political response to surrogate motherhood in New York? First, because the task force membership was diverse, including religious leaders, feminist lawyers, philosophers, medical practitioners, and patient advocates, their findings were likely viewed as unbiased and therefore valid.[30] Also, since the task force existed prior to its charge to study surrogacy, its members could not be seen as having been selected specifically because of their known views on the issue. Commenting on the group's influence, one member explained, "[T]he task force has developed a reputation, so it's trusted. It doesn't have any agendas, it's nonpartisan. It's respected nationally and internationally, so . . . its reputation has enhanced its authority."[31] Furthermore, the task force's unanimous policy decision most likely added weight to their conclusions. That is, the agreement of such a diverse group of people on what to do with the problem of surrogate motherhood ("baby selling") meant that their recommendations (ban commercial surrogacy) must be the appropriate policy response to the phenomenon. The task force was keenly aware of the possibility of this effect. The preface to the final report states: "The Task Force hopes that the consensus forged among its diverse membership will serve as a catalyst for public resolution."[32]

After the task force's report was released, two additional policy reports were produced by New York governmental agencies. The first, *Contract Motherhood: Ethical and Legislative Considerations,* was prepared in 1991 by a staff member of Assemblyman Roger L. Green (D), chairman of the Legislative Commission on Science and Technology.[33] Although this document did not provide a particular policy recommendation, it reviewed the task force's earlier policy suggestions, taking a very critical stance toward commercial surrogacy. For instance, despite acknowledging the "plight of infertile couples," the report's closing lines indicate a preference for approaching the problem of surrogate motherhood using a "baby-selling" frame: "State sanction of the practice gives implicit approval to the conception of children for others in exchange for money, and to such a use of women's reproductive capabilities. . . . [T]he question for legislative consideration is whether the needs of a few individuals could justify the creation of a market in birth mothers and children with the attendant social risks and ethical pitfalls of commodifying the reproductive capabilities of underprivileged women and their children."[34] This report was not undertaken in response to any particular bill or legislative proposal, but the analysis it provided suggests that in the early 1990s government agencies in New York were still leaning heavily toward understanding surrogacy as a form of commodified reproduction.

Another report, published in early 1992 by the New York State Department of Health, encouraged legislative support of the anti–commercial surrogacy bill then under consideration. This report, *The Business of Surrogate Parenting,* explicitly opposed commercial surrogacy. In fact, its tone was quite alarmist with regard to the consequences of the state's continued lack of legislation on surrogacy: "Government inaction in New York State is particularly troubling in light of a recent New York State Department of Health investigation of surrogate parenting. The investigation found that New York State has become the national center for surrogate parenting. As other states and nations have taken steps to limit or prohibit commercial surrogacy, the practice has flourished within New York's borders."[35] The report warned that "[i]n the absence of legislation, the practice of commercial surrogacy will continue to flourish in New York State, guided solely by commercial and contractual standards."[36]

The agency's support for a "baby-selling" frame and a ban on commercial surrogacy is indicated by the detailed review the report provides of the task force's 1988 study and by the positive appraisal given to that group's policy proposals.[37] A copy of the antisurrogacy proposal then under consideration in the legislature, a bill explicitly derived from the task force's recommendations, was included in the appendix of the Department of Health report. Additionally, the report highlighted Noel Keane's prominent and problematic role in surrogacy arrangements: "Noel Keane, the country's most active commercial broker, also bases his business in New York State. Keane first gained national attention as the broker for the Baby M case. He has been the center of more commercial surrogacy litigation than any other broker."[38] Besides referencing the Baby M case, the report documented two other disputed surrogacy cases in which Keane was involved.[39]

As with the report of the task force, New York papers took note of the Department of Health's report. On the day of its release, the *New York Times* ran a story entitled "New York Is Urged to Outlaw Surrogate Parenting for Pay," which emphasized the study's image of New York as "'the surrogate-parenting capital of the nation' because it had not joined other states in outlawing commercial baby-brokering."[40] A month later, in its editorial endorsement of the antisurrogacy bill, the *New York Times* also used research from the Department of Health report to support its position, quoting the reports' description of New York as the "capital" of surrogacy transactions.[41] The Department of Health's description of New York as the "surrogate-parenting capital of the nation" was also referred to in the editorial endorsements of the anti–commercial surrogacy bill in two other local papers, the *Daily News* and *Newsday*.[42]

In the end, more than these two widely publicized and respected governmental reports on surrogate parenting legitimated the definition of surrogacy in New York state as a practice that involved "baby selling." What makes the two studies especially important is that each was reported and commented on by the press, thereby making salient their framing of the issue, and each was used by opponents of commercial surrogacy as evidence that the appropriate policy approach was to ban the practice. The significant effect of these publications in New York contrasts with the role of investigations of surrogate parenting undertaken by state actors and agencies in California.

As in New York, the first state investigation in California took a generally positive approach in assessing the practice of surrogate parenting. In March 1988, the state's deputy attorney general wrote a memorandum for the Department of Justice that provided an overview of surrogacy arrangements in California and reviewed the potentially relevant existing state laws. In the memo's final section, "The Need for Legislation," the author acknowledged concerns about commodification but seemed to lean toward a "plight of the infertile" framing of the practice:

> If anything is clear, it is that legislation must be enacted to prevent exploitation of the parties and the commercialization of what could under certain circumstances be a socially redeeming practice. Although the simplest approach would be to ban paid surrogacy arrangements altogether, it would appear that the rising rates of infertility, the long wait for adoption and some couple's *[sic]* firm commitment to have their "own" child at any cost will result in clandestine arrangements. Therefore, appropriate regulation to protect against the dangers inherent in the commercialization of such a private and emotional arrangement and to protect the child, the natural parents, the adoptive parents and society at large would seem to be in order.[43]

Notably, this memorandum was written while the Baby M case was still receiving media attention and during the same year as the New York task force's highly critical report was published. Although the deputy attorney general's recommendations do not seem to have had much direct effect on the legislative process in California, his memo does indicate that government actors were favorably inclined toward regulating surrogacy, even at a time when there was a national backlash against the practice.

In September 1988, the California legislature approved a resolution, proposed by Assemblywoman Sunny Mojonnier (R), to create the Joint Legislative Committee on Surrogate Parenting to study the issue of surrogate motherhood (see chapter 1 for additional information about the committee). A committee-appointed advisory panel of experts was directed to investigate the issue of surrogate parenting. Unlike the New York State Task Force on Life and the Law, however, this group was not a standing committee representing diverse interests. Instead, the panel was formed solely to deal with the issue of surrogate parenting, and its members were chosen by legislators with established positions on surrogacy. The joint committee's chair was the resolution's sponsor, Assemblywoman Mojonnier, who was also the legislature's most vocal surrogacy opponent. She selected Alexander Capron, a University of Southern California law professor known for his antisurrogacy views, as chair of the advisory panel.[44] After Mojonnier's appointments were criticized as stacking the panel against surrogate parenting, other legislators on the committee with more favorable attitudes toward the practice selected additional members.[45] Yet concerns about bias persisted, as indicated by the following excerpt from a letter to Assemblywoman Mojonnier written by a legislative advocate who supported surrogacy: "At least one member of the Advisory Task Force announced at the first Task Force meeting that he would not be swayed from an anti-surrogacy stance regardless of how much empirical data was submitted which would support surrogacy."[46]

The advisory panel's final report, issued in 1990, shows the effects of the appointment process. Unlike New York's task force, this advisory panel did not achieve consensus. Internal divisions resulted in the preparation of *two* reports. The majority report, whose signers were Mojonnier's appointments, came down strongly against commercial surrogacy, recommending that it be prohibited and justifying their position in terms of a "baby-selling" frame. The minority report took a more positive approach toward surrogate parenting, proposing that the state provide regulations to clarify the legal relations of the parties involved. Their different policy recommendation came from a rejection of a "baby-selling" frame in favor of a "plight of infertile couples" frame. "[S]urrogate parenting does not represent commercialization of reproduction, as alleged in the Majority Report. . . . Further, and as the evidence indicates, surrogate parenting as practiced in the State of California and in the United States has not led to any significant harm to the women who act as surrogates, or the children or couples involved. At the same time, surrogate parenting has produced substantial benefit in the form of new families."[47] The advisory panel's split opinion diminished the significance accorded to its final report. Although the majority of the members concluded that the state should ban commercial surrogacy arrangements, the lack of unanimity left room for competing frames of surrogate parenting to persist.

Senator Watson's chief of staff spent hours discrediting the panel majority's position.[48] Additionally, numerous letters were written to legislators criticizing the way some advisory panel members conducted their study of surrogacy. Critics included various chapters of RESOLVE (a national infertility association), California NOW, the Organization for Parenting Through Surrogacy (OPTS), and the National Association of Surrogate Mothers (NASM). Most of these letters expressed strong dismay over the failure to include infertile couples, surrogate mothers, and women's rights organizations as either panel members or witnesses. These critiques of the majority report made use of cultural discourses concerning women, families, and infertility, and notions of "expert" status and representation, to present their concerns. As a spokesperson for OPTS stated, "I am writing to express my outrage that public funds were used by a legislative committee to conduct a debate on surrogate parenting without including any representatives of the infertile community (one in six couples), surrogate mothers, or professionals having direct experience with surrogate parenting."[49] Given the lack of input from these groups, "OPTS respectfully urges the Committee to seriously question the validity of the Advisory Panel's majority report and recommendation regarding surrogate parenting."[50] The letters from RESOLVE chapters expressed similar concerns: "Due to the fact that we were excluded from discussion or informational input, it seems doubtful that any conclusions this committee may have reached were the result of careful scrutiny of all sides of the issue. Certainly, the fact that no infertility organizations were included cast aspersions on any representation of the infertile interest. Surely, since we are the population for whom this innovation was designed, our concerns should have been taken into consideration."[51] Similarly, California NOW expressed its "deep concern and disappointment in the manner in which the Advisory Panel to the Joint Committee on Surrogate Parenting was constituted, administered and consequently, its likely conclusions."[52] California NOW echoed others' criticisms of the panel's failure to include the views of all interested parties: "Despite the importance of this debate, your panel failed to include even the most basic viewpoints involved: surrogate parents and infertile people, and the people who help those two groups find each other. It's a bit like naming a panel to discuss civil rights and failing to include people of color."[53] Jan Sutton, spokesperson for the National Association of Surrogate Mothers, submitted a similar complaint. Her specific concerns stemmed from the panel's failure to consult with women's rights groups: "How can such important legislation regarding a woman's fundamental rights of procreation, privacy and self-determination be written and have validity without including a voice from the segment of society it presumes to protect, women?"[54]

The panel's lack of consensus and the criticism leveled at its makeup and at its methods of inquiry seem to have undermined its overall legitimacy. The majority's recommendation to ban commercial surrogacy did not seem to carry the same weight as that of the similar recommendation made by the New York task force. The panel's sponsoring body, the Joint Committee on Surrogate Parenting, did not adopt the recommendations offered in either the majority or the minority report. And, unlike the *New*

York Times editors, who responded swiftly and positively to the final report of the Task Force on Life and the Law, the editorial staff of the *Los Angeles Times* apparently considered the recommendations of the joint committee's panel of too little importance to warrant comment.

Whereas state agencies in New York became important claims makers for the "baby-selling" framing of surrogacy, the lack of any such strong claims from state actors in California created the space in which the "plight of the infertile" framing could become more dominant. This suggests that certain social actors and institutions had more legitimacy and/or were more effective in making claims about surrogacy. An examination of the particular legislators and interest groups, and the divisions and alliances among them, reveals additional layers in the complex dynamics that characterized the legislative debates over surrogacy policy in New York and California. The credentials these social actors brought to the table and the rhetorical strategies they used to define the problem of surrogate motherhood shaped the political landscapes and opportunity structures of surrogacy politics and policies in the two states.

FACES OF SURROGACY: TWO PROCHOICE FEMALE LEGISLATIVE SPONSORS

In both New York and California, female legislators were at the forefront in shaping the social policy response to surrogate motherhood in their respective states. Assemblywoman Helene Weinstein's and Senator Diane Watson's sponsorship of the New York and California bills, respectively, seems to have been important in influencing the outcome of surrogacy legislation in each state. (See also chapter 1.)[55] Both women devoted extensive time and energy to the passage of their bills, and both could legitimately claim to represent women's interests and reproductive rights, a strong advantage in the debates over how to understand and respond to the issue of surrogate motherhood. (See chapter 2.)

Helene Weinstein was first elected to the New York State Assembly in 1980. In 1994 she became the first woman to chair the prestigious Assembly Judiciary Committee, a position she continues to hold more than a decade later. As an assemblywoman, Weinstein has championed an array of women's issues, including bills on domestic violence and child support. She also has sponsored bills that allow officials to use gender-neutral or gender-specific titles; that prohibit private clubs from barring members on the basis of race, creed, color, national origin, sex, disability, or marital status; that forbid sex offenders from plea-bargaining; and that recommend clemency for battered women who kill or attack their assailants in self-defense.[56]

Furthermore, Weinstein has held prominent leadership positions in women's organizations. She was chair of the Assembly Task Force on Women's Issues, a group devoted to legislation dealing with women, for seven years, beginning in 1987.[57] She also headed the Legislative Women's Caucus, a group formed in 1983 to provide combined support and strategy for the state's female legislators.[58] Weinstein was involved, as well, with groups such as the State Commission on Child Support, the Governor's Task Force on Domestic Violence, and the Governor's Task Force on Displaced Homemakers.[59] In sum, she brought extensive credentials as an expert on women's issues to her role in the legislature as an advocate for anti–commercial surrogacy legislation. Comments Weinstein's colleague, Assemblyman Richard Brodsky (D), made during the floor debate on the 1992 antisurrogacy bill underscore just how widely accepted the assemblywoman's credentials were: "Anybody who thinks it does not matter that women are in positions of responsibility in public debate [should] realize it is highly unlikely that this issue would have gotten to this point without the respect and concerns that have been raised by Ms. Weinstein and some of her female colleagues."[60]

Senator Diane Watson (D) was Weinstein's West Coast counterpart. Watson joined the legislature in 1978, becoming the first black woman to be elected to the California State Senate.[61] In 1981, she was appointed to the California Commission on the Status of Women. She also chaired the Health and Human Services Committee and was a member of the Committees on Budget and Fiscal Review, Education, Judiciary, and Public Employment and Retirement. Like Weinstein, Watson was a prominent women's rights advocate, participating in events from the first National Women's Town Meeting to a panel against domestic violence. As chair of the Health and Human Services Committee, she was a strong supporter of women's health issues. In 1987 she successfully introduced a bill on informed consent for hysterectomies, and in 1991 she co-sponsored a resolution declaring breast cancer an epidemic and calling for action on both the state and federal level. Senator Watson also sponsored legislation that required the state

Office of Family Planning to test women for chlamydia, the most common bacterial sexually transmitted disease in the United States. Her activities on behalf of women's issues also included co-chairing an advisory committee that documented the existence of gender bias throughout California's judicial system and sponsoring a bill that put a bond measure on the California ballot to provide working parents with more safe and good-quality child care centers.[62]

Given the use of choice rhetoric to define the problem of surrogate motherhood (see chapter 2), it is also significant that both Watson's and Weinstein's credentials as women's rights supporters extended to their strong support of abortion rights. A Weinstein staff member described her as "very prochoice."[63] Similarly, a member of Watson's staff described her as "the most outspoken defender of the prochoice position in the legislature."[64] Indeed, Watson had a particularly long public record of work on behalf of women's rights to abortion. In 1985 she sponsored a bill that was signed into law, making it a felony to bomb a health clinic or an office of a pro- or antiabortion group. In 1989, in the wake of a Supreme Court decision in favor of a Missouri law that restricted abortions, Watson introduced a resolution reaffirming abortion rights in California and the requirement that Medi-Cal pay for abortions. Later in 1989, she unsuccessfully led a campaign, along with then-Assemblywoman Maxine Waters (D), to provide emergency funds to prevent the closure of family planning clinics throughout California. Watson also helped defeat a measure in 1990 that prohibited abortions after twenty-four weeks of pregnancy. In 1991 she sponsored a joint resolution stating that the California legislature opposed the "gag rule," a Supreme Court decision that curbed the rights of clinics receiving federal funds to inform pregnant women of abortion as an option. Later that year she also supported the distribution of the French-made abortion pill RU486 in the United States.[65]

The fact that Assemblywoman Weinstein and Senator Watson were female and were prochoice advocates may have aided in the relative success of the divergent surrogacy legislation each sponsored. Their long histories of engagement with women's issues made it possible for them to legitimately claim ownership of this new social problem.[66] This was certainly the view of one of Weinstein's staff members. In that person's opinion, Weinstein's history as a strong women's rights advocate allowed other people in the legislature to trust her as representing the "woman's position."[67] Similarly, Watson's extensive women's rights record, and in particular her activism on behalf of reproductive rights, probably would have increased her regulatory bill's legitimacy as legislation that truly reflected women's interests. Her sponsorship of regulatory surrogacy legislation may have been additionally influential because it neutralized the concerns of many critics of commercial surrogacy, particularly academic feminists, regarding the possible exploitation of poor women and women of color.[68] Watson not only was a women's rights advocate but also was widely known for her advocacy on behalf of the poor.[69] Furthermore, she represented a predominantly lower-class minority community—her district's population was 43.3 percent black and 36.5 percent Latino, with 24 percent of the residents earning below the official poverty level.[70] Watson's endorsement of a practice that her constituents most likely would not have the financial resources to benefit from could not be as effectively criticized for discriminating against the poor and minorities. Indeed, given the racialized nature of reproductive politics more generally, and surrogacy in particular, Watson's support of the practice, as a black woman, is significant.

The sponsors of the surrogacy legislation on both coasts seem to have played a significant role in shaping the fate of the bills addressing this issue. At the same time, in both states, those closely involved with the surrogacy debates often commented on the "personal" nature of these debates and the individualized way in which legislators voted. As the sections below will make clear, their positions on surrogacy cost both Weinstein and Watson the support of many of their usual liberal and feminist allies. The fact that in the New York State Assembly and in both the California Senate and Assembly Democrats and Republicans voted on both sides of the issue also indicates the unusual splits as well as alliances made with regard to this new social problem. This implies that who sponsored a particular surrogacy bill may have been less important in shaping how individual legislators voted than is typical in legislative politics.[71] And this in turn reinforces the fact that reproductive politics does not always correspond to the usual patterns and cleavages found in the political arena.

In Senator Watson's case, regardless of how strongly her sponsorship assisted the passage of surrogacy regulatory bill SB 937 through the legislature in 1992, her political background probably hurt the bill in the end. As a liberal and vocal Democratic legislator, she had no political capital with or ties to the state's then-governor, Republican Pete Wilson. As a result, she had no power or persuasive ability to prevent his eventual veto of the bill. As one informant put it, "[T]he fact that Diane Watson was against it [the veto]—Diane Watson is against everything Pete Wilson does anyways. So for him to screw over Diane Watson, no harm, no foul."[72] The legislative outcome in California suggests that apart from the effects of individual sponsors, in both states, the activities and positions of other interested groups might also have shaped the dominant framing of surrogacy and the divergent policy responses. The next section examines alliances made and not made among and between groups that represented women's/reproductive rights and organizations representing other interests. These ties and divisions affected what social movement theorists refer to as the "political opportunity structure"[73] surrounding the bills, thus influencing their eventual fates.

WOMEN'S GROUPS: UNITY VERSUS DIVISIONS

Assemblywoman Weinstein's sponsorship of New York's anti–commercial surrogacy legislation was an important factor in the bill's successful passage, but so, too, was the active involvement of an array of women's groups whose members testified at hearings, wrote letters, and mobilized on the issue in defense of women's rights. In fact, the extent and prominence of women's organizations' participation in these debates probably help account for the successful claiming of surrogacy as a women's issue. (See chapter 2.) The Assembly's Task Force on Women's Issues (with Weinstein as chair) co-sponsored the largest public hearing on surrogacy in the late 1980s—and it was on the basis of this hearing that the assemblywoman formulated her policy response.

Representatives from several women's rights organizations attended the many public hearings held in the late 1980s as the New York legislature was trying to determine the most appropriate policy response to this new social issue. A representative of the Coalition on Women's Legislative Issues (COWLI), for instance, testified against surrogate motherhood on more than one occasion.[74] Testimony from these hearings reveals COWLI's particular concern about the effect commercial surrogacy would have on women. The testimony reflects the group's use of the "baby-selling" frame to understand the problem of surrogacy: "To use and pay a woman as a breeder is the ultimate in dehumanization. Poor women and third world women could be exploited by the wealthy, and surrogacy could become a new form of prostitution."[75] Speaking on behalf of the Institute of Women and Technology, radical feminist Janice Raymond also testified against surrogacy at a public hearing and emphasized her organization's concern with the impact of surrogate practices on women's rights. Likewise, a representative of New York State NOW spoke out against the Dunne-Goodhue regulatory bill at a 1987 hearing, attesting to her group's primary goal of advocating on behalf of women. Similar to the other women's groups, New York State NOW's opposition to surrogate motherhood was framed around concerns about reproductive freedom and the effects of surrogacy practices on women's rights to privacy. (See also chapter 2.) It seems, then, that women's groups were vocal and important actors in shaping the dominant framing of "baby selling" and the resulting policy approach to surrogate parenting taken by New York State in 1992.

The involvement of women's groups was still very visible when Weinstein's bill was up for vote in the Assembly and subsequently put on the governor's desk. The Women's Division of the State of New York and the Women's Bar Association of the State of New York both sent letters to Governor Mario Cuomo in support of the anti–commercial surrogacy bill.[76] Support for the bill from a government agency and a professional women's organization further signaled that the "women's position" was anti–commercial surrogacy and as a result probably affected the dominance of the "baby-selling" frame. The involvement of the Women's Bar Association was particularly interesting since its members were not directly affected by, or particularly organized around, the specific issue of surrogate parenting. Yet the group represented, simultaneously, two types of expertise: as women the members were experts on "women's issues," and as lawyers they were experts on legal issues. Furthermore, by the early 1990s, the Women's Bar Association had a sixty-year history of fighting for gender equality and issues of concern to women and families. This background probably legitimated their position on surrogate motherhood as a women's rights position, since they could claim expert status on and thus ownership of women's issues.

Other women's rights experts also lobbied on behalf of the 1992 legislation. Although no letter of support from New York State NOW is in the bill file, Weinstein's office did list the group as an organization in support of her anti–commercial surrogacy bill. Additionally, in her remarks on the Assembly floor and in an internal memo listing organizations that backed her bill, Weinstein mentioned the support of the New York State National Women's Political Caucus.[77] COWLI, too, was included on Weinstein's list of organizations in support of the bill (see table 7).

The fact that these women's groups testified against and wrote letters in opposition to commercial surrogacy is significant for two reasons. First, in their support of the 1992 anti–commercial surrogacy bill, they represented a visible, united force of experts on women who definitively opposed surrogate motherhood. Second, these groups also represented an alliance among diverse types of feminists (e.g., liberal and radical) who often do not see eye to eye. Those in the liberal feminist camp, for instance, often endorse the widest array of choices and thus, in the case of surrogacy, were sometimes reluctant to have the practice banned (see Introduction). The convergence between and agreement among different types of feminist organizations despite such reservations, along with the endorsement of institutions such as the state's Women's Division and the Women's Bar Association, probably further legitimated the antisurrogacy position in New York as the women's rights position.

This is not to say that only those who opposed surrogacy relied on women's rights to support their position. As chapter 2 explained, groups in New York who opposed a ban on commercial surrogacy also used women's rights rhetoric. For instance, when women who had acted as surrogate mothers testified against a ban—as individuals and in groups (e.g., Surrogates by Choice)—they often punctuated their arguments with references to feminist notions of bodily rights, choice, and equality. Similarly, legislators, infertile couples (individually and as part of groups such as the National Infertility Network Exchange), and personnel from commercial surrogate parenting programs used women's rights rhetoric in defending the practice.

Assemblyman Alan Hevesi's (D) comments during the Assembly floor debate on the proposed ban clearly highlighted the tension over what policy position best reflected women's interests: "Well, I still remain convinced, even if some of my friends in the women's movement or in the civil rights movement are not convinced in this case that a woman should have those rights to decide for herself what is right for her life, when to have a baby, when not to have a baby, even to have a baby as an act of love for another

TABLE 7. Interest Groups, by Position Taken on New York's S 1906/A 7367 (1992)

Support	Oppose
American Jewish Congress	None
Council on Children and Families, State of New York	
Department of Health, State of New York	
Department of Social Services, State of New York	
Division for Women, State of New York	
National Coalition Against Surrogacy	
National Committee for Adoption	
National Council for Adoption	
National Organization for Women—New York State	
New York Civil Liberties Union	
New York National Women's Political Caucus	
New York State Catholic Conference	
New York State Coalition on Women's Legislative Issues	
New York State Interfaith IMPACT	
Surrogate Association of the State of New York	
United Jewish Appeal—Federation of Jewish Philanthropies of New York	
Women's Bar Association of the State of New York	

SOURCES: New York State Bill Jacket, 1992, S 1906/A 7437; documents from Assemblywoman Weinstein's files, in author's files.

couple, I believe that should be her right. I believe this bill destroys that right, and I'm going to vote against it."[78] Assembly member Deborah Glick (D), an openly gay legislator who has worked with the National Organization for Women, the Women's Political Caucus, and the National Abortion and Reproductive Rights Action League,[79] also voted against the bill. Her remarks during the Assembly floor debate reflected a distinct "plight of the infertile" framing of the practice as shaping her position on the problem of surrogacy: "I also know many people who must, who absolutely must use extraordinary means in order to have their families. Many of my friends, lesbian and gay men, all have to use some extraordinary means in order to have the families they deeply desire to have. So, it has given me great pause in the deliberations on this issue to think that we might close the door to some who want to have children of their own and are not able to do so."[80] Glick's split with Weinstein on the issue was unusual enough to draw notice. As one activist commented, "Helene Weinstein . . . and Deborah Glick usually have the same point of view, so for them to differ on that [the ban] was . . . interesting."[81]

Clearly, there was a minority view regarding what social policy best reflected women's interests and reproductive rights during the legislative debates in New York. However, in New York, no organization explicitly devoted to women's issues or women's rights opposed the 1992 bill. Many women's organizations were involved in some way in the New York legislative debates over surrogate motherhood. Despite different approaches to some of the issues involved, *all* of these organizations supported the type of bill that was eventually enacted. Since these groups could legitimately portray themselves as representatives of women's interests and experts on such matters, their consensus regarding a ban can be viewed as partially responsible for the passage of an anti–commercial surrogacy bill in New York in 1992.

In California, on the other hand, various divisions in and among women's organizations seem to have contributed to the partial success of a very different legislative response to surrogate motherhood. First, in contrast to New York, women's groups in California did not achieve consensus on the regulatory bill. A member of Senator Watson's staff described the state's women's organizations as "strong and divided."[82] One informant in California described the women's groups in California as "totally split down the middle." "Where some feminists think this is a woman's fundamental right to do with her body what she wishes," this informant explained, "the other one says paying a woman to have a child for someone else is inherently exploitation, worse than prostitution."[83]

The division among feminists and women's rights advocates in California manifested itself in two ways. One was at the intraorganizational level. Internally, many of the women's organizations were torn and divided on the issue of surrogate parenting. A lobbyist for Planned Parenthood told a Watson aide that their membership was split fifty-fifty on the issue. As a result, the organization did not take an official position on the bill. Planned Parenthood's reluctance to take a stance was also affected by the fact that Senator Watson was an important prochoice advocate in the legislature and thus the group did not want to jeopardize the strong ties they had to her.[84] The fact that other groups that did not support Watson's regulatory legislation (e.g., California NOW, ACLU) usually considered her an ally on reproductive rights and other women's issues probably tempered their opposition as well. For instance, Watson was only one of four state senators who received an "A" in California NOW's "1991 Legislative Report Card."[85] This again suggests that Watson's sponsorship of the surrogacy regulatory bill was significant, since it affected the level of interest groups' involvement—deterring it altogether or tempering opposition.

The second division among women's organizations occurred at the interorganizational level. While most California women's and women's rights groups did not take official positions due to a lack of consensus within their organizations, two important groups did become involved. However, they took opposing positions on Senate Bill 937. As previously noted, California NOW did not support Watson's regulatory bill. Their opposition, however, was not due to a fundamental rejection of surrogate parenting arrangements. In 1988, when California NOW opposed a bill that would have prohibited and criminalized surrogacy arrangements, the group explained its opposition this way: "We support the right of every woman to set the terms of their sexuality, including the right to choose if and when to bear children. A law that would deny a woman the right to be a contract birth mother is simply unacceptable to our organization."[86] Their concerns about the 1992 bill stemmed not from worries over the commercial aspects of surrogacy but rather from concerns over four specific aspects of the bill: (1) it did not include a grace period during which a surrogate could change her mind; (2) it would regulate only genetic surrogate births (as opposed to all surrogate births) under adoption law; (3) it did not ensure that children born through surrogate arrangements would have open access to adoption records; and (4) it included language that suggested that the infertile couple did not have to take custody of the child if the surrogate was found in violation of what could be a very restrictive contract.[87] California NOW's opposition may have hurt the bill's chances of getting through the legislature since, as chapter 2 showed, surrogate motherhood was successfully claimed as a "women's issue," and California NOW was an important women's rights lobbying organization in the state. Expressing his view that Watson's reputation as a reproductive rights activist was crucial to the bill's passage, one informant remarked, "It's like one of those things, like only Nixon could go to China; only Diane [Watson] could go against NOW and prevail. Because her standing in that community is without question."[88]

On the other hand, the regulatory bill did have the support of the California Commission on the Status of Women. This body was established by the California legislature in 1965 and became a permanent, state-funded agency in 1971.[89] The commission, which has repeatedly selected reproductive rights as a primary focus of its legislative efforts, reaffirmed that top-priority commitment in 1991. Senator Watson first introduced Senate Bill 937 during the 1991 legislative session; the commission supported the proposed legislation, designating it as a priority one bill for that session.[90] The commission's support and California NOW's opposition to SB 937 created a visible schism in the women's rights position regarding the appropriate state policy response to surrogacy. Even though a Republican governor, George Deukmejian, had appointed several of the commission's public members, both California NOW and the commission were considered "liberal" women's rights organizations and tended to support the same sort of issues.[91] For instance, of the ten bills used by California NOW in 1991 for their "Legislative Report Card," eight received priority one or two status from the Commission on the Status of Women.

The commission's institutional place in government can be compared to the legislative role of the New York State Assembly Task Force on Women's Issues. Both groups had members who were in the legislature. And the sponsors of each bill—Watson and Weinstein—were members of the legislative women's organizations in their state. The result in California was a divide between two well-known, liberal women's rights groups. The commission's support of Watson's bill might have helped legitimate this legislation as considerate of women's interests for two reasons. First, the commission's position as a body of experts on issues that concerned women was widely accepted. Second, the visible absence of a large contingent of other such women's experts lobbying against the legislation meant that there was no significant and united counterclaim that opposition to the 1992 bill was a mark of support for women's rights.

Women's groups were strategically placed to shape the legislative debates about surrogacy, but the involvement of other interest groups, and the particular arguments they brought to the table, also affected how reproductive politics over the problem of surrogate parenting played out in New

York and California. The next section discusses the roles played by other key groups.

STRANGE BEDFELLOWS: ALLIANCES BETWEEN WOMEN'S GROUPS AND RELIGIOUS ORGANIZATIONS

Surrogate motherhood raises many ethical concerns about the status of family, marriage, and kinship ties. Religious organizations, and in particular the Catholic Church, were generally opposed to surrogate parenting in all forms and were actively involved in shaping policy.[92] Many of those who tried to implement a regulatory approach to surrogacy claimed that the Catholic Church's opposition to surrogate motherhood was instrumental in defeating their bills.[93] In fact, in the early 1980s commentators linked the defeat of both versions of Assemblyman Roos's regulatory bills to religious opposition. (See chapter 1 for details about this legislation.)[94] The Catholic Church, along with other religious groups, continued to play a pivotal role in surrogacy politics in both states through 1992.

In New York, three religious interest groups, the Metropolitan Chapter of the American Jewish Congress, the New York Council of Churches, and probably most importantly, the New York State Catholic Conference, submitted letters in support of the 1992 anti–commercial surrogacy bill. The strength of Catholic lobbying organizations ensured that the religious viewpoint would be accorded legislative attention, but the fact that all three religious organizations endorsed the bill was important as well. These bodies represented a wide array of religious interest-group organizations. The Council of Churches, an interfaith group, is a very liberal organization. In stark contrast to the Catholic Church, it has supported a woman's right to an abortion. On the other hand, the Catholic Conference is the lobbying arm for the Council of Bishops and consequently represents the official views of the Catholic Church. Yet on the issue of surrogate parenting, these various groups' positions converged. The Catholic Conference's letter of opposition was an unequivocal attack on the practice and clearly framed the issue as being about "baby selling": "The practice of surrogate parenting amounts to nothing more than womb renting, baby selling, and the exploitation of the poor. It damages the lives of children and destroys the integrity of marriage."[95] The American Jewish Congress's framing of the issue and the reasons provided for their opposition to surrogacy were very similar: "While Jewish tradition approves efforts to overcome infertility, the commercialization of surrogacy, which leads to womb renting, baby selling and the exploitation of the poor by the rich, is religiously problematic for the Jews. It violates human dignity and demeans the sanctity and infinite value of human life."[96]

A second and perhaps more crucial factor in the role played by religious organizations was the somewhat unusual alliance between feminists and Catholics in New York. A legislator involved with the debate over surrogacy attributed the success of the 1992 anti–commercial surrogacy bill to the powerful coalition between women's groups and the church.[97] A staff member in Weinstein's office described their alliance with the Catholic Conference as involving a "strange bedfellow."[98] Similarly, an informant who advocated for the anti–commercial surrogacy bill remarked on the surprising alliance of interest groups: "Imagine that. The Coalition for Choice and the Catholic Conference."[99] Senator Mary Goodhue, also noting this seemingly unique coalition, quipped that it was the only issue "the pope and Gloria Steinem agreed on."[100] Indeed, the sponsors of the bill in each legislative house themselves represented this unusual alliance. The Senate sponsor of New York's 1992 ban, John Marchi, was antiabortion and was viewed as acting on behalf of the Catholic Conference.[101] On the other hand, as discussed above, the Assembly sponsor, Helene Weinstein, was a strong supporter of abortion rights.[102]

Working together on the issue of surrogate parenting, women's and religious groups appealed to a wide ideological and political spectrum. United, these two very different types of groups each legitimated the other's message. In particular, feminists and religious organizations shared a concern about commodified reproduction, and both promulgated a "babyselling" frame (see chapter 3). The report produced by the Senate Judiciary Committee for Senator Dunne elucidated the shared feminist and religious perspective toward and framing of surrogate parenting as an unacceptable and dangerous form of commodified reproduction: "[T]he most forceful public statements of opposition have been made by feminist theorists and spokesmen *[sic]* for religious groups. They believe that the practice is immoral and unethical because it violates the precept that human beings should not be bought and sold. . . . They fear that acceptance of the practice could lead to the full commercialization and dehumanization of reproduction."[103]

In addition to their condemnation of "baby selling," anti–commercial surrogacy feminists and religious groups shared a concern about maternal bonding. The feminist anti–commercial surrogacy position on bonding concerned women's incapacity to give informed consent on the revocation of parental rights prior to the birth of a child. Assemblywoman Weinstein argued during the Assembly floor debate that "[p]ublic policy must recognize that many women may not be able to give informed consent to relinquish a child in advance of the child's conception and birth."[104] Likewise, Father Kenneth Doyle of New York's Catholic Conference raised the issue of bonding as a primary factor in his organization's response against surrogacy: "The fundamental reason for our concern is that the practice fractures the parent/child bond."[105] These shared perspectives on the problems posed by surrogacy helped solidify the alliance between feminists and religious organizations. The support for a ban on commercial surrogate arrangements from these two large, strong, and diverse interest groups in turn boded well for the anti–commercial surrogacy bill's eventual passage in New York.[106]

In California no similar united front emerged, and consequently the dynamics of interest-group coalitions seem to have played out differently there. As in New York, many religious organizations in California lobbied against surrogacy. Not only did the powerful California Catholic Conference oppose the regulatory bill, but so did the California Association of Catholic Hospitals, the Committee on Moral Concerns, and California Right to Life. According to a member of Senator Watson's staff, this opposition was the toughest hurdle for SB 937. As this informant put it, "[The] Catholic Church plays rough. . . . [It's] not [a] gentle opponent."[107] In his view, Catholic opposition did hurt the regulatory bill, influencing some no votes and affecting its eventual veto. However, unlike in New York, religious organizations and women's groups in California did not form a powerful alliance against the California regulatory bill. Without the backing of large numbers of women's groups, the Catholic anti–commercial surrogacy contingent may have had less legitimacy. This, in turn, may have helped permit the regulatory surrogacy bill's passage through the California Senate and Assembly. That Catholic groups did not successfully block the bill in these two legislative bodies suggests the possible importance of coalition politics with women's groups when it comes to social problems that are successfully claimed as women's issues. In other words, as the next section will show, the story of surrogate motherhood was more than a straightforward and simplistic case of the triumph of strong and well-organized interest groups, as the situation in New York might lead some to conclude.

COALITION POLITICS AND THE POLITICS OF REPRODUCTION

Although the support of women's and religious groups was probably key, there were other important groups that advocated on behalf of the New York anti–commercial surrogate parenting bill. These included the National Committee for Adoption and the ACLU. The former group's backing was important because adoption and surrogacy involve similar issues (e.g., children's rights); the latter's group backing was important because the ACLU represents a legal and civil rights perspective. In the end, an impressive array of groups—including women's organizations, religious organizations, civil rights organizations, and children's advocates—unanimously supported the anti–commercial surrogacy bill in New York. Such broad-based backing seems likely to have assisted the passage of this legislation.

Furthermore, no major interest group expressed opposition to the ban (see table 7 for a complete list of the interest groups and their positions on the proposed legislation). This fact did not go unnoticed. During the Assembly debate on Weinstein's bill, Assemblyman Robert Wertz (R) commented on this combination of minor opposition to and vast and varied support for banning commercial surrogacy in the state: "I must tell you when I saw a memo which combined the Civil Liberties Union with the Catholic Conference, and now I said, this one is one in which you can vote yes and can't get in any trouble at all because everyone in the world is in favor of it."[108] In this sense, the political opportunity structure in New York was one that seemed to favor and aid the passage of the anti–commercial surrogacy bill. Indeed, many of those active in the surrogate parenting debates in New York attributed the success of anti–commercial surrogacy legislation to the absence of a strong, organized constituency in support of the practice. One informant said the 1992 bill was successful because only a limited group of people actually cared about surrogate motherhood, and this group did not have much political clout.[109] Similarly, a staff member of Assemblywoman Weinstein pointed out that what little support there was for regulating surrogate parenting came almost exclusively from people in the surrogacy business and the infertile couples who wanted to use the practice.[110] Additionally, Senator Mary Goodhue, who had co-sponsored regulatory legislation in the Senate in 1987, claimed that she did not pursue regulatory surrogacy legislation again after the failure of the bill she and Senator Dunne had sponsored in 1987 because "everyone" was against surrogate parenting.[111] At the same time, the predominantly white and middle-class status of these group members and activists rendered invisible implicit racial/class assumptions that were embedded in many of their arguments. (See chapter 3.)

At first glance, then, the case of New York seems to validate a pluralist account of politics—that is, the state responds to pressure exerted by the strongest and most active interest group(s). However, the preceding analysis of California's legislative response to surrogate motherhood belies such a simplified account of politics and social policy formation, particularly in the case of reproductive politics. In addition to the opposition of many religious organizations, other important interest groups opposed the California bill, and it still passed through both the State Assembly and the Senate (see table 8 for a complete list of the interest groups and their positions on the proposed legislation). Representing the same positions they took in New York, the ACLU and the National Coalition Against Surrogacy opposed California's regulatory legislation. The American Adoption Congress and the American College of Obstetricians and Gynecologists also opposed the bill.[112] Despite the similarity between this coalition of diverse interest groups and the alliances in New York, surrogacy opponents in California were unsuccessful in blocking the bill's passage through the two houses of the California legislature. In terms of the predictions of pluralist political theory, this is a particularly surprising outcome, since the number of organized groups in California opposed to regulating surrogacy was twice that of those supporting it.

However, unlike in New York, the other side—those in favor of the regulatory bill—did have the support of some significant organized groups, albeit many fewer than the number who opposed it. Four groups with direct interests in the legality of surrogacy—the Center for Surrogate Par-

TABLE 8. Interest Groups, by Position Taken on California's SB 937 (1992)

Support	*Oppose*
Center for Surrogate Parenting	American Adoption Congress
Commission on the Status of Women	American Civil Liberties Union
National Association of Surrogate Mothers	American College of Obstetricians and Gynecologists
Organization of Parents Through Surrogacy	California Association of Catholic Hospitals
RESOLVE	California Catholic Conference
State Bar of California	California National Organization for Women
	California Right to Life
	Committee on Moral Concern
	National Coalition Against Surrogacy
	Pacific Center for Health Policy and Ethics
	Women's Lobby

SOURCES: California Assembly Committee on Judiciary, "Bill Analysis: SB 937," August 12, 1992; California Bill File on SB 937, 1992; files from Senator Watson, in author's files.

enting, the National Association of Surrogate Mothers, the Organization of Parents Through Surrogacy, and RESOLVE—lobbied on behalf of the bill. In fact, CSP was listed as a co-sponsor on the bill analysis and was also responsible for hiring a professional lobbying firm, Nossaman, Gunther, Knox & Elliot, to facilitate the bill's passage.[113] As in New York, the predominantly white, middle-class background of those involved, personally or professionally, with surrogacy and infertility (as well as other interest groups) masked the class-race assumptions and interests of many of the social actors involved in the debate over surrogate parenting legislation in California.

The State Bar of California also formally supported Watson's regulatory bill. Their involvement was initiated by a lawyer from Orange County who became a mother through a surrogate parenting transaction arranged by CSP. The state bar's position did not go unchallenged—two lawyers filed lawsuits against the organization.[114] However, the legitimacy that the bar's support lent to the bill should not be dismissed. No similar legal organizations in New York took such an accepting position toward regulating surrogacy transactions. That the state bar, along with a minority of other organizations, offered a challenge to the dominant interest-group response in California (a challenge completely absent in New York) seems to have provided visible and important backing for Watson's bill, as well as for the "plight of the infertile" frame. At the same time, the success of the surrogate parenting legislation in California cannot be explained by the strength and number of interest groups in support of it, since, as noted, these groups were in the minority.

Rather, it seems that different policy approaches to surrogate parenting were able to take hold in California and New York because the political opportunity structure in each state differed. Interest-group politics may matter, but reproductive politics seems to involve more than simply which position is supported by the most organizations. It matters *who* takes a given position. Whereas the New York case was a story of "all against none," the comparison with California reveals that strength does not come from numbers alone. Although more interest groups opposed the California surrogacy regulatory bill than supported it, the bill still was passed by the state legislature. This may have occurred because of the split between women's groups and the consequent inability of religious organizations to represent themselves as concerned with women's rights. Explanations based on interest-group politics often are too simplistic to adequately account for observed outcomes. Yet in the politics of reproduction alliances and coalitions among usual adversaries may play a particularly important role, given the overlapping and contradictory interests and arguments that shape the contours of such debates.

Furthermore, in each state, there was only a very small constituency in support of or directly affected by surrogacy. Thus the amount of legislative attention given to this social problem suggests that in the end the symbolic nature of the issue mattered as much as, or even more than, interest-group strength and politicking.[115] That New York's and California's legislative process with regard to surrogate parenting was clearly not "politics as usual" is evidenced by cross-party alliances as well as the atypically long debates that ensued before voting occurred. As New York Assemblyman Michael Balboni, a fervent opponent of the anti–commercial surrogacy bill, commented during the 1992 debate, "This is not a Democratic issue. This is not a Republican issue. This is not a conservative or liberal issue. Look at the coalition of people who are going to get up on the floor today and look to see where the different divergent groups get up."[116] Later, he remarked: "This moment where we have spent over five hours discussing what I consider to be one of the most important issues I've ever considered makes me so proud to be a part of this Chamber."[117]

The fact that Balboni, and presumably many others, given the attention and time the topic garnered, considered surrogate parenting to be an especially important issue speaks to the symbolic politics that is fundamental to the politics of reproduction. Because of this symbolic element a key part of the political opportunity structure of reproductive politics is the cultural rhetoric available to name the issue in the first place. Preexisting political discourses—from women's and children's rights to the private nature of the family, reproductive freedom, and eugenic/racial assumptions about the future of the nation—shape the contours of reproductive politics, make some strategies more viable than others, and make certain speakers and alliances more or less authoritative in claiming ownership of the issue. At the same time, as the case of surrogate motherhood has shown, reproductive politics and interests do not form a predictable, linear continuum, and culture is constantly contested. Thus we can expect fluidity, ambivalence, overlap, and contradiction in the ongoing politics of reproduction.

Chapter 6 | A BRAVE NEW WORLD?

Reproductive Politics from the Past to the Present

Of all the institutions in America, the family is the one whose future is perhaps the most regularly described as being in jeopardy. Whether on the basis of real or imagined social trends and changes, the family repeatedly has been the focal point of general cultural anxieties and social conflict. Contemporary worries about the threat to the normative family, and to its place as the cornerstone of the nation, have parallels in the late-nineteenth- and early-twentieth-century alarm over women's declining fertility and the subsequent interventions to boost childbearing levels—ranging from the banning of birth control and abortion to the discouragement of higher education for women.[1] And much as in the late 1800s, contemporary reproductive politics is characterized by race- and class-specific concerns. Early-twentieth-century consternation about declining fertility was focused on the declining fertility of white, middle-class women and the concomitant rise in immigration from southern and eastern Europe. These fears fueled a campaign against "race suicide." More recent concerns about issues such as delayed marriage and childbearing, increased infertility, and the lack of "adoptable" babies also are clearly focused on the reproduction of white, middle-class families.[2] Evidence of "stratified reproduction"[3] can be seen in attempts in the last decade to legislate infertility coverage that benefits typically white, middle-class workers who have health insurance but whose policies typically do not include contraceptive coverage. Meanwhile, Medicaid funds contraception, including sterilization, for the poor, who are disproportionately people of color, yet denies coverage for assistance with infertility.[4] And, as the preceding chapters have shown, the debates over the problem of surrogacy also provide clear evidence that racial and class politics are intertwined with reproductive politics today no less than in the past.

Also integral to both past and present concerns over population and reproduction are gendered explanations for the (supposed) social trends of the time. In the late nineteenth century the decreased fertility of upper-class white women was traced to higher education.[5] Fast-forward to the more recent politics of reproduction over surrogacy in the late twentieth century. Again, gender issues mixed with racial anxiety are quite evident. For instance, a *Los Angeles Times* article about surrogate parenting attributed the crisis of too few adoptable white babies to two significant social trends involving women in the last decades of the twentieth century: the increased acceptability of single mothers and the legalization and subsequent rise in use of contraception (by women).[6] A *New York Times* editorial on surrogacy, meanwhile, linked the putative increase in infertility to three social trends related to changes in women's roles and behavior in the last decades of the twentieth century: the later age of childbearing associated with women's pursuit of careers, the increase in reproductive problems due to the use of birth control, and women's increased sexual behavior outside marriage.[7] Clearly, then, the politics of reproduction, including the legislative debates over surrogate parenting, is bound up with social conflicts about gender, particularly the role of motherhood in women's lives. The possibility that the significance of motherhood for women's identity is declining is a great source of worry for some groups, as is the seeming decoupling of motherhood from marriage.

Indeed, recent concerns about the family often take the institution of motherhood as their primary focus. Given motherhood's role, along with baseball and apple pie, as a symbol of America, it should not be too surprising that the inability to define motherhood, an issue central to the surrogacy debates, contributed to surrogate motherhood's emergence as a publicly perceived social problem. As sociologist Evelyn Nakano Glenn has pointed out, "[S]ome of the most heated social and political debates taking place in late-twentieth-century America turn out to revolve around disputed meanings of mothering and motherhood in contemporary society."[8]

Given these ties to debates over motherhood, surrogate parenting's successful emergence as a publicly perceived social problem was connected as well to the broader reproductive politics of the time. This book's examination of the legislative debates over surrogacy thus helps map the general social and cultural terrain of the United States at the turn of the twenty-first century. This landscape will definitely continue to influence the debates and policy responses to future developments in reproductive and genetic medicine.

CONCEIVING SURROGACY, CONTESTED CONCEPTIONS

In the preceding chapters, I explored why two analogous political bodies, the New York and California state legislatures, responded with two very different policy solutions to the problem of surrogate motherhood. I drew on constructionist approaches to social problems to show how and why different ways of framing surrogacy—"baby selling" versus "the plight of infertile couples"—became dominant in each state and how those dominant frames led to the states' disparate policy approaches. This analysis confirms the overall usefulness of the constructionist approach to social problems. The diverse interpretations of surrogate parenting are evidence of the indeterminateness of social problems, and the story of surrogacy reveals how particular cultural and political processes create the meaning attributed to a given issue. In particular, my analysis shows how the competing frames drew on ongoing societal contestations about families, motherhood, and paternity. As the members of the New York State Task Force on Life and the Law noted, "At stake in the debate is nothing less than the psychological, social and legal content of the terms 'mother,' 'father,' and 'parent.' Surrogate parenting . . . challenges society to assess the process by which parenthood is recognized."[9] Thus at the heart of the legislative debates over surrogacy was the question of what, socially and culturally speaking, constitutes familial relations. Surrogacy exposes the tentative and contingent nature of what are often assumed to be "natural" matters. For instance, it fragments maternity into three distinct components: genetic motherhood, birth motherhood, and social motherhood. In the Baby M case, as we saw, the birth (and genetic) mother was favored, while in the *Johnson v. Calvert* custodial dispute the genetic and intended (social) mother was favored.

At first glance, the outcome of the Baby M case seems to reinforce more traditional notions of family than does the outcome of the Johnson-Calvert case. Children belong to the women who give birth to them; to give them to someone else for a sum of money therefore constitutes baby selling and denigrates women's childbearing capacities. This is so because in our culture contractual and commercial transactions are held to have no place in the private, sanctified realm of family relations. Furthermore, to enforce a surrogacy contract against a surrogate's will is to tamper with an important and intrinsic maternal-infant bond that begins developing during pregnancy. The "baby-selling" frame that emerged from the Baby M case thus naturalizes and valorizes women's/mothers' relationships and envisions a version of the family that is definitionally and experientially separate from the public world of the marketplace.

Johnson v. Calvert supported the rights of genetic mothers over birth mothers and validated the use of contracts in the formation of families. Nevertheless, the "plight of the infertile" frame that became dominant in this case draws on notions about family that are no less traditional than those that underpin the Baby M frame. First, by dismissing Anna Johnson's solely gestational role in determining her relationship to the child she bore, the court valorized and legitimated genes as the marker of relatedness, giving them primacy over the important social relations that can exist between non–biologically related children and adults. This case thus reinforces a narrow notion of kinship based on genetics and "blood ties." Second, by supporting parental claims to a child through genetic links and by affirming the "need" for a couple to have custody of such a child, the ruling reinforced another traditional image of the family, namely that a complete and "natural" family consists of a marriage that produces biological children, and, in particular, children racially similar to their parents. Characterizations of surrogacy that drew on the frame of the plight of infertile couples were therefore just as immersed in traditional notions of family as were the characterizations associated with the frame of baby selling. Both frames reinforced normative constructs of family and kinship.

These competing frames of surrogacy share an additional important similarity. Lurking behind the two surrogacy disputes and their related framings of surrogate parenting were particular understandings regarding the rights of men as fathers. Surrogate parenting often pits two women against each other over claims to maternal rights (e.g., Is motherhood a social or biological determination? What constitutes biological motherhood?). Neither men's genetic nor their legal claims to paternity were contested in either the Baby M or Johnson-Calvert disputes. In traditional surrogacy cases such as Baby M, the birth mother and genetic father were considered to have equally valid biological claims to the child. This is why surrogacy is a "no-win" situation: a dispute over the resulting child can result in a custodial tug-of-war between two families with similarly legitimate claims to parental rights. Although the father may be frowned on for paying a woman to produce his child ("baby selling"), there is never any question that the baby is "his" child. Likewise, in gestational surrogacy cases such as *Johnson v. Calvert,* the man's genetic contribution to the child produced positioned him as the sole claimant of father. His unchallenged paternal claims reinforced the maternal claims made by his wife. Infertile couples who use gestational surrogacy face a potentially nightmarish plight, however: a "genetic stranger" can attempt to lay claim to "their" child. Both ways of framing surrogate motherhood, then, used common notions regarding fathers' rights. Thus, in both cases, a distinctively male standard of parenthood—genetics—was applied to both men and women. In this manner, gender ideology regarding the roles and rights of fathers and mothers, as well as genetically deterministic notions of kinship, informed policy reactions to surrogate parenting arrangements.

The fact that despite their differences the two frames drew on traditional gender ideology regarding constructs of motherhood, fatherhood, parenting, and kinship highlights a key—and unexpected—finding of this study: there is much ideological agreement among those with divergent positions on surrogate motherhood. Thus, instead of a "culture war" of mutually exclusive opposing viewpoints, the discursive politics over surrogacy legislation suggests that the slow legal response in the United States to the phenomenon of surrogate motherhood arises just as much from ideological agreements as from disagreements regarding the status, value, and norms of children, mothers, and families. In particular, and what should be of interest to feminist scholars, is that both opponents and supporters of surrogate motherhood drew on culturally dominant notions of the family as a private sphere that should not be interfered with by outside forces. Those on both sides of the debate were trying to protect family relations from outside intrusions, and thus the rhetoric used by both supporters and detractors of surrogacy drew on and reproduced the dominant ideology of a public/private divide. Which frame (and policy) represents "the" feminist position and which frame is more or less likely to naturalize reproductive practices therefore are not clearly evident. Indeed, the cultural frames, or idioms, that we come to use to understand and respond to developments in reproductive technologies can simultaneously reinforce and challenge our notions of kinship. Thus a common critique of surrogate parenting—that it has commodified motherhood—may or may not serve the complex interests of differently situated women in the long term. Drawing solely on this characterization of surrogacy reinforces the very boundaries and dichotomies (i.e., the false separation of public and private) that feminists, critical-race scholars, and others have long challenged. The challenges posed by new reproductive technologies and assisted reproduction to notions of motherhood and family as existing outside a supposed private domain represent *both* dangers and potentials for a revisioning of kinship relations. It is this dual potential that feminists must address.[10]

GENDER, REPRODUCTIVE POLITICS, AND SOCIAL PROBLEMS

Recent studies on the relation between women and the state have drawn attention to women's agency in social policy. My analysis of surrogate parenting legislation in New York and California contributes to this growing body of scholarship by focusing on the effect of female political mobilization on social policy outcomes.[11] One limitation of existing studies is their authors' tendency to take for granted what constitutes a "women's issue" and how a given problem becomes defined this way. Labeling some social issues, such as the ERA, sexual harassment, and child care, as women's issues is relatively straightforward; assigning the label to other issues, such as welfare, homelessness, health care, and employment policies, is more problematic and has met with varying degrees of success. We should not assume that there are particular, objective qualities of a social problem that lead to its being defined as a women's issue. Instead, we should closely examine the social and political processes by which a new social problem is constituted as a women's issue or, indeed, as a problem at all.

This study undertook just such an examination. The story of surrogate parenting legislation in New York and California exposes the successful claiming of surrogate motherhood as a women's issue through the dominant use of women's rights rhetoric. In particular, we saw that the language of prochoice discourse was used by *both* detractors and supporters of surrogacy. This strategic use of abortion rights discourse indicates the institutionalization of feminist rhetoric in the legislative arena as a potentially effective political tool. Indeed, the legislative debates on surrogacy reveal that talking about women's rights and gender equality was accepted as a legitimate and appropriate way to support one's position on surrogacy.

This institutionalization of feminist rhetoric bodes well for the claiming of new social issues as women's issues—whether the problems are ones traditionally recognized as women's issues or not. This in turn suggests the real possibility of successfully integrating feminist/women's perspectives into a wide array of social issues, including those brought about by advances in biomedicine. Of course, an important caveat is that surrogate motherhood is a *new* social problem. Issues with longer histories, such as abortion and welfare, might not be so easily influenced, since the line dividing the two sides is already deeply drawn. Likewise, an appeal to women's rights might be less successful on issues with more direct fiscal impact on state expenditures, such as welfare.

Nevertheless, surrogate motherhood is an important empirical site in which to examine what happens to a social problem defined as a women's issue when advocates for different policy responses claim to represent women's rights.[12] The contested nature of surrogate motherhood as a women's issue also adds evidence to support the assertion of a "greater plasticity" with respect to gendered social problems.[13] That is, social problems defined as women's issues become entangled in ongoing conflicts over appropriate gender roles and the role of motherhood in particular. At the same time, the debate over which side represents a feminist/women's rights position on surrogacy is evidence that feminism itself is a contested terrain.

Indeed, schisms within the ranks of feminists over surrogacy mimic the larger debates about gender equality and the status of motherhood among diverse women's rights supporters, as well as among the general public. In particular, reactions to surrogate motherhood were connected to debates over how best to legislate gender equality. From a legal perspective, the question of how to address pregnancy poses a conundrum for gender equality, since only women can experience this biological event. Academic and legal debates abound over whether treating women "the same" or "differently" from men will help or hinder gender equality.[14] The legislative debates chronicled in chapter 2 reveal the simultaneous existence of consensus about securing women's rights and conflict about how to obtain and measure such ends, particularly when pregnancy is involved.

A second hurdle in shaping women-friendly social policy is the question of whether to valorize the link between women and their children. Underlying the feminist (and nonfeminist) disputes over surrogate parenting are conflicts over women's status as mothers. Should women's ties and relations to children be cherished and valued? Or should they be seen as merely one possible aspect of women's identities?[15] These questions had special weight in the surrogacy battles because the debates took place within the context of rising rates of female labor force participation, divorce, and single-parent households, as well as increasing levels of visibility for gay and lesbian families. These changes sparked concern not only about women but about the status of children and families as well. At the heart of feminist debates about surrogacy, then, were disagreements over how best to protect women's rights in general, and reproductive rights in particular, during a historical moment when family relations and the rights and responsibilities of family members were undergoing fundamental shifts and transformations. At the same time, the past and present inequalities experienced by different communities within the United States made (and continue to make) it difficult to achieve a societal consensus on what (if any) part the state should play in institutionalizing family roles and relations.

For those of us concerned with advancing women and women's perspectives in politics, particularly with regard to new reproductive technologies, my findings offer cause for both concern and optimism. First, since not all women share the same interests, it is difficult for any self-designated and/or self-appointed women's rights advocate to represent all women's interests. The debates over surrogate motherhood clearly reveal that no consensus exists on what position reflects women's interests. Given the historical race and class bias exhibited in various priorities of the reproductive rights movement in the United States,[16] it is important that women's diverse and conflicting interests be taken into account in responses to the challenges posed by advances in reproductive medicine.[17]

Second, even on women's issues, the political efficacy of female activism is affected by the stance taken by other interested parties. Given the importance of coalition politics, links that women's organizations forge with other groups are likely to enhance their political sway. At the same time, such alliances can compromise the pursuit of women's interests. In the context of the battles over surrogacy, this occurred when feminist advocates and Catholic lobbyists joined forces, but the primacy of women's rights also was jeopardized when these rights were pursued in conjunction with children's rights. Both cases suggest, however, that alliances are a political necessity. This, in turn, indicates the limited power of claims making on behalf of women's rights alone. Furthermore, since claims to feminism are now politically useful, the co-optation of feminist rhetoric is nearly inevitable. My research indicates that the use of feminist rhetoric has become a valuable discursive strategy in the political arena. Thus those who are not concerned with women's best interests can and may manipulate the discourse of women's rights for their own political ends.[18] This suggests limits to the effectiveness of women's groups in shaping the legislative agenda toward issues that are successfully claimed as concerning and affecting women.

Finally, even when a policy is determined to be relevant to women's rights, groups representing women are not necessarily the only interested parties. Many issues that pertain to women, including surrogate motherhood, also intersect with larger debates about family, children, and the rights and obligations of parents. On the one hand, women's groups can challenge the authority of others involved with these issues, such as religious groups, to influence policy choices if these others' stances are not normally associated with the women's rights position. On the other hand, as was the case in the surrogacy debate in New York State, a formidable alliance can be forged when two different types of organizations agree on specific legislation. Similarly, we saw that the alignment of women's and children's interests can be politically powerful and strategic. In both cases, the influence of women's groups over problems successfully claimed as women's issues was enhanced by coalition building. Two important questions linger, however: (1) How much influence do women's groups have in the absence of alliances with other powerful groups? and (2) Although seemingly effective, do such coalitions exact a cost? These are questions that deserve exploration in future research.

BEYOND THE REPRODUCTIVE POLITICS OF SURROGACY

The last three decades have witnessed the rapid growth of reproductive technologies and genetic medicine, from the first so-called "test tube" baby in 1978 to the more recent, highly publicized birth of septuplets in Iowa in the 1990s. These advances in reproductive medicine shatter naturalized notions of reproduction, making possible children with as many as ten different legally recognized parents![19] Not surprisingly, there are diverse reactions to new reproductive technologies and surrogate parenting. Some welcome the plethora of reproductive choices that these advances in biomedicine open up. Others are concerned about the brave new world these technologies create—including the potential for the re-emergence of eugenics, the commodification of children, and the possible erosion of women's reproductive rights.

Of course, the debates about surrogate motherhood and new reproductive technologies do not occur in a cultural or social vacuum. As we have seen, they are linked to ongoing debates about the future of the family, which many see as beleaguered, owing to the rising rates of divorce, blended families, single mothers, and working mothers. Furthermore, the growing attention to and concern over problems of infertility has caused fears about the reproduction of the American family itself—meaning, of course, the white middle-class family. Additionally, setbacks to abortion rights and the growing attention to fetal abuse that began in the late 1980s have created a climate of concern among advocates of women's reproductive rights.

Meanwhile, the use of new reproductive technologies remains largely unregulated in the United States. The deep divisions over how best to address the rapid developments in biomedicine have proven difficult to resolve, perhaps because of their unique combination of ideological overlap and contradiction. Consequently, new and different reproductive and procreative arrangements continue to be pursued without a clear sense of what rights and responsibilities accrue to the various parties involved. At present, approximately one thousand women in the United States undergo IVF per week, and over eleven thousand women give birth annually to children conceived by some form of assisted reproductive technology. Fertility assistance has become a $2 billion a year industry. Although many states have started to specify the rights of the parties involved in assisted reproduction, there is still much legal uncertainty when it comes to the use of others' genetic materials. For instance, only twenty-two states specifically deny legal paternity to sperm donors, while only five states withhold parental rights and/or obligations from egg donors. Only seventeen states and Washington, D.C., have specific laws regarding surrogate motherhood, and only two states have enacted legislation since 1992. In the meantime, in the last decade not only has gestational surrogacy become more common, but surrogate parenting centers have begun to accommodate single fathers and gay couples.[20]

It is not likely that the societal conflict over the appropriate relations within families—between mothers, fathers, and children—that feeds policy debates over surrogate parenting and related assisted reproductive technologies will subside soon. Similarly, advances in reproductive technologies—such as the freezing of a human egg and the birth of siblings seven years apart that came from embryos developed at the same time—show no signs of tapering off. And since the successful cloning of a sheep in 1996 there has been much discussion in both lay and scientific communities about the possibility of human cloning, as well as the use of stem cells and reproductive cloning for biomedical research. Yet no new comprehensive legislation has been enacted to regulate this proliferation of biomedical and genetic technologies.

The preceding chapter's comparison of New York and California's legislative responses to surrogate parenting suggests several observations regarding the societal response to new reproductive technologies more generally. For instance, how we respond to advances in new reproductive technologies and biomedicine can be very much affected by the dramatic events that come to represent these issues to the wider public, thus giving the media an important claims-making role. My comparison of the coverage and content of local media has shown how regional incidents can affect policy responses to the same issue in different places. Thus the (local) media are an important part of framing because they choose what events to report and what degree of coverage to give to a specific issue. It is also important to acknowledge that government agencies, when they are presented and perceived as experts, can be influential claims makers with regard to the framing of new reproductive technologies and practices. In particular, government task forces' success in framing a new social issue is contingent on several factors: the respectability of the agency writing the report, the ability of task force members to reach a consensus, the diversity of the group recommending a particular policy solution, and the news stories that publicize the group's findings and recommendations. The general nature of these findings should make them useful in future explorations of controversies that arise in response to new forms of assisted reproduction—from human cloning to the freezing of eggs and embryos.

Investigating the frames used in reproductive politics is an essential part of understanding how we as a society respond to developments in reproduction and biomedicine. Frames influence the political resources that shape what and how legislative strategies are pursued. This in turn shapes what social actors can and cannot achieve in the political arena. As we have seen, the very evocative and powerful frames that were used in the legislative debates over surrogate motherhood allowed certain actors to have more power than others, made certain alliances more viable than others, and rendered the possible achievement of consensus more or less likely. Thus the story about the politics of reproduction with respect to surrogacy is necessarily a multilayered, causal one. In the end, how we as a society react to advances in reproductive technology is not predetermined. The diverse and competing framings of and responses to surrogacy are evidence of the plasticity of social problems. If we are to understand issues such as surrogacy and related new reproductive technologies, we need to recognize the diversity of possible interpretations, uses, and political reactions to these social problems.

At the same time, I would suggest that new reproductive technologies are more likely to be permitted and tolerated when they are associated with acts of reproduction rather than with acts of consumption. That is, although we live in a consumer-oriented culture (and this is a major reason why new reproductive technologies have flourished more in the United States than elsewhere), as a society we remain averse to equating kinship formations with commercial transactions. Furthermore, we need to recognize the influence and power of various claims makers and discursive claims making to shape our responses, as well as the limits imposed by our culturally and socially shaped imaginations. The findings presented in this book demonstrate that these issues are currently being negotiated in terms of their social, cultural, and political meanings and that women's participation in this process is critical with respect to the conceptualization, representation, and institutionalization of interests for differently situated women.

Appendix A | A NOTE ON METHODS AND DATA

The research for this book involves a dual-site, multimethod comparison. A comparison of two states allows for an in-depth and nuanced look into the specific dynamics behind the legislative outcomes in each state. Employing comparative analysis allows for a more precise evaluation of the dynamic interplay between structure and agency as I seek to uncover the effect of political mobilization, as well as the limits imposed on such activity by institutional structures. The methodological design of comparative analysis permits findings in one case to be checked against another. Consequently, comparative research creates built-in tests of causal relationships.

California and New York make for a useful comparison, as my dependent variable of state response/legislative outcome is different.[1] Furthermore, this comparison is highly controlled because New York and California share many similarities: (1) large populations; (2) politically diverse populations; (3) prominent surrogacy centers and brokers; (4) highly professionalized legislatures; (5) strong interest groups; and (5) highly publicized court cases involving both states.[2] A comparison of New York and California is also of substantive interest because both these states are known for innovation with regard to their adoption of new programs.[3]

Most of my research involves the use of detailed content analysis of a wide assortment of primary materials. One data set consists of all newspaper articles on surrogacy in the *New York Times,* the *Los Angeles Times,* and the *Washington Post* between 1980 and 2002.[4] Over 725 newspaper articles and editorials were read and coded: 213 from the *Washington Post,* over 286 from the *New York Times,* and over 226 from the *Los Angeles Times.*[5] I used this data source to reflect national and local media coverage of surrogate parenting (see chapter 4 for more discussion of the media). While the print media are not the only, or primary, media source for public knowledge of events, these three papers have been documented to play an important agenda-setting role given their stature. Furthermore, newspapers (and particularly the three examined) do play an important role in shaping the views and behavior of public officials and other activists—the political actors on which this book focuses.[6] This media data source is also used to chronicle the views and opinions of interested parties in the debates over surrogacy through analysis of the descriptive coverage of their activities and interviews with them.

I also made use of a large collection of documents produced by and for the California and New York state governments, including (1) letters of support and opposition, (2) transcripts from public hearings, (3) committee analyses, (4) legislative research reports, (5) transcripts from floor debates, and (6) bill files. These textual data served two purposes. One was informational; I was provided with specific dates, names, time lines, and the like that aided in my reconstruction of events. The other use was analytical; the bulk of my findings derive from a careful and detailed interpretation of these materials as historical texts. In particular, I use these source documents to analyze how specific political actors framed their position on surrogate motherhood—the focus of this book.

To supplement my primarily textual data, I also conducted semistructured interviews with prominent activists in the legislative debates over surrogacy. I first identified such key actors by locating the names of sponsors and witnesses who are listed on committee analyses and from newspaper accounts. After conducting these first interviews, I employed a snowball-like sampling, asking this first set of interviewees to identify other pivotal players in these debates. Informants were asked questions about their involvement in the legislative process, the history of the bill under question, key supporters and opponents, and the reasons that led them to a particular policy position. I conducted a total of eleven interviews, seven in New York and four in California. These included five current or former legislators, three legislative staff members, two surrogacy program directors, and one legislative consultant.[7] When permitted, interviews were tape-recorded and transcribed. Extensive notes were taken after each interview as well.

Appendix B | A MULTISTATE COMPARISON OF THE IMPACT OF SPONSOR'S GENDER AND ABORTION POSITION ON THE SUCCESS OF SURROGACY BILLS

A comparison of surrogate parenting legislation in New York and California suggests the important role of female legislators and women's rights advocates in the fate of bills dealing with new social problems that are defined as women's issues. But a question to ask is whether these findings are idiosyncratic to these two case studies. Data from the total population of bills introduced in state legislatures nationally provide important information about the effect of the gender and the politics of the bill's sponsor on surrogacy bills' outcomes.[1]

In the 1991–92 legislative sessions, a total of thirty-four bills were introduced into sixteen state legislatures across the country. Of these, seventeen permitted and regulated surrogacy contracts and seventeen prohibited surrogacy contracts in whole or in part or rendered them unenforceable by the courts.[2] Male legislators introduced 82 percent of these bills, female legislators 18 percent. Since women accounted for 17 percent of state representatives in the early 1990s, the proportion of bill introductions by gender is proportionate to their presence in state governments.[3] This finding is contrary to other research that has found that women legislators are more likely than their male counterparts to introduce legislation on issues dealing with women, children, and families.[4]

Are women, though, more likely to be *successful* in their sponsorship of surrogate parenting legislation? This is an important question, as my

TABLE 9. Passage Rates of State-Level Surrogacy Bills by Gender of Sponsor, 1991–92

Gender of Sponsor	*Total Number of Bills Introduced*	*Percentage of Bills That Passed*
Female Sponsor	6	50.0
Male Sponsor	27	15.0

analysis of New York and California suggests that part of the success of the two surrogacy bills in each state was attributable to the fact that the sponsor of each bill was a woman. As table 9 shows, having a female sponsor did not guarantee the success of surrogate parenting bills introduced between 1991 and 1992, but it did make passage more likely: 50 percent of the bills introduced by women during this time period did pass through their respective legislatures. In absolute terms, this is a very high success ratio. For instance, in New York State legislators introduce approximately sixteen thousand bills during a legislative session. Of these, approximately one thousand (less than 10 percent) are eventually signed into law, and another hundred are vetoed.[5] In California the success rate of bills is higher, yet only about one-third are eventually signed into law, with over one-half dying in committee.[6]

Women's success rate in sponsoring legislation on surrogate motherhood was not just high in absolute terms; it was also high relative to men's. Whereas 50 percent of surrogate parenting bills introduced by women between 1991 and 1992 passed through their respective legislatures, only 15 percent of surrogacy bills introduced by men were as fortunate (see table 9). This 35 percent difference in rates of success between women and men sponsors is substantially significant.

But women's greater success with sponsorship of surrogacy legislation may have less to do with the fact that they are women than with the type of legislation they sponsor. In other words, women's higher success rate may be the result of introducing different types of bills on surrogate motherhood than men introduce. For instance, legislation that is antisurrogacy may be more likely to pass, and women may be more likely than men to introduce antisurrogacy bills. Indeed, of the eleven bills introduced by women between 1990 and 1992, seven were antisurrogacy.[7] On the other hand, just over half (n = 16) of the thirty-one bills introduced by men

TABLE 10. Passage Rates of State-Level Surrogacy Bills by Gender of Sponsor and Content of Bill, 1990–92

Gender of Sponsor	*Content of Bill*	*Total Number of Bills Introduced*	*Percentage of Bills That Passed*
Female Sponsor	Prosurrogacy	4	50.0
	Antisurrogacy	7	42.8
Male Sponsor	Prosurrogacy	15	13.3
	Antisurrogacy	16	12.5

during this same time period were antisurrogacy in content. However, women's success rate (42.8 percent) for antisurrogacy bills was slightly lower than their success rate (50.0 percent) for prosurrogacy bills. At the same time, men's success rates for anti- and prosurrogacy legislation were nearly identical at 12.5 percent and 13.3 percent respectively. For both women and men, then, success of surrogate parenting legislation was not related to the content of the bill. This indicates that irrespective of bill content, female legislators have a higher passage rate for surrogacy bills than their male counterparts (see table 10). These findings support my analysis of the two bills in California and New York; these different bills were successful, in part, because *both* were sponsored by a woman.

My analysis of Senator Watson's and Assemblywoman Weinstein's roles also suggests that a sponsor's advocacy on behalf of women can positively affect the legislative outcome of surrogate parenting bills. In particular, a sponsor who has a history of supporting women's reproductive rights has a higher chance of passing legislation on surrogate motherhood because of his or her expert status. What do we find? Of the nineteen bills introduced by prochoice sponsors during the 1991–92 legislative session, five bills passed through their respective legislatures, for a success rate of 26.3 percent.[8] This compares to a success rate of 13.3 percent for antichoice sponsors, who had only two of their fifteen bills pass through their respective legislatures during the same time period (see table 11). While the abortion position of the sponsor does not have as dramatic an effect on the success of surrogate parenting legislation as the sponsor's gender, prochoice sponsors' 13 percent greater rate of success still marks a significant difference. These findings confirm that a history of advocacy on behalf of women is important when it comes to legislation dealing with surrogate motherhood.

TABLE 11. Passage Rates of State-Level Surrogacy Bills by Sponsor's Abortion Position, 1991–92

Sponsor's Abortion Position	*Number of Bills Introduced*	*Percentage of Bills That Passed*
Prochoice	19	26.31
Antiabortion	15	13.33

TABLE 12. Passage Rates of State-Level Surrogacy Bills by Sponsor's Abortion Position and Content of Bill, 1991–92

Sponsor's Abortion Position	*Content of Bill*	*Number of Bills Introduced*	*Percentage of Bills That Passed*
Prochoice	Prosurrogacy	11	27.0
	Antisurrogacy	8	25.0
Antiabortion	Prosurrogacy	7	0.0
	Antisurrogacy	8	25.0

But is this difference in success rates attributable to the fact that prochoice sponsors are more likely to sponsor antisurrogacy legislation? To the contrary, 58 percent ($n = 11$) of the bills introduced by prochoice sponsors were prosurrogacy (i.e., regulatory); on the other hand, slightly more than half ($n = 8$) of the bills introduced by antichoice sponsors were antisurrogacy. Although slight, do these differences in the proportion of types of bills introduced by pro- and antichoice sponsors affect their success rates with surrogacy legislation? This does not seem to be the case for prochoice sponsors. Regardless of the content of the bill, prochoice sponsors had nearly equivalent success with their bills; 27 percent and 25 percent of their pro- and antisurrogacy bills, respectively, passed.

However, the content of the bill has a significant effect on passage rates for antichoice sponsors. Whereas 25 percent of their antisurrogacy bills passed, *none* of the seven prosurrogacy bills introduced by antichoice sponsors passed through their respective legislatures (see table 12). These findings also back up the story I have presented about the success of the New York and California bills. First, different bills were successful in the two states, in part, because *both* were sponsored by a women's rights advocate.

Second, a prosurrogacy bill was able to pass through the California legislature in part because it had a prochoice sponsor. This suggests the particular importance of an "expert" status when pushing a less popular legislative solution.

Overall, these findings lend support to the story I presented regarding the New York and California cases. That is, when a new social problem is defined as a women's issue—as was surrogate motherhood—the gender of those who formulate social policy matters with regard to the chances of legislative success because female legislators can more successfully claim ownership of such issues. This in turn indicates the existence of some political space for women in positions of political authority. Furthermore, advocacy on behalf of women's reproductive rights seems to be a crucial characteristic of sponsors of regulatory surrogacy bills. This indicates that not only gender but political perspective matters when it comes to legislation on social problems that are claimed as women's issues.

NOTES

INTRODUCTION

1. *Jaycee B. v. The Superior Court of Orange County,* 42 Cal. App. 4th 718 (1996); quotes in the epigraph are from 722. See also the California Court of Appeal's decision on this case, *In re the Marriage of Buzzanca,* 61 Cal. App. 4th 1410 (1998).
2. I use the terms *surrogacy* and *surrogate motherhood* because these are the terms most commonly used and recognized. See Purdy (1992) for a discussion of why this terminology is inadequate and misleading. Her alternative, *contract pregnancy,* is not adequate for my purposes, since I do not want to limit this study to commercial pregnancy. See Strathern (2002) for a discussion of how the use of the term *surrogacy* presumes that the birth mother is not the mother of the child.
3. Davan Maharaj, "Surrogate Ruling Leaves a Girl, 2, Legally Parentless," *Los Angeles Times,* September 9, 1997, A:1,19. Using the standard of intentionality that the California Supreme Court developed in their 1993 decision *Johnson v. Calvert* (discussed in chapters 1 and 4), a California Court of Appeal ruled in 1998 that John Buzzanca was the legal father of Jaycee, and he was ordered to pay child support. The California Supreme Court denied his appeal of this decision.
4. Franklin (1993, 128).
5. Gestational surrogacy involves the process of in vitro fertilization (IVF).

The contracting couple's sperm and ova (or gametes that are purchased from a third party) are fertilized ex utero, and the resulting embryo is implanted in the surrogate mother, who then gestates the fetus. The practice by which a woman bears a child who is genetically related to her is now being called traditional surrogacy. In this book, I generally do not distinguish between the two; I use the term *surrogacy* to refer to both types of arrangements. When I am focusing on one specific practice, I use the terminology associated with that practice.

6. Dolgin (1997).
7. Peirce (1972).
8. Ginsburg and Rapp (1995); Brown and Ferree (2005).
9. Blake (1974); Morell (1994).
10. On lesbian parenting, see, for instance, Lewin (1995), Weston (1997), and Agigian (2004).
11. See Chesler (1990), Field (1988), and Office of Technology Assessment (1988).
12. See chapter 4 for more on the media response to the Baby M case.
13. See, for instance, Ginia Bellafante, "Surrogate Mothers' New Niche: Bearing Babies for Gay Couples," *New York Times,* May 27, 2005, A:1. Unfortunately, there is no accurate or precise way to determine the number of surrogacy births. There is no official recording of this statistic, and it is estimated that half of such births are arranged informally, without a third-party intermediary. In 1992, a report by the New York State Department of Health estimated that there were at least twenty-nine surrogate parenting centers in the United States. See *The Business of Surrogate Parenting* (Albany: New York State Department of Health, 1992), 3. On the other hand, an author of another study estimated that as of 1992 there were eight surrogate programs in the United States, supplemented by various part-time, small operations run by an assortment of lawyers and doctors (Ragoné 1994, 4). See also Office of Technology Assessment (1988) and E. Roberts (1998a, 1998b). According to the Centers for Disease Control, surrogate births doubled between 1997 and 2000, and in 2002 there were 548 surrogate births (see Amy Argetsinger, "Surrogate Returns Couple's Hope for a Child Fivefold," *Washington Post,* April 14, 2005, A:1). Meanwhile, according to the Organization of Parents Through Surrogacy, there have been ten thousand surrogate births since the 1970s. See "Information about OPTS," 2002, www.opts.com/informat.htm (accessed September 22, 2006).

14. The country's largest surrogate program reports that over 50 percent of all their arrangements involve this form. See Ragoné (1994, 1998, 1999).

15. Andrews (1992).

16. See chapter 1 for a summary of state laws on surrogate parenting.

17. See chapter 1 for further discussion of the two states' bills.

18. See Appendix A for a description of methods and data.

19. Engels (1884).

20. See Mills (1959).

21. On prenatal testing, see Browner and Press (1995), Markens (2002), Rapp (1999b), Rothman (1986), and Kolker and Burke (1994). On ultrasound, see Taylor (1992) and Mitchell and Georges (1997). On infertility, see Becker (2000), Sandelowski (1991, 1993), Thompson (2005), Greil (1991), and Lasker and Borg (1994). On fetal surgery, see Casper (1998). On neonatal intensive care, see Anspach (1993) and Heimer and Staffen (1998).

22. See, for example, Evans (2002), Mulkay (1993, 1997), Richardt (2003), and Franklin (1993). One of the only sociological studies on a macro policy level that places an analysis of gender centrally is Blankenship et al.'s (1993) research on U.S. court cases involving reproductive technologies. Their research assesses whether state regulation of reproductive technologies represents an instance of state control of women's reproductive lives or a mechanism that enhances women's reproductive freedom. They argue that social context is crucial in how the meaning of reproductive technologies and their regulation is derived and that the meaning of these technologies is a product of struggles over them. Their study starts to address how regulation and/or lack of regulation affects women. However, their exclusive focus on court decisions limits the extent to which the gendered dynamics of the debates over and struggles surrounding the use of new reproductive technologies and practices can be explored.

23. See, for example, Andrews (1989), Bartels et al. (1990), Dolgin (1997), Field (1988), Gostin (1990), and Tong (1995).

24. Helena Ragoné's anthropological study (1994; see also Ragoné 1998, 1999) investigates what motivates the parties involved in a surrogacy arrangement. Her work illuminates how surrogate mothers' "conservative" motivations—their emphasis on traditional values of family and their fulfillment through their roles as mothers—have quite radical potentials in terms of the relation between genetics and parenthood: they help sever biological motherhood from social motherhood. A similar study by Elizabeth Roberts

(1998a, 1998b) shows how surrogates embrace the view of themselves as vessels, therefore challenging assumptions that they are merely suffering from false consciousness. Likewise, in her case study, Gillian Goslinga-Roy (1998) reveals the complexity of a surrogate's agency. Elly Teman's (2001, 2003a, 2003b) research into gestational surrogates in Israel reveals the way that surrogates and intended mothers collaborate in medicalizing processes to define the latter's intuitive embodied knowledge of the pregnancy and biogenetic connection as constitutive of "real" motherhood.

25. According to Malcolm Spector and John Kitsuse (1977), social problems are "the activities of individuals or groups making assertions of grievances and claims with respect to some putative conditions" (75). See also Best (1989, 1991), J. Schneider (1985), and Gusfield (1981).

26. Best (1989).

27. See chapter 1 for information regarding media and legislative attention given to surrogacy.

28. Gailey (2000).

29. Gamson and Modigliani (1987, 143).

30. Social problems theorist Joel Best (1989) terms this process of determining cause and assigning blame "typification" and describes it as "an integral part of social problem construction. Claims-makers inevitably characterize problems in particular ways: They emphasize some aspects and not others; they promote specific orientations; and they focus on particular causes and advocate particular solutions" (xxi).

31. Ferree (2005). See also Taylor (1996) for a discussion of discursive politics.

32. Ferree et al. (2002); Linders (1998); Saguy (2003).

33. Consider, for instance, research on the following four gendered social problems: women's dependency, teenage pregnancy, premenstrual syndrome (PMS), and cocaine-addicted mothers. Misra, Moller, and Karides (2003) show that throughout the twentieth century media depictions of welfare became less concerned with men's dependency and much more concerned with women's dependency as the population of single-female households and teen mothers grew. Luker (1996) argues that teenage pregnancy became defined as a problem in the 1970s—despite falling birth rates—because of the rise in premarital sex, numbers of abortions, and out-of-wedlock births throughout the U.S. population. PMS emerged as a social problem in the early 1980s, Rittenhouse (1991) asserts, because murder cases against two British women who used PMS as a mitigating factor in

their defense served as dramatic events and because cultural beliefs concerning women's reproductive capacities and appropriate roles were undergoing change at the end of the 1970s. Finally, according to Gómez (1997), "crack mothers" became a national issue as concerns about violent crime and drugs were rising and fetal personhood emerged as a cultural issue in both the lay and medical imagination.

34. See, for example, Popenoe (1996) and Stacey (1996).

35. Dolgin (1997).

36. In 1960, 9 out of 1,000 married women divorced; in 1979, the rate was 23 per 1,000. By the late 1980s, it was still relatively high at 21 per 1,000. These and the following demographic statistics are from DaVanzo and Rahman (1993).

37. In the late 1970s and early 1980s, the fertility rate reached a low of 1.8; the 1989 fertility rate, at 2.0, was still remarkably lower than the 1955 rate of 3.6.

38. For instance, in 1980, 10 percent of women aged 40–44 had no children, a figure that rose to 16 percent by 1990.

39. Although the proportion of teen births to all births had actually fallen from one-sixth in 1970 to one-eighth in 1989, alarm over teenage mothers grew, in part because they accounted for a full 68 percent of unmarried mothers in 1990, whereas in 1960 the figure had been 15 percent. Although many social scientists have questioned the extent of the "teen mom" problem, its hold on public and political discourse endures (Luker 1996). These aggregate statistics also do not convey the differences that exist between racial/ethnic groups.

40. See, for instance, Markens, Browner, and Press (1997), Litt (2000), Hochschild (1989), Hays (1996), and Blum (1999).

41. See Ladd-Taylor and Umansky (1998), Gómez (1997), Blum (1999), and Taylor (1996).

42. See, for example, Collins (1990), B. Roth (2004), Reese (2005), Davis (1981), and Colen (1995).

43. See, for example, Blum (1999), Daniels (1993), Gómez (1997), Litt (2000), Petchesky (1984/1990), D. Roberts (1997), and Solinger (1992).

44. Petchesky (1984/1990).

45. Voluntary motherhood meant that women would decide on sexual encounters; they had the right to choose when to be pregnant. Therefore, a fundamental condition of birth control was seen in a woman's right to refuse sex. The strategy of voluntary motherhood was definitively anti-

contraception; fears of promiscuity and associations with prostitution spurred this female opposition to birth control. See Gordon (1974/1990).

46. See Luker (1984). The story of abortion activism is also complicated by race. For instance, black women's relationship to the abortion rights movement has been complex and ambivalent, owing mainly to sterilization abuse and a history of eugenic control over women of color. See Davis (1981) and D. Roberts (1997).

47. See Ginsburg (1989).

48. See, for instance, Davis (1981, 1993), Gordon (1990), D. Roberts (1997), and Petchesky (1984/1990).

49. Gordon (1990); Piven (1990); Laslett and Brenner (1989); Mink (1990); Nelson (1990); Orloff (1991); Reese (2005); Skocpol (1992).

50. Nelson (1990, 138); Skocpol (1992, 424–79).

51. Orloff (1991, 252).

52. Skocpol (1992, 479).

53. Gordon (1990, 25).

54. T. Kaplan (1982); Ginsburg (1989).

55. See Stacey (1991), Blum (1999), Taylor (1996), and Blee (1991).

56. Ginsburg (1989).

57. See D. Roberts (1997), Davis (1981), Blum (1999), Beisel and Kay (2004), Reese (2005), and Petchesky (1984/1990).

58. Armstrong (2003); Blum (1999); Gómez (1997); Hays (1996); Taylor (1996).

59. Armstrong (2003, 18).

60. Mosher and Pratt (1991).

61. On the stability of infertility rates, see Hirsch and Mosher (1987), Mosher and Pratt (1990, 1991), and Office of Technology Assessment (1988); on the perception of their rise, see Scritchfield (1989).

62. Mosher and Pratt (1990, 1991).

63. Office of Technology Assessment (1988, 5). At the same time, the women who fit this demographic profile were most likely to be white and educated.

64. Sandelowski (1993).

65. Greil (1991); Sandelowski (1991); Scritchfield (1989).

66. Greil (1991, 197).

67. See Dolgin (1997), Franklin (1995), McNeil and Franklin (1993), Robertson (1994), and Stanworth (1987).

68. See Greil (1991), King and Meyer (1997, 10), Mosher and Pratt (1990), Pfeffer (1987), and Sandelowski (1991, 30; 1993, 8–9).

69. Scritchfield (1989, 106).

70. Rothman (1989); Schmidt and Moore (1998).

71. King and Meyer (1997); Ragoné (1994); Jan Hoffman, "Egg Donations Meet a Need and Raise Ethical Questions," *New York Times,* January 8, 1996, A:1, 10; "Cost of Test Tube Babies Averages $72,000," *New York Times,* July 28, 1994, A:16.

72. Dolgin (1997).

73. See Thompson (2002) for a discussion of shifting feminist attitudes toward new reproductive technology and infertility treatments.

74. See, for example, Arditti, Klein, and Minden (1984), Corea (1985), and Corea et al. (1987).

75. Corea (1985).

76. Dworkin (1983).

77. Rothman (1989).

78. Davis (1993).

79. Andrews (1989); Purdy (1992).

80. Rapping (1990); Sawicki (1991); Stanworth (1987).

81. Sawicki (1991).

82. See, for instance, Luker (1984) regarding worldviews. See Hunter (1991) regarding culture wars.

1. THE NEW PROBLEM OF SURROGATE MOTHERHOOD

1. Time/Yankelovich Poll, release date January 21, 1987, Public Opinion Online, Roper Center at University of Connecticut, 1989, accessed at web.lexis-nexis.com, copies in author's files; Family, Marriage & Current Affairs Poll, release date June 21, 1987, Public Opinion Online, Roper Center at University of Connecticut, 1989, accessed at web.lexis-nexis.com, copies in author's files; Roper/U.S. News & World Report Poll, release date April 1, 1987, Public Opinion Online, Roper Center at University of Connecticut, 1989, accessed at web.lexis-nexis.com, copies in author's files; Gallup Poll, release date April 13, 1987, Public Opinion Online, Roper Center at University of Connecticut, 1989, accessed at web.lexis-nexis.com,

copies in author's files; CBS New/New York Times Poll, release date April 1987, Public Opinion Online, Roper Center at University of Connecticut, 1989, accesed at web.lexis-nexis.com, copies in author's files; U.S. News & World Report/CNN poll, release date April 1, 1987, Public Opinion Online, Roper Center at University of Connecticut, 1989, accessed at web.lexis-nexis.com, copies in author's files.

2. National Conference of State Legislatures, Denver, CO, "Surrogacy Contract Bill Introductions: 1990 Legislative Sessions," November 8, 1990, in author's files; National Conference of State Legislatures, Denver, CO, "Surrogate Parenting Contract Legislation Enacted: 1987, 1988, and 1989 Legislative Sessions," *State Legislative Report* 15 (January 1990): 1–10; National Conference of State Legislatures, Denver, CO, "Surrogacy Contract Bill Introductions: 1991 Legislative Sessions," November 22, 1991, "Surrogacy Contract Bill Introductions: 1992 Legislative Sessions," November 30, 1992, and "Regarding Surrogacy Bills, 1992–2005: Lexis Legislation Search," memo, March 16, 2005, all in author's files.

3. See Ferree et al. (2002) and Taylor (1996) regarding critical discourse moments.

4. See Gómez (1997) regarding the institutional phase of a social problem.

5. See New York State Department of Health, *The Business of Surrogate Parenting* (Albany: New York State Department of Health, 1992), Lorio (1999), and Steven Greenhouse, "French Supreme Court Rules Surrogate Mother Agreements Illegal," *New York Times,* June 1, 1991, I:17. Although commercial surrogacy contracts are not recognized in the United Kingdom, there is a centralized board that people must go through to make noncommercial arrangements. In 1996, Israel became the first country to legalize and regulate noncommercial surrogacy (Teman 2003a; Kahn 2000).

6. See, for example, Warnock (1985); Ontario Law Reform Commission, *Report on Human Artificial Reproduction and Related Matters,* vol. 2 (Ontario: Ministry of the Attorney General, 1985); Surrogate Parenthood Act, Queensland, Australia (1988), Reprint 1995 (Reprint No. 1), prepared by the Office of the Queensland Parliamentary Counsel; and Infertility Treatment Act, Victoria, Australia (1995), Act. No. 63/1995, Victorian Consolidated Legislation.

7. Lorio (1999); ISLAT Working Group (1998).

8. Pierce (1985).

9. Pierce (1987, 1442).

10. See "Bill Set on Surrogate Mothers," *New York Times,* February 2, 1989, A:23; Rae (1994).

11. National Conference of Commissioners on Uniform State Laws (NCCUSL), "Uniform Status of Children of Assisted Conception Act," 1988, www.law.upenn.edu/bll/ulc/fnact99/uscaca88.htm (accessed August 16, 2006); Friedman (1992); Pretorius (1994). The NCCUSL is a nonprofit association that works for uniformity in state laws by drafting and proposing legislation. The conference can only propose laws; it is up to specific state legislatures to enact them

12. Dolgin (1997).

13. Morgan (2001); NCCUSL, "Uniform Parentage Act," www.law.upenn.edu/bll/ulc/upa/upasty1020.htm (accessed August 16, 2006).

14. As quoted in "Surrogate Mother-to-Be Fights to Keep Unborn Child," *New York Times,* March 24, 1981, A:12.

15. As quoted in Elizabeth Mehren and Bob Drogin, "Judge Awards Father Full Custody of Baby M," *Los Angeles Times,* April 1, 1987, I:1.

16. *J.F. v. D.B.,* Common Pleas Court of Erie County, Pennsylvania. 66 PA.D. & C.4th 1; 2004 Pa. D. & C. Lexis 21. Exhortations of judges ruling on surrogacy cases in New York and California are reviewed in the second half of this chapter.

17. Additionally, in two states, Oklahoma and Oregon, the state attorney generals have written opinions claiming that commercial surrogacy contracts are void and unenforceable. Brandel (1995); New York State Department of Health, *Business of Surrogate Parenting,* 11.

18. In 2005, the Illinois legislature amended the law to further simplify the nonadoption procedure for the issuing of a birth certificate to the genetic (and intended) parents.

19. See, for example, Robertson (2004) regarding the "open" U.S. approach to assisted reproductive technologies.

20. Field (1988); National Conference of State Legislatures, "Surrogacy Contract Bill Introductions: 1990," "Surrogacy Contract Bill Introductions: 1991," "Surrogacy Contract Bill Introductions: 1992," and "Regarding Surrogacy Bills"; Pierce (1987).

21. Brandel (1995). Criminal penalties include fines and jail time.

22. Andrews (1992); Brandel (1995); National Conference of State Legislatures, "Surrogate Parenting Contract Legislation Enacted."

23. Bill Billiter, "State May Set Rules on Motherhood," *Los Angeles Times,* June 20, 1982, I:3.

24. Transcribed interview with former California Assembly member, Los Angeles, February 1996. To protect the privacy of my informants, the names of all interviewees in the book are withheld, with the exception of one person who is deceased.

25. Of note, Handel's Center for Surrogate Parenting was a key co-sponsor of the regulatory bill that passed through both houses in 1992.

26. Andrews (1992, 46).

27. In California a legislative session is one year. As a result, bills expire at the end of the year and have to be reintroduced on an annual basis. To make comparisons to New York, I have therefore combined sessions to mimic New York's two-year sessions (see n. 33 below).

28. California Assembly Committee on Judiciary, "Bill Analysis: SB937," August 12, 1992, 1.

29. California Assembly Committee on Judiciary, "Surrogate Parenting Contracts," Whittier College Law School, Los Angeles, Hearings of November 19, 1982.

30. Bill Billiter, "Surrogate Mothers Bill Dead for Session," *Los Angeles Times.* August 5, 1982, II:2; see chapter 5 for further discussion of the role of the Catholic Church and other religious groups.

31. Transcribed interview with former California Assembly member, Los Angeles, February 1996.

32. It is common in California for there to be an outside sponsor of bills to help conduct research and to serve as a public relations expert.

33. New York legislative sessions consist of two years, unlike California. As a result, bills can stay alive for two calendar years before needing to be resubmitted.

34. New York State Assembly Judiciary Committee and New York Senate Judiciary Committee, *Hearing on Surrogate Parenthood and New Reproductive Technologies,* October 16, 1986, 30–38.

35. New York State Department of Health, *Business of Surrogate Parenting,* 10.

36. Transcribed interview with former New York State senator, Albany, NY, March 1996.

37. This is a conservative estimate of bill introductions. I derived the figure of twenty-one bills from bill introductions in the Assembly; this total does

not include the five bills introduced in the Senate, since all five bills had an identical companion bill in the Assembly.

38. New York State Assembly Judiciary Committee and Senate Judiciary Committee, *Hearing on Surrogate Parenthood and New Reproductive Technologies,* October 16, 1986, 4.

39. New York State Senate Judiciary Committee, *Surrogate Parenting in New York: A Proposal for Legislative Reform* (Albany, NY: New York State Senate Judiciary Committee, 1986), 3.

40. See chapter 5 for further discussion of this and other state reports produced by New York and California state agencies.

41. New York State, *Hearing in the Matter of Surrogate Parenting,* April 10, 1987; New York State Senate Standing Committee on Child Care, *Surrogate Parenting Hearing,* May 7, 1987.

42. New York State Task Force on Life and the Law, *Surrogate Parenting: Analysis and Recommendations for Public Policy* (New York: New York State Task Force on Life and the Law, 1988), 125.

43. Hevesi (1975); Zimmerman (1981).

44. New York State Assembly Standing Committee on Judiciary, Assembly Task Force on Women's Issues, *Public Hearing on Surrogate Parenting,* December 8, 1988, 9.

45. California Senate Committee on Health and Human Services, *Hearing on Surrogate Parenting,* Los Angeles, December 11, 1987, unpaginated document in author's files.

46. See Pierce (1987) about the pre– and post–Baby M legislative response to surrogacy.

47. This committee consisted of Senators Robert Presley (D), Diane Watson (D), and Ed Davis (R) and Assembly members Jackie Speier (D), Mike Roos (D), and Sunny Mojonnier (R-Chair).

48. California Joint Legislative Committee on Surrogate Parenting, *Commercial and Noncommercial Surrogate Parenting* (Sacramento: Joint Publications Office, 1990), 154–65.

49. Ibid., M-49.

50. California Assembly Committee on Judiciary, "Bill Analysis: SB 937."

51. Hevesi (1975, 17).

52. New York State Legislative Commission on Science and Technology, *Contract Motherhood: Ethical and Legal Considerations* (Albany: New York

State Legislative Commission on Science and Technology, 1991). The aim of the commission is "to provide objective scientific and technical analyses that will be useful to legislative decision-makers as they weigh the many varied factors and interests that must be considered in establishing public policy" (ii).

53. See New York State Department of Health, *Business of Surrogate Parenting*, 12–13.

54. The announcement of the Department of Health's report appeared in the May 13, 1992, issue of the *New York Times*. See chapter 5 for additional details.

55. Mario Cuomo, memorandum filed with SB 1906, State of New York, Executive Chamber, 1992, in author's files.

56. Andrews (1992).

57. Andrews (1992); Leo C. Wolinsky and Jerry Gillam, "Bill Passed to Bar Surrogate Parent Pacts," *Los Angeles Times*, May 24, 1988, I:1.

58. *Johnson v. Calvert*, 5 Cal. 4th 84 (1990).

59. Philip Hager, "State High Court to Rule in Child Custody Case," *Los Angeles Times*, January 24, 1992, A:1.

60. *Johnson v. Calvert*, 5 Cal. 4th 84, 19 Cal. Rptr. 2d. 494, 851 P2d. 776 (1993); for a thorough discussion of the Johnson case, see chapter 4.

61. Catherine Gewertz, "Genetic Parents Given Sole Custody of Child," *Los Angeles Times*, October 23, 1990, A:1.

62. *Johnson v. Calvert*, 5 Cal. 4th 84 (1990), 14.

63. Quoted in Robert R. Walmsley to Governor Pete Wilson, September 10, 1992, in author's files.

64. Hager, "State High Court," A:1.

65. Transcribed interview with California Senate staff member, Sacramento, CA, June 1996.

66. Andrews (1992).

67. California Assembly Committee on Judiciary, "Bill Analysis: SB 937."

68. Transcribed interview with surrogacy program director, Los Angeles, May 1996; transcribed interview with California Senate staff member, Sacramento, CA, June 1996.

69. Transcribed interview with California legislative aide, Sacramento, CA, June 1996.

70. Cited in Walmsley to Wilson, September 10, 1992.

71. *Johnson v. Calvert* has also been referred to by courts in other states and thus serves as an important precedent nationally as well.

72. In *In re the Marriage of Moschetta,* 25 Cal. App. 4th 1218 (1994), a surrogacy dispute that went through the California court system around the same time as *Johnson v. Calvert,* the birth mother and genetic father were given joint custody of a child born through a traditional surrogacy arrangement. The intended/adoptive mother was not given any parental rights to the child. Meanwhile, the California Court of Appeal decision *In re the Marriage of Buzzanca,* 61 Cal. App. 4th 1410 (1998), showed the important precedent of the Johnson case by its reinforcement of intention to determine parental rights in surrogacy cases. Given the courts' willingness to recognize surrogacy contracts in California, many see this as the state most open to the practice. That half of all surrogacy contracts take place in California validates this assessment. At the same time, without a countermovement to ban surrogacy practices, proponents no longer see a pressing need to pass legislation on it. This may account for the lack of bills on surrogacy since the early 1990s.

73. *In re the Marriage of Moschetta,* 25 Cal. App. 4th 1218 (1994), 1235; *Jaycee B. v. The Superior Court of Orange County,* 42 Cal. App. 4th 718 (1996), 732.

2. "CHOICE" AND THE "BEST INTERESTS OF CHILDREN"

1. U.S. House of Representatives, *Surrogacy Arrangements Act of 1987: Hearing before the Subcommittee on Transportation, Tourism, and Hazardous Materials of the Committee on Energy and Commerce, October 25, 1988* (Washington, DC: U.S. Government Printing Office, 1988), 119.

2. Quoted in Gary Abrams, "Surrogates Support Baby M Ruling," *Los Angeles Times,* October 15, 1987, V:2.

3. New York State Senate Standing Committee on Child Care, *Surrogate Parenting Hearing,* May 7, 1987, 120.

4. New York State Assembly, floor debate on A 7437/S 1906, June 26, 1992, 264.

5. Ibid., 238.

6. Ibid., 129.

7. *Webster v. Reproductive Health Services,* 492 U.S. 490 (1989).

8. Garrow (1994); Joffe (1995); Solinger (1998a); National Abortion and Reproductive Rights Action League, "Supreme Court Decisions Concerning Reproductive Rights: A Chronology, 1965–2002," January 17, 2003, www.naral.org/facts/socutus_decisions_choice.cfm (accessed June 30, 2003).
9. Wilder (1998, 85).
10. Ginsburg (1989); Condit (1990); Garrow (1994); Wilder (1998).
11. Ginsburg (1998).
12. Faludi (1991); Ginsburg (1998); Solinger (1998a); Wilder (1998).
13. Ginsburg (1998); Wilder (1998).
14. Garrow (1994); Ginsburg (1998).
15. *Planned Parenthood v. Casey*, 505 U.S. 833 (1992); Karen DeWitt, "Huge Crowd Backs Right to Abortion in Capital March," *New York Times,* April 6, 1992, A:1; Robin Toner, "Right to Abortion Draws Thousands to Capital Rally," *New York Times,* April 10, 1989, A:1.
16. Ginsburg (1998).
17. Daniels (1993, 1997); R. Roth (1993); Gómez (1997); Markens, Browner, and Press (1997); Petchesky (1987); Pollitt (1998).
18. Daniels (1993, 1997); Gómez (1997); R. Roth (1993).
19. Daniels (1993); R. Roth (1993); Pollitt (1998).
20. Daniels (1993). See *UAW v. Johnson,* 680 F. Supp. 309 (E.D. Wis. 1988) and *UAW v. Johnson,* 886 F.2d 871 (7th Cir. 1989).
21. This case was ultimately a victory for reproductive rights, as it was eventually taken to the Supreme Court, which ruled in favor of the plaintiffs. See *UAW v. Johnson,* 499 U.S. 187 (1991).
22. Blank and Merrick (1995).
23. Tsing (1990); McNeil and Litt (1992); Daniels (1993); Gómez (1997); Oaks (2001); Armstrong (2003); Bordo (1994).
24. McNeil and Litt (1992).
25. On efforts to discourage smoking during pregnancy, see Oaks (2001); on campaign for breast-feeding, see Blum (1999); on fetal surgery, see Richard (1995) and Casper (1998); on genetic and medical monitoring, see Browner and Press (1995), Rapp (1999b), and Markens (2002); on pregnancy advice manuals, see Georges and Mitchell (2000); on emphasis on diet during pregnancy, see Markens, Browner, and Press (1997).
26. Petchesky (1987); J. Taylor (1992); Duden (1993).

27. Dolgin (1997); Luppino and Miller (2002); Mintz and Kellogg (1988).

28. On child abuse, see Johnson (1989), Pfohl (1977), and Scheper-Hughes and Stein (1998); on childhood poverty, see Harrington (1963); on children's rights, see Mintz and Kellogg (1988).

29. New York State Assembly, floor debate on A 7437/S 1906, June 26, 1992.

30. Ibid., 259.

31. Ibid., 217–18; emphasis mine.

32. California Senate Committee on Health and Human Services, *Hearing on Surrogate Parenting,* Los Angeles, December 11, 1987, n.p.; emphasis mine.

33. New York State Assembly Standing Committee on Judiciary, Assembly Task Force on Women's Issues, *Public Hearing on Surrogate Parenting,* December 8, 1988, 404; emphasis mine.

34. Organization of Parenting Through Surrogacy to Senator Watson, June 17, 1992, in author's files; emphasis in original.

35. This was the center involved in the Baby M dispute.

36. New York State Assembly Standing Committee on Judiciary, Assembly Task Force on Women's Issues, *Public Hearing on Surrogate Parenting,* December 8, 1988, 574.

37. New York State Senate Standing Committee on Child Care, *Surrogate Parenting Hearing,* May 7, 1987, 35.

38. New York State Assembly Standing Committee on Judiciary, Assembly Task Force on Women's Issues, *Public Hearing on Surrogate Parenting,* December 8, 1988, 467.

39. New York State Senate Standing Committee on Child Care, *Surrogate Parenting Hearing,* May 7, 1987, 158.

40. California Senate Committee on Health and Human Services, *Hearing on Surrogate Parenting,* Los Angeles, December 11, 1987, n.p.; emphasis mine.

41. Ragoné (1994).

42. New York State Assembly, floor debate on A 7437/S 1906, June 26, 1992, 264, emphasis mine.

43. Ibid., 273, emphasis mine.

44. New York State Senate Standing Committee on Child Care, *Surrogate Parenting Hearing,* May 7, 1987, 168; emphasis mine.

45. Betty Friedan et al., "Feminists on Commercialized Childbearing: Adapted from a Friend of the Court Brief in the Baby M Case," in author's files; emphasis mine.

46. California Assembly Committee on Judiciary, *Hearings on Surrogate Parenting Contracts,* Whittier College Law School, Los Angeles, November 19, 1982, 68, emphasis mine.

47. Ibid., 222.

48. Transcribed interview with New York legislative consultant, New York, NY, April 1996; emphasis mine.

49. New York State Assembly Standing Committee on Judiciary, Assembly Task Force on Women's Issues, *Public Hearing on Surrogate Parenting,* December 8, 1988, 383.

50. Ibid., 382.

51. New York State Assembly, floor debate on A 7437/S 1906, June 26, 1992, 151. That Hevesi can legitimately consider himself a "friend to the women's movement" is documented by an endorsement he received from the Westchester Coalition for Legal Abortion in 2002, when he ran for state comptroller. In explaining their endorsement, the coalition described Hevesi as "the leader of legislators who sided with the pro-choice movement" and as "deeply involved in women's issues on many levels" See Westchester Coalition for Legal Abortion, "Alan Hevesi Was There Back When," summer 2002, www.choicematters.org/02_summer/hevesis.there.html (accessed September 24, 2006).

52. Mary Goodhue, transcribed interview, March 1996; emphasis mine.

53. New York State, *Hearing in the Matter of Surrogate Parenting,* April 10, 1987, 108–9.

54. Ibid., 110.

55. California Assembly Committee on Judiciary, *Hearings on Surrogate Parenting Contracts,* Whittier College Law School, Los Angeles, November 19, 1982, 222; emphasis mine.

56. See Introduction for a brief overview of various feminist academic approaches to surrogacy.

57. Priscilla Alexander, memorandum to National NOW Board, Surrogate/Contract Birth Mothering," April 27, 1988, in author's files; emphasis mine.

58. New York State Assembly Standing Committee on Judiciary, Assembly

Task Force on Women's Issues, *Public Hearing on Surrogate Parenting,* December 8, 1988, 381.

59. New York State Senate Standing Committee on Child Care, *Surrogate Parenting Hearing,* May 7, 1987, 20.

60. New York State, *Hearing in the Matter of Surrogate Parenting,* April 10, 1987, 21.

61. California Senate Committee on Health and Human Services, *Hearing on Surrogate Parenting,* Los Angeles, December 11, 1987, n.p.

62. California 1992 Bill File on SB 937, in author's files.

63. Office of Helene Weinstein, "Important Principles Underlying the Surrogate Parenting Bill—A. 7367," memo, in author's files.

64. New York State Assembly Judiciary Committee, Senate Judiciary Committee, *Hearing on Surrogate Parenthood and New Reproductive Technologies,* October 16, 1986, 132.

65. New York State Assembly Standing Committee on Judiciary, Assembly Task Force on Women's Issues, *Public Hearing on Surrogate Parenting,* December 8, 1988, 250.

66. Ibid., 437; emphasis mine.

67. "Child's Interest Is Paramount," *Los Angeles Times,* October 23, 1990, B:6. See chapters 1 and 4 for details regarding the Johnson case.

68. New York State Task Force on Life and the Law, *Surrogate Parenting: Analysis and Recommendations for Public Policy* (New York: New York State Task Force on Life and the Law, 1988), 71.

69. California Joint Legislative Committee on Surrogate Parenting, *Commercial and Noncommercial Surrogate Parenting* (Sacramento, CA: Joint Publications Office. 1990), 152; emphasis mine. See chapters 1 and 5 for further information regarding the panel's majority and minority reports.

70. New York State Assembly, floor debate on A 7437/S 1906, June 26, 1992, 306; emphasis mine.

71. Ibid., 96; emphasis mine.

72. Diane Watson, "Statement to the Senate Judiciary Committee Re: SB 937," May 22 1991, in author's files.

73. Child Welfare League of America, "Surrogacy: Guidelines for Child Welfare Agencies," memo from David S. Liederman, Executive Director, April 4, 1989, in author's files.

74. California Senate Committee on Health and Human Services, *Hearing on Surrogate Parenting,* Los Angeles, December 11, 1987, n.p.

75. New York State Assembly Standing Committee on Judiciary, Assembly Task Force on Women's Issues, *Public Hearing on Surrogate Parenting,* December 8, 1988, 18–19.

76. New York State Assembly Standing Committee on Judiciary, Assembly Task Force on Women's Issues, *Public Hearing on Surrogate Parenting,* December 8, 1988, 386–87; emphasis mine. (Mary Beth Whitehead divorced and remarried after the initial custody battle and became Whitehead-Gould.)

77. New York State Bill Jacket S 1906/A 7437, 1992, in author's files.

78. Ibid.

79. California 1992 Bill File on SB 937, in author's files.

80. New York State Assembly Standing Committee on Judiciary, Assembly Task Force on Women's Issues, *Public Hearing on Surrogate Parenting,* December 8, 1988, 82; emphasis mine.

81. New York State Assembly, floor debate on A 7437/S 1906, June 26, 1992, 274–75; emphasis mine.

82. New York State Assembly Judiciary Committee, Senate Judiciary Committee, *Hearing on Surrogate Parenthood and New Reproductive Technologies,* October 16, 1986, 39.

83. New York State Assembly Standing Committee on Judiciary, Assembly Task Force on Women's Issues, *Public Hearing on Surrogate Parenting,* December 8, 1988, 171; emphasis mine.

84. California Senate Committee on Health and Human Services, *Hearing on Surrogate Parenting,* Los Angeles, December 11, 1987, n.p.

85. New York State Senate Standing Committee on Child Care, *Surrogate Parenting Hearing,* May 7, 1987, 13.

86. Ibid., 547.

87. New York State Assembly, floor debate on A 7437/S 1906, June 26, 1992, 282; emphasis mine.

88. California Joint Legislative Committee on Surrogate Parenting, *Commercial and Noncommercial Surrogate Parenting,* M15; emphasis mine.

89. Transcribed interview with California Senate staff member, Sacramento, CA, June 1996.

90. New York State Bill Jacket S 1906/A 7437, 1992, in author's files.

91. Vicki Michel, introduction to testimony on SB 937 before the California Senate Judiciary Committee, May 21, 1991, in author's files; emphasis mine.

92. New York State Assembly, floor debate on A 7437/S 1906, June 26, 1992, 209. See chapter 5 for a lengthier examination of Weinstein's long history of activism on behalf of women, families, and reproductive rights.

93. Joan Byalin, memo to Assembly member Weinstein re: Surrogacy Show, April 19, 1992, in author's files.

94. New York State Bill Jacket S 1906/A 7437, 1992, in author's files.

95. New York State Assembly Standing Committee on Judiciary, Assembly Task Force on Women's Issues, *Public Hearing on Surrogate Parenting*, December 8, 1988, 216.

96. Institute on Women and Technology, "Women and Children Used in Systems of Surrogacy: Position Statement," n.d., in author's files; emphasis mine.

97. On child care, see Michel (1999); on the medicalization of pregnancy, see, for example, Markens, Browner, and Press (1997) and Bordo (1994).

98. Hays (1996).

99. Zelizer (1985).

100. Faludi (1991).

101. Ladd-Taylor and Umansky (1998).

102. See Petchesky (1984/1990) and Solinger (1998b).

3. "MORAL CONUNDRUMS AND MENACING AMBIGUITIES"

1. See the excerpt from the testimony of Monsignor William Levada provided at the beginning of this chapter. (California Assembly Committee on Judiciary, *Hearings on Surrogate Parenting Contracts,* Whittier College Law School, Los Angeles, November 19, 1982, provides the full testimony.) At a New York State hearing in 1986, Agudath Israel of America's general counsel David Zweibel objected to surrogate parenting on the grounds that it "would tell society that there is nothing wrong with reproduction outside the marital context." New York State Assembly Judiciary Committee and Senate Judiciary Committee, *Hearing on Surrogate Parenthood and New Reproductive Technologies,* October 16, 1986, 225.

2. New York State Senate Standing Committee on Child Care, *Surrogate Parenting Hearing,* May 7, 1987, 295. Holka, who had been on a committee in Michigan that studied surrogacy, was fiercely opposed to commercial surrogate parenting arrangements.
3. George F. Will, "For Surrogate Mothering, Lots of Supposes," *Los Angeles Times,* December 15, 1980, II:11.
4. California Senate Committee on Health and Human Services, *Hearing on Surrogate Parenting,* Los Angeles, December 11, 1987, n.p.
5. New York State Assembly Judiciary Committee and Senate Judiciary Committee, *Hearing on Surrogate Parenthood and New Reproductive Technologies,* October 16, 1986, 179.
6. California Senate Committee on Health and Human Services, *Hearing on Surrogate Parenting,* Los Angeles, December 11, 1987, n.p.
7. New York State Senate Standing Committee on Child Care, *Surrogate Parenting Hearing,* May 7, 1987, 167.
8. New York State Task Force on Life and the Law, *Surrogate Parenting: Analysis and Recommendations for Public Policy* (New York: New York State Task Force on Life and the Law, 1988), 78.
9. Rochfort and Cobb (1993).
10. Best (1991).
11. Elizabeth Mehren and Bob Drogin, "Judge Awards Father Full Custody of Baby M," *Los Angeles Times,* April 1, 1987, I:1.
12. Nadine Brozan, "Surrogate Mothers: Problems and Goals," *New York Times,* February 27, 1984, C:12.
13. Don Colburn, "Redefining 'Mother' and 'Father,'" *Washington Post,* February 24, 1987, Z:6.
14. Martin Kasindorf, "And Baby Makes Four," *Los Angeles Times Magazine,* January 20, 1991, 10.
15. Sonni Efron, "Bill to Legalize Surrogacy Is Introduced," *Los Angeles Times,* April 28, 1991, B:1.
16. "Church Hits Surrogacy," *Washington Post,* July 16, 1987, A:9.
17. See, respectively, Philip J. Hilts, "N.Y. Ban Urged on Surrogate-Mother Deals," *Washington Post,* May 30, 1988, A:4, and Elizabeth Mehren, "A Capital Site for a Surrogate Parent Center," *Los Angeles Times,* April 19, 1983, V:1.
18. Quoted in Efron, "Bill to Legalize Surrogacy."

19. Quoted in Dennis Hevesi, "Surrogate-Parenthood Measures Sought," *New York Times*, April 2, 1987, B:2.

20. "Gestation, Inc.," *New York Times*, November 23, 1980, 4:20.

21. Judy Mann, "Surrogate Motherhood: The Inevitable Conflict," *Washington Post*, March 25, 1981, C:1.

22. Claudia Levy, "Surrogate Mom Gives Up Baby after Dispute," *Washington Post*, April 23, 1988, G:1.

23. U.S. House of Representatives, *Surrogacy Arrangements Act of 1987: Hearing before the Subcommittee on Transportation, Tourism, and Hazardous Materials of the Committee on Energy and Commerce, October 25, 1988* (Washington, DC: U.S. Government Printing Office, 1988), 101.

24. New York State Assembly Judiciary Committee and Senate Judiciary Committee, *Hearing on Surrogate Parenthood and New Reproductive Technologies*, October 16, 1986, 253.

25. Ibid., 225.

26. U.S. House of Representatives, *Surrogacy Arrangements Act of 1987*, 8.

27. New York State Assembly, floor debate on A 7437/S 1906, June 26, 1992, 81.

28. Ibid., 187.

29. New York State Assembly Standing Committee on Judiciary, Assembly Task Force on Women's Issues, *Public Hearing on Surrogate Parenting*, December 8, 1988, 211. Initial concerns about the development of a "breeder" group of lower-class women do not seem to have been borne out. Although surrogates tend not to be as wealthy as the couples who commission them, they usually are not from extremely disadvantaged classes or countries. See Ragoné (1994, 1998).

30. Mann, "Surrogate Motherhood," C:1.

31. Josh Getlin, "Surrogate Motherhood-for-Pay Is Argued," *Los Angeles Times*, October 16, 1987, I:4.

32. Beverly Beyette, "Bar's Family Law 'Think Tank' Tackles Surrogate Motherhood Issue," *Los Angeles Times*, January 21, 1987, V:1.

33. Initially, not all surrogacy advocates were savvy enough to distance their endorsement of surrogate parenthood from a commodified and commercialized view of reproductive processes. For instance, Harriet Blankfeld, founder of a surrogacy program in the Washington, D.C., area, frankly stated that she wanted her agency to become the "Coca-Cola of

the surrogate parenting industry." See Ellen Goodman, "Wombs for Rent: New Era of the Reproduction Line," *Los Angeles Times,* February 8, 1983, II:5, and Carol Krucoff, "The Surrogate Baby Boom," *Washington Post,* January 25, 1983, C:5.

34. Krucoff, "Surrogate Baby Boom," C:5.

35. Angel Castillo, "When Women Bear Children for Others," *New York Times,* December 22, 1980, B:6.

36. Elizabeth Kolbert, "Baby M Adds Urgency to Search for Equitable Laws," *New York Times,* February 15, 1987, 4:22.

37. The use of the "gift" metaphor has been viewed as reflecting societal ambivalence over and discomfort with the commodification of reproduction. See Kaplan (1999), Layne (1999), Ragoné (1999), and Rapp (1999a) for further discussion of the "gift" metaphor with regard to assisted reproductive technologies.

38. California Senate Committee on Health and Human Services, *Hearing on Surrogate Parenting,* Los Angeles, December 11, 1987, n.p.

39. See Zelizer (1985).

40. Itabari Njeri, "The Pain of Infertility: One Couple's Choices," *Los Angles Times,* March 22, 1987, VI:12.

41. New York State Assembly Standing Committee on Judiciary, Assembly Task Force on Women's Issues, *Public Hearing on Surrogate Parenting,* December 8, 1988, 455.

42. Diane Baker to Governor Pete Wilson, August 31, 1992, in author's files.

43. Getlin, "Surrogate Motherhood-for-Pay," I:4.

44. Art Harris, "Stand-In Mother," *Washington Post.* February 11, 1980, A:1.

45. New York State, *Hearing in the Matter of Surrogate Parenting,* April 10, 1987, 79.

46. Kasindorf, "And Baby Makes Four," 10.

47. Iver Peterson, "Baby M, Ethics and the Law," *New York Times,* January 18, 1987, I:1.

48. "A.B.A.'s 2 Models for 'Baby M' Laws," *New York Times,* February 9, 1989, C:13.

49. "On Bearing Someone Else's Baby," *New York Times,* August 28, 1986, A:22.

50. "The Surrogate's Baby Comes First," *New York Times,* January 26, 1987, A:34.

51. New York State Assembly, floor debate on A 7437/S 1906, June 26,1992, 92.

52. "Baby Sales," *New York Times,* February 8, 1983, A:20.

53. "Surrogate's Baby Comes First," A:34.

54. New York State Assembly Standing Committee on Judiciary, Assembly Task Force on Women's Issues, Public Hearing on Surrogate Parenting, December 8, 1988, 581.

55. See Ortiz and Briggs (2003) regarding the construction of a crisis in white "adoptable" babies.

56. Walter Goodman, "New Reproduction Techniques Redefine Parenthood," *New York Times,* November 16, 1984, A:21.

57. Dava Sobel, "Surrogate Mothers: Why Women Volunteer," *New York Times,* June 29, 1981, B:5.

58. Quoted in Harris, "Stand-In Mother," A:1.

59. See D. Schneider (1980) about the significance of "blood ties" in American kinship. See Finkler (2000) about the geneticizing of family relations.

60. Brozan, "Surrogate Mothers," C:12.

61. Njeri, "Pain of Infertility," VI:12.

62. Malcolm Andrews, "Steps to Control Surrogate Births Rekindle Debate," *New York Times,* June 26, 1988, 1:1.

63. Donald T. DiFrancesco, "Government and Surrogate Parenthood," *New York Times,* June 28, 1987, 11:26.

64. U.S. House of Representatives, *Surrogacy Arrangements Act of 1987,* 6.

65. New York State Assembly, floor debate on A 7437/S 1906, June 26, 1992, 120.

66. Ibid., 175.

67. U.S. House of Representatives, *Surrogacy Arrangements Act of 1987,* 112.

68. Duster (1990); Nelkin and Lindee (1996); Rothman (1998); Alper et al. (2002).

69. For information regarding alternative family constructions, see, for example, Collins (1990) and Stack (1974). Both Collins and Stack discuss the importance in the black community of family-like relations among persons not related by biology.

70. D. Roberts (1997); also see Beisel and Kay (2004) and Solinger (1992).

71. California Senate Committee on Health and Human Services, *Hearing on Surrogate Parenting,* Los Angeles, December 11, 1987, n.p.

72. U.S. House of Representatives, *Surrogacy Arrangements Act of 1987,* 126.

73. Ibid., 1–2.

74. New York State Assembly, floor debate on A 7437/S 1906, June 26, 1992, 269.

75. Ibid., 275.

76. New York State Task Force on Life and the Law, *Surrogate Parenting,* 118.

77. New York State Assembly, floor debate on A 7437/S 1906, June 26, 1992, 85–86.

78. California Senate Committee on Health and Human Services, *Hearing on Surrogate Parenting,* Los Angeles, December 11, 1987, n.p.

79. Charles Krauthammer, "The Hired Incubator: There Ought to Be a Law," *Washington Post,* January 16, 1987, A:23.

80. New York State Assembly, floor debate on A 7437/S 1906, June 26, 1992, 85–86.

81. California Joint Legislative Committee on Surrogate Parenting, *Commercial and Noncommercial Surrogate Parenting* (Sacramento, CA: Joint Publications Office, 1990), 139–40.

82. New York State Assembly Judiciary Committee and Senate Judiciary Committee, *Hearing on Surrogate Parenthood and New Reproductive Technologies,* October 16, 1986, 277.

83. New York State Senate Judiciary Committee, *Surrogate Parenting in New York: A Proposal for Legislative Reform* (Albany: New York State Senate Judiciary Committee, 1986), 49.

84. New York State Assembly Standing Committee on Judiciary, Assembly Task Force on Women's Issues, *Public Hearing on Surrogate Parenting,* December 8, 1988, 173.

85. New York State Assembly, floor debate on A 7437/S 1906, June 26, 1992, 299.

86. Ibid., 217–18.

87. New York State Assembly Standing Committee on Judiciary, Assembly Task Force on Women's Issues, *Public Hearing on Surrogate Parenting,* December 8, 1988, 164.

88. New York State Assembly, floor debate on A 7437/S 1906, June 26, 1992, 97.

89. Robert Walmsley to Governor Wilson, September 10, 1992, in author's files; emphasis in original.

90. New York State Assembly Standing Committee on Judiciary, Assembly Task Force on Women's Issues, *Public Hearing on Surrogate Parenting,* December 8, 1988, 284.

91. The delicate balance that some surrogacy supporters had to maintain in supporting a policy to regulate the practice in order to ensure reproductive rights while at the same time not relinquishing their overall theme that the state should not interfere too much in this private arena is visible in some criticisms made by surrogate parenting proponents of particular aspects of regulatory legislation. Prosurrogacy advocate Lori Andrews, for example, was careful to acknowledge the limits of state policy to regulate the practice in one of her few criticisms of Senators Dunne and Goodhue's proposed regulatory bill in New York in the mid-1980s: "I think that one thing I would object to is I would not require genetic screening. . . . I would hate to see the State get involved in mandated testing." New York State, *Hearing in the Matter of Surrogate Parenting,* April 10, 1987, 48.

92. Novelle and Rob Myerhoff to Governor Pete Wilson, August 21, 1992, in author's files.

93. Holiday Jackson to Governor Pete Wilson, 1992, in author's files.

94. California Senate Committee on Health and Human Services, *Hearing on Surrogate Parenting,* Los Angeles, December 11, 1987, n.p.

95. New York State Assembly, floor debate on A 7437/S 1906, June 26, 1992, 83.

96. Lasch (1977).

97. Zelizer (1985).

98. Hays (1996).

99. Stevens (2001).

100. Boris (1994).

4. COMPETING FRAMES OF SURROGACY

1. Park (1940).

2. McCombs and Shaw (1972); Park (1940); Rogers and Dearing (1988); Shaw and McCombs (1977).

3. McCombs and Shaw (1972).

4. Cook et al. (1983).

5. See Fishman (1980), Gans (1979), and Tuchman (1978) for accounts of how the institutional structure of the media affects what news is reported.
6. Edelman (1988, 91).
7. Burstein (1991); Johnson (1989); Rittenhouse (1991).
8. Best (1989, xxi).
9. Print media allow for more in-depth coverage than does broadcast journalism. I chose to examine the *New York Times,* the *Los Angeles Times,* and the *Washington Post* because their readership implies a national-level influence. Furthermore, the *Los Angeles Times* is considered the most authoritative paper in California, and the *New York Times* is the most frequently cited paper (Best 1991). These distinctions suggest that these two papers would play important roles in setting the policy agenda in each state. See Appendix A for further discussion of methods and data.
10. Many aspects of surrogate parenting transactions could be viewed as "horrors." I limited the coding of newspaper horror stories to accounts of particular surrogacy arrangements that went awry or, at the least, did not proceed smoothly, and thus the media accounts necessarily include reports of a problem. The vast majority of stories so coded involve cases where the custody and/or parentage of a child is disputed; however, incidences involving questions regarding the main parties' motives and qualifications also are included (e.g., the case of a single man who killed his surrogate child a few weeks after it was born).
11. See Ferree et al. (2002) and Gamson and Stuart (1992).
12. A few years later, she changed her mind and became an active opponent of surrogacy. In a 1987 congressional hearing prompted by the Baby M case, Kane was among those who testified against commercial surrogacy.
13. "Giving Love, or Selling Life?" *New York Times,* January 9, 1987, A:26.
14. "The Case of Baby M," *Los Angeles Times,* January 25, 1987, V:4.
15. Erik Eckholm, "Designing an Ethical Frame for Motherhood by Contract," *New York Times,* January 11, 1987, 4:6.
16. Iver Peterson, "Baby M's Future," *New York Times,* April 5, 1987, 4:1.
17. Robert Hanley, "Mother Said to Change Her Mind at Baby M's Birth," *New York Times,* January 8, 1987, B:1.
18. Robert Hanley, "Surrogate Mother Seemed 'Perfect' Father of Baby M Testifies," *New York Times,* January 6, 1987, B:1.

19. Richard Cohen, "The Battle for Baby M," *Washington Post,* January 15, 1987, A:21.
20. Ruth Marcus, "Baby M Fight Goads Legislatures," *Washington Post,* March 31, 1987, A:1.
21. E. J. Dionne Jr., "Sex and Politics: Tough Decisions along a New Ethical Frontier," *New York Times,* March 15, 1987, 4:1.
22. Carol Lawson, "Surrogate Mothers Grow in Number Despite Questions," *New York Times,* October 1, 1986, C:1.
23. Myrna Oliver, "Baby M: Old Story but the Legal Issues Remain," *Los Angeles Times,* April 5, 1987, I:3.
24. *In re Baby M,* 109 N.J. 396 (1988), 412.
25. Ibid.
26. "On Bearing Someone Else's Baby," *New York Times,* August 28, 1986, A:22.
27. "All Questions, No Answers," *Los Angeles Times,* April 5, 1987, 5:4.
28. "Excerpts from Decision by New Jersey Supreme Court in the Baby M Case," *New York Times,* February 4, 1988, B:6.
29. Mary McGrory, "Dispensing Pain in the Baby M Case," *Washington Post,* March 17, 1987, A:2.
30. Elizabeth Mehren, "Surrogate Births: Is Mother Bound by a 'Contract'?" *Los Angeles Times,* January 10, 1987, I:1.
31. Margot Hornblower, "'Just Wanted My Child,' Surrogate Mother Says," *Washington Post,* January 9, 1987, A:3.
32. Conversely, it could be argued that Stern's "Jewishness" may have undermined his ability to fully tap "white privilege" as a resource in generating public sympathy.
33. Hornblower, "'Just Wanted My Child,'" A:3.
34. McGrory, "Dispensing Pain," A2.
35. George F. Will, "The 'Natural' Mother," *Washington Post,* January 22, 1987, A:21.
36. Judy Mann, "The Motherhood Contract," *Washington Post,* February 18, 1987, B:3.
37. Richard Cohen, "The Battle for Baby M," *Washington Post,* January 15, 1987, A:21.
38. *In re Baby M,* 109 N.J. 396 (1988), 412.

39. As quoted in Robert Hanley, "Father of Baby M Thought Mother Had Been Screened," *New York Times,* January 14, 1987, B:2.

40. Ibid.

41. Lois Timmick, "Surrogate Mother Wins Fight to Keep Custody of Infant Son," *Los Angeles Times,* June 5, 1981, I:3. See also "Surrogate Mother-to-Be Fights to Keep Unborn Child," *New York Times,* March 25, 1981, A:12; "Baby's Father Agrees to Withdraw His Suit over Surrogate Birth," *New York Times,* June 5, 1981, A:12. Although surrogacy is now often promoted as a legitimate option for gay couples and there are several agencies that specialize in helping gay men, this early case reveals that surrogate parenting frequently reproduces normative family formations. Nontraditional families (and transgendered persons) are seen as deviant and thus as having less valid claims to the children born of surrogate transactions.

42. "Surrogate's Baby Born with Deformity Rejected by All," *Los Angeles Times,* January 22, 1983, I:17; "Man Who Hired 'Surrogate Mother' Isn't Child's Father," *Los Angeles Times,* February 3, 1983, I:17; "Baby Does Get Home," *New York Times,* February 3, 1983, I:16.

43. New York State Department of Health, *The Business of Surrogate Parenting* (Albany: New York State Department of Health, 1992), 8.

44. Judy Mann, "Nature Too Chancy for Contracts," *Washington Post,* April 22, 1988, C:3.

45. James Risen, "Michigan Outlaws Surrogate Maternity Contracts; Ban Aimed at 'Baby M' Clinic," *Los Angeles Times,* June 28, 1988, I:4.

46. "7 States Prohibit Surrogacy for Pay," *Los Angeles Times,* March 6, 1989, 5:5.

47. See, for example, Ragoné (1994).

48. Philip J. Hilts, "N.Y. Ban Urged on Surrogate-Mother Deals," *Washington Post,* May 30, 1988, A:4.

49. As quoted in James Risen, "Lawyer Runs Surrogate Baby Boom," *Los Angeles Times,* March 12, 1987, I:1.

50. Anne Taylor Fleming, "Our Fascination with Baby M," *New York Times,* March 29, 1987, 6:33.

51. Risen, "Lawyer Runs Surrogate Baby Boom," I:1.

52. Forty-one articles pertaining to surrogacy appeared in the *New York Times, Los Angeles Times,* and *Washington Post* in 1990, the same amount as in 1986, when the Baby M case began.

53. *Johnson v. Calvert,* 5 Cal. 4th 84 (1990), 3–4; emphasis mine.

54. Catherine Gewertz, "Genetic Parents Given Sole Custody of Child," *Los Angeles Times,* October 23, 1990, A:1; emphasis mine.

55. Richard Paddock and Rene Lynch, "Surrogate Has No Rights to Child, Court Says," *Los Angeles Times,* May 21, 1993, A:1; emphasis mine.

56. "Genetic Parents Awarded Custody of Test-Tube Baby," *Washington Post,* September 22, 1990, A:8; emphasis mine.

57. Catherine Gewertz, "Surrogate's Custody Fight Opens," *Los Angeles Times,* October 10, 1990, A:3.

58. "Profit Is the Wrong Motive," *Los Angeles Times,* October 12, 1990, B:6.

59. Ramona Ripston, "One Baby, Three Parents: Whose Rights Prevail?" *Los Angeles Times,* October 17, 1990, B:7.

60. Catherine Gewertz, "Surrogate Parent Trial Nears End; Judge Is Likened to Solomon," *Los Angeles Times,* October 18, 1990, A:3.

61. Catherine Gewertz, "Witness Doubts Surrogate's Claim of Bonding," *Los Angeles Times,* October 12, 1990, A:39.

62. *Johnson v. Calvert,* 5 Cal. 4th 84 (1990), 5; emphasis mine.

63. Ted Rohrlich, "Ruling Brightens Aspect of Surrogate Parenting," *Los Angeles Times,* October 23, 1990, A:24.

64. Sonni Efron, "Genetic Parents Get Baby," *Los Angeles Times,* October 22, 1990, A:1.

65. Catherine Gewertz, "Genetic Parents Given Sole Custody of Child," *Los Angeles Times,* October 23, 1990, A:1; emphasis mine.

66. Seth Mydans, "Surrogate Denied Custody of Child," *New York Times,* October 23, 1990, A:14.

67. See, for example, Effron, "Genetic Parents Get Baby," and Gewertz, "Genetic Parents Given Sole Custody."

68. Effron, "Genetic Parents Get Baby," A:1.

69. Mydans, "Surrogate Denied Custody," A:1.

70. Philip Hager, "State High Court to Rule in Child Surrogacy Case," *Los Angeles Times,* January 24, 1992, A:1.

71. See *Johnson v. Calvert,* 5 Cal. 4th 84 (1990), 21: "And so if it's agreeable that they be paid for that service, *they are not selling a baby,* they are selling, again, the pain and suffering, the discomfort, that which goes with carrying a child to term. And if they can get good feelings and feel like they've done something for someone who can't have a child and they've

already had a child hopefully already, they know what it's like, how rewarding it is, *to help a couple that is desperate and longing for their own genetic product*" (21, emphasis mine). In *Johnson v. Calvert,* 5 Cal. 4th 84, 19 Cal. Rptr. 2d. 494, 851 P2d. 776 (1993), the California Supreme Court decision noted, "As discussed above, Anna was not the genetic mother of the child. The *payments to Anna under the contract were meant to compensate her for her services* in gestating the fetus and undergoing labor, rather than for giving up 'parental' rights to the child" (96, emphasis mine).

72. Catherine Gewertz, "Surrogate Mother Sues to Keep Couple's Child," *Los Angeles Times,* August 14, 1990, A:1; emphasis mine.

73. See Gewertz, "Surrogate Mother Sues," A:1, "Surrogate Parent Trial," and "Parents of Child Born to Surrogate Face Final Challenge," *Los Angeles Times,* April 17, 1992, A:3; Martin Kasindorf, "And Baby Makes Four," *Los Angeles Times Magazine,* January 20, 1991, 10.

74. Jay Matthews, "California Surrogate Stirs Dispute," *Washington Post,* September 20, 1990, A:8; emphasis mine.

75. Gewertz, "Parents of Child," A:3.

76. The common description of this baby as white also can be viewed as tapping into dominant cultural norms by elevating the child's worth and supporting the processes that produced him. See D. Roberts (1997) for a discussion of the racialized discourses surrounding new reproductive technologies.

77. Research on gestational surrogates has found that they often prefer to give birth to a child of a different race precisely because it further deemphasizes any "relatedness" between themselves and the child (Ragoné 1998). See Hartouni (1997), D. Roberts (1997), and Van Dyck (1995) for other analyses of the role of race in the Johnson-Calvert case.

78. "Profit Is the Wrong Motive," B:6.

79. "Surrogate Parenting: The Bioethical Issue," *Los Angeles Times,* August 20, 1990, B:4; "Give the Baby to the Genetic Parents," *Los Angeles Times,* September 22, 1990, B:6.

80. Catherine Gewertz, "Surrogate Mother in Custody Fight Accused of Welfare Fraud," *Los Angeles Times,* August 16, 1990, A:3.

81. See Collins (1990).

82. Kasindorf, "And Baby Makes Four," 11.

83. Dolgin (1997). This is similar to the Baby M case when Mary Beth Whitehead's working-class background was used against her in the lower court's determination of parental fitness.

84. See, for example, "Babies: No Sale," *Los Angeles Times,* February 4, 1988, II:6, and Harrison (1987).

85. Andrews (1992). The Calverts did sue Bill Handel for letting them have access to what a contract would look like, but Handel distanced himself from the transaction, as his agency did not screen Johnson or arrange their particular agreement; see Kasindorf, "And Baby Makes Four."

86. Gewertz, "Surrogate Mother Sues," A:1.

87. Dana Parsons, "It's Time to Conceive Baby-Trafficking Laws," *Los Angeles Times,* April 12, 1991, B:1. See also Kasindorf, "And Baby Makes Four."

88. Robert Hanley, "Brokers Play Down Surrogacy Case," *New York Times,* February 5, 1988, B:5.

89. Garry Abrams, "A Setback for Surrogate Parenting?" *Los Angeles Times,* February 4, 1988, V:1. Another *Los Angeles Times* story contrasted the blemish-free records of CSP and a second surrogacy program in the area with the Baby M case: "Neither the surrogate center in Beverly Hills nor the one in West Los Angeles has been involved in a dispute like the Baby M case." Itabari Njeri, "Surrogate Motherhood: A Practice That's Still Undergoing Birth Pangs," *Los Angeles Times,* March 22, 1987, VI:1.

90. Njeri, "Surrogate Motherhood," VI:1.

91. Abrams, "Setback for Surrogate Parenting?" V:1.

92. Hanley, "Brokers Play Down Surrogacy Case," B:5.

93. Daniel Coleman, "Motivations of Surrogate Mothers," *New York Times,* January 20, 1987, C:1.

94. Oliver, "Baby M," I:3.

95. See Parsons, "It's Time." In this same article, a co-director of the program was quoted as saying that although "some less reputable surrogate operations 'act pretty much as a dating service,' the overwhelming number of surrogate cases work out. . . . But that doesn't stop Fagen [CSP co-director] from advocating state legislation" (B:1).

96. CSP was a key sponsor of the regulatory prosurrogacy legislation in California; Watson's bill, SB 937, was modeled on the center's own practices. See chapter 1 for details regarding the development and passage of the bill.

97. As of 1992, the year the California legislature passed a surrogacy regulatory bill, no surrogacy arrangement brokered by Handel had ever resulted in a custodial court battle. See Andrews (1992).

98. For an analysis of selection bias in newspaper coverage, see Myers and Caniglia (2004).

99. Additional evidence of the role the location of a horror story can play in shaping media coverage and public and political reaction is provided in editorials from other New York area papers. These, too, indicate the dominance of the "baby-selling" definition of surrogacy in the state by 1992. The editorial from the *Daily News* in support of the 1992 bill ran with the heading "Wanna Buy a Baby?" (May 19, 1992). Similarly, in their endorsement of the anti–commercial surrogacy bill, *Newsday* titled their opinion "Womb to Rent" (June 11, 1992).

100. The impact of geography can also be found in other surrogacy "horror story" coverage. For instance, only one article appeared in the *New York Times* regarding the lesser-known California case *In re the Marriage of Moschetta,* which went to trial in 1991, whereas the *Los Angeles Times* covered the case with both articles and editorials (this coverage is discussed further later in this chapter). The Alejandra Munoz case, which occurred around the same time as the Baby M trial, received no coverage in the *New York Times,* whereas the *Los Angeles Times* published six pieces on this "horror story" of a Mexican woman allegedly compelled by family members to act as a surrogate. And *Jaycee B. v. The Superior Court of Orange County,* the most recent precedent-setting California court case on surrogate motherhood, similarly received no attention from the *New York Times,* while the *Los Angeles Times* published seven pieces about the case. (*Jaycee* is described in the Introduction and is discussed later in this chapter as well.)

101. See, for example, Sigal (1973).

102. See Van Dyck (1995) for an account of Gewertz's conflict of interest between her role as reporter and witness during the trial. Gewertz was called to testify during the custody trial, as she had reported on Johnson's lack of bonding to the baby during pregnancy in one of her articles.

103. More evidence concerning the impact of geography specifically on editorial coverage is that the *Washington Post* published only four editorials on surrogate parenting between 1980 and 2002. Additionally, while the New York Times editorial page did not comment on surrogacy after 1992, the Los Angeles Times editorial page published four more editorials in the 1990s: two in 1993 in response to *Johnson v. Calvert* and one each in 1996 and 1998 as *Jaycee* went through the California court system (see Introduction for discussion of *Jaycee*).

104. "On Bearing Someone Else's Baby," A:22.

105. "The Surrogate's Baby Comes First," *New York Times,* January 26, 1987, A:34.

106. Ibid.; "Now, What about Babies N, O and P?" *New York Times,* April 30, 1987, A:30.

107. "Giving Love, or Selling Life?" A:26.

108. "Surrogate's Baby Comes First," A:34 .

109. "Nothing Surrogate about the Pain," *New York Times,* March 9, 1987, A:14.

110. "Baby M: Groping for Right and Law," *New York Times,* April 2, 1987, A:30.

111. "Nothing Surrogate," A:14.

112. Ibid. This editorial also weakened claims to a "plight of infertile couples" frame of surrogate motherhood by cynically noting the class bias regarding whose infertility problems are likely to be alleviated through use of this practice: "Above all, we've been forcefully reminded that surrogacy is not a solution to the problem of female infertility, only to the problem of female infertility among the affluent."

113. "Baby M: Groping for Right," A:30.

114. "Justice for All in the Baby M Case," *New York Times,* February 4, 1988, A:26, emphasis mine.

115. "It's Baby-Selling, and It's Wrong," *New York Times,* June 4, 1988, 1:26.

116. "Making Money by Making Babies," *New York Times,* June 10, 1992, A:22.

117. "All Questions, No Answers," *Los Angeles Times,* April 1, 1987, 5:4.

118. Ibid. It should be noted that during the 1980s abortion rates actually declined slightly. See Finer and Henshaw (2003). False claims about climbing rates of abortion can be viewed as yet another way in which the adoption epidemic was falsely constructed in public discourse.

119. "Case of Baby M."

120. "Babies: No Sale," II:6; emphasis mine.

121. "Surrogate Parenting," B:4.

122. "Give the Baby," B:6.

123. "Surrogate Parenting," B:4.

124. "Profit Is the Wrong Motive," B:60.

125. "Child's Interest Is Paramount," *Los Angeles Times,* October 23, 1990, B:6.

126. "Surrogate Parenting," B:4.

127. "Child's Interest Is Paramount," B:6; emphasis mine.

128. "Stand-in Moms: What's the Law?" *Los Angeles Times,* January 27, 1992, B:4.

129. "Surrogate Case: A Good Ruling," *Los Angeles Times,* May 24, 1993, B:6.

130. "Surrogate Parenting," B:4.

131. "Stand-in Moms," B:4.

132. *In re the Marriage of Moschetta,* 25 Cal. App. 4th 1218 (1994). This case was also written about once each in 1992 and 1995.

133. "It's Kramer vs. Kramer vs. Somebody Else," *Los Angeles Times,* April 22, 1991, B:4.

134. "The Tangled Web of Surrogacy Issues," *Los Angeles Times,* September 28, 1991, B:5.

135. A 1992 editorial critical of an early version of Senator Diane Watson's regulatory bill also supported the claims of nongenetic parents. In denouncing the bill's proposal to give more extensive rights to genetic than nongenetic mothers, the editors warned, "And make no mistake, the couple seeking to have the child must have first claim of parenthood. Anything else would be bad public policy. To those concerned about the emotional attachment developing in a birth mother, the answer is simple: Nobody should agree lightly to be a surrogate." "An Invitation to Further Chaos," *Los Angeles Times,* February 28, 1992, B:6.

136. "New Clarity in Surrogacy Cases," *Los Angeles Times,* March 12, 1998, B:8.

137. See, for example, Blum (1999); Daniels (1993); D. Roberts (1997); Solinger (1992).

138. Transcribed interview with surrogacy program director, Los Angeles, May 1996.

5. UNITY, DIVISIONS, AND STRANGE BEDFELLOWS

1. Gray (1973); Preston (1984); Walker (1969).

2. Transcribed interview with California Senate staff member, Sacramento, CA, June 1996.

3. Glendon (1989, 188–89).

4. Leiter (1993).

5. Leiter (1993).

6. Additionally, both states require that a physician perform the insemination in order for their respective laws regarding the establishment of paternity to apply (Henry 1993).

7. Henry (1993).

8. Given the New York legislature's involvement in the early 1980s with adoption reform when the surrogacy debate emerged, it is possible that the earlier debates about adoptees' right to know, and thus the whole adoption process, and ideas of kinship subsequently affected legislators' reaction to surrogate parenting legislation. See Judy Lembesrud, "Mothers Find the Children They Gave Up," *New York Times,* August 29, 1983, B:5, on the New York legislation regarding opening adoption records. Similarly, in 1970, New York experienced one of the first highly publicized adoption custody battles, *People ex rel. Scarpetta v. Spence-Chapin Adoption Serv.,* 28 N.Y. 2d 185 (N.Y. 1971) (commonly known as the Baby Lenore case), in which a birth mother changed her mind. As a result of this case, New York changed its adoptions laws in 1970 from a birth mother having absolute right to revoke consent prior to court finalization of adoption to a more qualified right to change her mind once consent has been signed.

9. Solinger (1998b).

10. See Guttmacher Institute, "State Facts about Abortion," 2005, www.agi-usa.org/pubs/sfaa.html (accessed August 21, 2006).

11. See National Conference of State Legislatures, "50 State Summary of State Laws Related to Insurance Coverage for Infertility Therapy," July 2006, www.ncsl.org/programs/health/50infert.htm (accessed August 21, 2006). New York mandates coverage, while California requires that it be offered. See Fertility Lifelines, "State-Mandated Benefits," 2006, www.fertilitylifelines.com/paying/insurance/statemandate.jsp (accessed September 24, 2006).

12. Andrew Pollack, "Measure Passed, California Weighs Its Future as a Stem Cell Epicenter," *New York Times,* November 4, 2004, C:1.

13. Mike McIntire, "Fearing New York May Fall Behind, Senator Proposes Stem Cell Institute," *New York Times,* January 17, 2005, B:4.

14. California's policy is much more extensive and, unlike New York, also implements a domestic partner registry. Lambda Legal, "State by State: Domestic Partnership," 2005, www.lambdalegal.org/cgi-bin/iowa/states/domesticpart-map (accessed August 21, 2006).

15. California law explicitly outlaws discrimination against gays in fostering and adoption. See Lambda Legal, "Overview of State Adoption Laws," www.lambdalegal.org/cgi-bin/iowa/documents/record2.html?record = 1923 (accessed September 23, 2006).

16. Entman (1991); Gitlin (1987); Herman and Chomsky (1988); Manoff (1989).

17. New York State Senate Judiciary Committee, *Surrogate Parenting in New York: A Proposal for Legislative Reform* (Albany: New York State Senate Judiciary Committee, 1986), 3.

18. Ibid.

19. Ibid., 59.

20. Ibid., 9.

21. See chapter 1, table 4.

22. The Dunne-Goodhue bill (S 1429) died in the Senate Child Care Committee, while its companion bill in the Assembly (A 4748), co-sponsored by Assemblymen Koppell (D) and Albert Vann (D), died in the Assembly Judiciary Committee.

23. Robert Hanley, "Seven-Week Trial Touched Many Basic Emotions," *New York Times,* April 1, 1987, B:2.

24. See New York State Department of Health, "The History of the Task Force," www.health.state.ny.us/nysdoh/taskfce/taskbio.thm, and "Task Force on Life and the Law—Fact Sheet," www.health.state.ny.us/nysdoh/taskforce/factsht.htm (both accessed September 23, 2006).

25. New York State Task Force on Life and the Law, *Surrogate Parenting: Analysis and Recommendations for Public Policy* (New York: New York State Task Force on Life and the Law, 1988), 125–26.

26. Ibid., 121, 123.

27. "It's Baby Selling, and It's Wrong," *New York Times,* June 4, 1988, I:26.

28. "Ban Commercial Surrogacy," *Buffalo News,* June 11, 1989; "Surrogate Parenting: Put the Child's Interest First," *Newsday,* June 21, 64. The governor is presented a bill file when asked to sign a bill. The materials in the file include items such as a copy of the bill being considered, who voted for it in the Assembly and Senate, letters and positions statements sent to the governor and legislators, and news stories.

29. New York State Bill Jacket S 1906/A 7437, 1992.

30. For instance, in their letter of support for the bill, derived from the find-

ings of this report, the New York Civil Liberties Union remarked on the diverse background of the task force's members: "This bill is consistent with the principal recommendations made by the *broadly representative* Task Force" (ibid.); emphasis mine.

31. Transcribed interview with New York legislative consultant, New York, NY, April 1996.

32. New York State Task Force on Life and the Law, *Surrogate Parenting,* i.

33. In 1987, a year before the task force issued its final report, the Commission on Science and Technology published a research note on all surrogate parenting legislation introduced in New York to that point.

34. New York State Legislative Commission on Science and Technology, *Contract Motherhood: Ethical and Legal Considerations* (Albany: New York State Legislative Commission on Science and Technology, 1991), 61.

35. New York State Department of Health, *The Business of Surrogate Parenting* (Albany: New York State Department of Health, 1992), 1.

36. Ibid., 15.

37. Ibid., 12–13.

38. Ibid., 3.

39. Ibid., 7–8.

40. Kevin Sack, "New York Is Urged to Outlaw Surrogate Parenting for Pay," *New York Times,* May 13, 1992, B:5.

41. "Making Money by Making Babies," *New York Times,* June 10, 1992, A:22. See chapter 4 for longer excerpts from this editorial.

42. "Wanna Buy a Baby?" *Daily News,* May 19, 1992 ; "Womb to Rent," *Newsday,* June 11, 1992.

43. California Department of Justice, "Memorandum: Surrogate Parenting Arrangements," March 1988, in author's files.

44. In an opinion piece that appeared in the *Los Angeles Times* a year before his appointment to the panel, Capron wrote that "for-profit brokering of surrogate contracts should be seen for the illegal and undesirable activity that it is." Alexander Morgan Capron, "Surrogate Contracts: A Danger Zone," *Los Angeles Times,* April 7, 1987, II:5.

45. Transcribed interview with California Senate staff member, Sacramento, CA, June 1996.

46. Margaret Catzen, to Assembly member Sunny Mojonnier, February 2, 1990, in author's files.

47. California Joint Legislative Committee on Surrogate Parenting, *Commercial and Noncommercial Surrogate Parenting* (Sacramento, CA: Joint Publications Office, 1990), M2–M3.

48. Transcribed interview with California Senate staff member, Sacramento, CA, June 1996.

49. Organization for Parenting Through Surrogacy to Senator Diane Watson, February 13, 1990, in author's files.

50. Ibid.

51. For instance, RESOLVE of Los Angeles to Senator Diane Watson, February 9, 1990, Northern California RESOLVE to Senator Diane Watson, February 7, 1990, and RESOLVE of Orange County to Senator Diane Watson, February 7, 1990, all in author's files.

52. California National Organization for Women to Assembly member Sunny Mojonnier, February 12, 1990, in author's files.

53. Ibid.

54. National Association of Surrogate Mothers to Senator Diane Watson, February 7, 1990, in author's files.

55. Transcribed interview with California Senate staff member, Sacramento, CA, June 1996; transcribed interviews with former New York State senator and with New York State Assembly staff member, both in Albany, NY, March 1996. According to others involved, Assemblyman Phil Eisenberg (D) was also pivotal in getting the California bill through the legislature in 1992. In New York, the attorney Barbara Shack, through her involvement in the task force, as well as her position on several key advocacy groups, also appears to have influenced the legislative outcome in that state. In addition, Senator John Marchi (R), who sponsored legislation identical to Weinstein's in the New York Senate, was viewed as "very effective" by an informant involved in the New York legislative debates. Marchi's leadership was seen as consequential because, as an antiabortion Republican, he "effectively" and "unremittingly" pushed the Catholic antisurrogacy position. I do not focus on Marchi's role because S 1906, the Senate version of the antisurrogacy bill, provoked no controversy. The unanimous vote in favor of S 1906 was taken without any prior debate. In contrast, when the same bill was put up for vote on the Assembly floor, the debate lasted over five hours—a very rare occurrence—and a significant minority of the Assembly voted against it.

56. Kathleen Cholewka, "Breaking the Silence on Violence," *Newsday*, Oc-

tober 27, 1994; Maureen Fan, "'Breakthrough' on Club Bill," *Newsday,* March 10, 1994, 17; Charles Mahtesian, "Don't Scoff: Sexual Titles Saved Time," *San Francisco Examiner,* February 27, 1994, B:9; Manuel Perez-Rivas, "College Upgrade Sought," *Newsday,* February 8, 1994, 33; Barbara Reach, letter to the editor, *New York Times,* June 1, 1984, A:30; Sam Roberts, "Metro Matters: Trying to Give Equal Justice to Jailed Women," *New York Times,* March 4, 1991, B:1; Vivienne Walt, "State Lawmakers Eye Rape Bills," *Newsday,* May 5, 1991, 43; Catherine Woodward, "State Pushes for More Child Support," *Newsday,* May 16, 1988, 19.

57. This task force was established in 1981 to work on issues of concern to women that can be dealt with via legislation; its membership consists of legislators and their staff. The task force is reactive as well as proactive; it reviews legislation's impact on women, conducts hearings on timely issues, and initiates and promotes new legislation. See New York State Assembly Task Force on Women's Issues, *Annual Report* (1987), 1.

58. Elizabeth Kolbert, "In Legislature, Women Make Quiet Strides," *New York Times,* January 28, 1987, B:1.

59. "For the Assembly," *Newsday,* November 4, 1990.

60. New York State Assembly, floor debate on A 7437/S 1906, June 26, 1992, 127.

61. Watson remained a state senator until 1998, when term limits prevented her from running for office again. Since 2001, she has served as member of the U.S. Congress representing the 33rd Congressional District. See "Meet Congresswoman Diane Watson," 2006, www.house.gov/watson/meet_congresswoman.shtml (accessed August 21, 2006).

62. Harriet Chiang, "Sexism Pervades State's Courts," *San Francisco Chronicle,* March 24, 1990, A:1; Susan Duerksen, "McCarthy Campaigning for Breast-Cancer Funds," *San Diego Union-Tribune,* December 19, 1991, A:4; Colleen O'Connor, "Seeking Equality by the Year 2000," *Dallas Morning News,* October 27, 1993, C:5; Allan Parachini, "A Clouded Crusade," *Los Angeles Times,* September 1, 1998, IV:1; "New Bill Requires State Office to Test for Chlamydia," *San Francisco Chronicle,* August 3, 1993, C:14; Yumi Wilson, "A Call for Unity in Effort to Halt Domestic Violence," *San Francisco Chronicle,* October 14, 1995, A:15.

63. Transcribed interview with New York State Assembly staff member, Albany, NY, March 1996.

64. Transcribed interview with California Senate staff member, Sacramento, CA, June 1996.

65. In recognition of this extensive record, in 1989 she was honored by the ACLU for her work in defending women's rights to reproductive freedom. See Daniel C. Carson, "Deukmejian Signs, Vetoes Bills in Rush to Meet Deadline," *San Diego Union-Tribune,* October 3, 1985, A:3; Robert B. Gunnison and Greg Lucas, "Senate Wants French Abortion Pill to Be Available," *San Francisco Chronicle,* September 12, 1991, A:19; "Civil Liberties Union to Honor Three Activists at Garden Party," *Los Angeles Times,* June 2, 1989, 5:14; "Anti-Abortion Bill Soundly Defeated," *Los Angeles Times,* April 19, 1990, A:2; Richard C. Paddock, "Republicans Stop Bid to Save Clinics," *Los Angeles Times,* November 5, 1989, A:51; Ron Roach, "Three State Senators Push Measure on Abortion Rights," *San Diego Union-Tribune,* July 6, 1989, A:3; Daniel M. Weintraub, "Watson Seeks to Reaffirm Abortion Rights," *Los Angeles Times,* July 6, 1989, 1:24.

66. See Gusfield (1981) regarding ownership of social problems. See Appendix B for a multistate analysis of this finding.

67. Transcribed interview with New York State Assembly staff member, Albany, NY, March 1996.

68. Corea (1985), Rothman (1989); Davis (1993); D. Roberts (1997).

69. Jennifer Warren, "With No Apologies, Watson Fights On," *Los Angeles Times,* March 16, 1997, A:1, 32–33.

70. Ibid.

71. A member of Watson's staff commented: "[Usually] who supports a proposal before the legislature is critical to its success or failure and [to] who opposes it. I don't think so here. This was something that the members looked to their own personal values and their own kind of intuitive judgment, and I don't think people were swayed by the list of opposition or support." Transcribed interview, Sacramento, CA, June 1996.

72. Transcribed interview with surrogacy program director, Los Angeles, May 1996.

73. Meyer and Minkoff (2004, 1457) describe the premise of political opportunity structure as "Exogenous factors enhance or inhibit prospects for mobilizations, for particular sorts of claims to be advanced rather than others, for particular strategies of influence to be exercised." See also McAdam, McCarthy, and Zald (1988) and Tarrow (1994).

74. COWLI, a statewide organization whose members are primarily female lawyers, is involved in issues of concern to women. New York State Assembly Standing Committee on Judiciary, Assembly Task Force on

Women's Issues, *Public Hearing on Surrogate Parenting,* December 8, 1988, 532.

75. New York State Senate Standing Committee on Child Care, *Surrogate Parenting Hearing,* May 7, 1987, 174.

76. The Women's Division argued against the practice because of its repercussions for women, invoking concerns of commodified reproduction and maternal bonding: "The practice reinforces the notion that women and children are chattel. It attempts to alienate a woman from her reproductive organs and alienate any connection she might be developing with her growing fetus." The New York Women's Bar Association similarly argued in a letter to the governor in support of the anti–commercial surrogacy bill that "New York should act to prevent this state from becoming the brokering capital of the country by adopting this proposal which bans surrogate parenting brokers from doing business here" (New York State Bill Jacket S 1906/A 7437, 1992).

77. New York State Assembly, floor debate on A 7437/S 1906, June 26,1992, 78. The National Women's Political Caucus, founded in 1971, was a grassroots organization devoted to getting women elected to political office.

78. Ibid., 151.

79. See "Assemblymember Deborah J. Glick," 2006, http://assembly.state.ny.us/mem/?ad = 066 (accessed August 21, 2006).

80. New York State Assembly, floor debate on A 7437/S 1906, June 26, 1992, 304.

81. Transcribed interview with New York legislative consultant, New York, NY, April 1996.

82. Transcribed interview with California Senate staff member, Sacramento, CA, June 1996.

83. Transcribed interview with surrogacy program director, Los Angeles, May 1996.

84. Transcribed interview with California Senate staff member, Sacramento, CA, June 1996.

85. California NOW, "1991 Legislative Report Card," 1992, in author's files.

86. California NOW to Assembly member Sunny Mojonnier, May 24, 1988, in author's files.

87. California NOW to Senator Diane Watson, June 27, 1991, in author's files.

88. Transcribed interview with California Senate staff member, Sacramento,

CA, June 1996. Another, considerably less significant women's group, the Women's Lobby, also opposed Watson's regulatory bill. Unlike NOW, this group is known as a conservative, "antifeminist" organization. Its founder, Barbara Alby, has a Christian Right background and extreme antiabortion views. As head of the Women's Lobby, Alby had lobbied against bills on child care and comparable worth for women because she believed such measures encouraged women to abandon their traditional role as housewife and to take jobs outside the home. Therefore, although Alby and the Women's Lobby were on record as against the regulatory bill, neither represented a "prochoice" or equal rights position on women's issues that legislators would consult to help define the new social issue of surrogate motherhood from a "prochoice," equal rights perspective.

89. California Commission on the Status of Women, *1989–1990 Biennial Report,* July 1991, 2. The commission is not a grassroots organization, but over half of the seventeen commissioners are public members. Seven members are appointed by the governor with the consent of the Senate, and one member each is appointed by the Speaker of the Assembly and the Senate Rules Committee. The remaining commissioners consist of three legislative members each from the state Assembly and Senate, the superintendent of Public Instruction, and the state labor commissioner. Watson was one such legislative commission member.

90. California Commission on the Status of Women, *Digest of Pending Legislation,* no. 1, April 11, 1991.

91. Transcribed interview with California Senate staff member, Sacramento, CA, June 1996. In 1985, both Watson and Assemblywoman Maxine Waters were disturbed by "the increasingly conservative policies of the commission that have developed since Deukmejian began making appointments." Douglas Shuit, "State Senate Oks a Budget It Knows Must Be Cut Back," *Los Angeles Times,* May 25, 1985, II:1. The commission's executive director, of whom the assemblywomen were especially critical, was replaced in 1986 (California Commission on the Status of Women, *1989–1990 Biennial Report*). Also of note, two public members of the commission, June Horton Gable and Gloria Godell, were a former president of the Sacramento chapter of NOW and a board member of the Southern California ACLU, respectively– two groups that opposed Watson's bill (California Commission on the Status of Women, *Digest of Pending Legislation*).

92. In March 1987, the Vatican issued a forty-page document called "Instruction on Respect for Human Life in Its Origins and on the Dignity of

Procreation—Replies to Certain Questions of the Day,'" in which most forms of assisted reproductive technology, including surrogacy, were denounced as immoral. Human procreation should, according to church doctrine, result only from the sexual union of married couples. See Roberto Suro, "The Vatican on Birth Science," *New York Times,* March 11, 1987, A:1.

93. Transcribed interview with former California Assembly member, Los Angeles, February 1996; transcribed interview with former New York State senator, Albany, NY, March 1996. Interestingly, Dunne's co-sponsor had not expected him to be a supporter of prosurrogacy legislation, as he is a "good Catholic" (Mary Goodhue, transcribed interview, March 1996). According to one informant, Catholic friends were also surprised at his position.

94. See Bill Billiter, "Surrogate Mothers Bill Dead for Session," *Los Angeles Times,* August 5, 1982, II:1.

95. New York State Bill Jacket S 1906/A 7437, 1992.

96. Ibid.

97. Phone interview with former New York State Assembly member, notes, New York, NY, December 1995.

98. Transcribed interview with New York State Assembly staff member, Albany, NY, March 1996.

99. Transcribed interview with New York legislative consultant, New York, NY, April 1996.

100. Goodhue, interview.

101. Transcribed interview with former New York State senator, Albany, NY, March 1966; transcribed interview with New York State Senate staff member, Staten Island, NY, December 1995.

102. Marchi's and Weinstein's sponsorship parallels the unusual alliance between Henry Hyde and Barbara Boxer in the U.S. Congress on this same issue (see chapter 1).

103. New York State Senate Judiciary Committee, *Surrogate Parenting in New York,* 21.

104. New York State Assembly, floor debate on A 7437/S 1906, June 26, 1992, 82.

105. New York State Senate Standing Committee on Child Care, *Surrogate Parenting Hearing,* May 7, 1987, 144.

106. Similar to this analysis of interest-group involvement and alliances in surrogacy politics is the view that the opposition to divorce reform in the state by both Catholic and women's groups is largely responsible for New York State's more conservative divorce laws. See Leslie Eaton, "A New Push to Loosen New York's Divorce Law," *New York Times,* November 30, 2004, A:1.

107. Transcribed interview with California Senate staff member, Sacramento, CA, June 1996.

108. New York State Assembly, floor debate on A 7437/S 1906, June 26,1992, 245.

109. Phone interview with former New York State Assembly member, notes, New York, NY, December 1995.

110. Transcribed interview with New York State Assembly staff member, Albany, NY, March 1996.

111. Goodhue, interview; she too voted for the anti–commercial surrogacy bill in 1992.

112. It should be noted that the American College of Obstetricians and Gynecologists originally wrote in support of SB 937 and later supported a similar bill introduced by Watson in 1993.

113. Andrews (1992); California Assembly Committee on Judiciary, "Bill Analysis: SB 937," August 12, 1992; transcribed interview with surrogacy program director, Los Angeles, May 1996.

114. Andrews (1992).

115. One informant described the experience of trying to get regulations passed in California as a lonely crusade: "We never had a huge constituency. . . . We were out there alone." Transcribed interview with surrogacy broker, Los Angeles, May 1996.

116. New York State Assembly, floor debate on A 7437/S 1906, June 26, 1992, 91.

117. Ibid., 294.

6. A BRAVE NEW WORLD?

1. Ehrenreich and English (1979); Petchesky (1984/1990); D. Roberts (1997).

2. See D. Roberts (1997), Blankenship et al. (1993), and Collins (1999).

3. See Colen (1995) and Ginsburg and Rapp (1995).
4. See for instance, King and Meyer (1997). Also see Davis (1981) about diverse needs for reproductive freedom among women of different racial/class groups.
5. Ehrenreich and English (1979).
6. Beverly Beyette, "Bar's Family Law 'Think Tank' Tackles Surrogate Motherhood Issue," *Los Angeles Times,* January 21, 1987, V:1.
7. "The Surrogate's Baby Comes First," *New York Times,* January 26, 1987, A:34.
8. Glenn (1994, 1).
9. New York State Task Force on Life and the Law, *Surrogate Parenting: Analysis and Recommendations for Public Policy* (New York: New York State Task Force on Life and the Law, 1988), 78.
10. Note, however, that an examination of family law reveals that government is intimately involved in regulating the so-called private sphere. What varies is the specific content of the laws.
11. See, for example, Gordon (1990), Orloff (1991), and Skocpol (1992).
12. Pornography is another issue over which such conflict occurs (e.g., Willis 1983).
13. See Gómez (1997).
14. See, for example, Eisenstein (1988), Littleton (1987), Vogel (1993), and Williams (1984–85).
15. See Glenn (1994).
16. See Davis (1981, 1993), Gordon (1974/1990), and D. Roberts (1997).
17. The fact that women are so much more successful than men in passing surrogacy legislation is also disturbing in as much as this may indicate an essentialization of womanhood. That is, just because a legislator or activist is a woman should not mean that she must be viewed as representing women's interests. Being a woman does not translate into being an expert on women. Additionally, female legislators should not be expected to introduce legislation on women and new reproductive technologies simply because they are women.
18. See Marshall's (1995) discussion of antifeminist organizations' co-optation of liberal feminist rhetoric.
19. The ten parents are the egg donor and her husband, the sperm donor and his wife, the surrogate and her husband, the intended mother and her husband, and the intended father and his wife.

20. See, for instance, Sue McAllister, "Firm Matches Gay Men, Surrogates," *Los Angeles Times,* February 22, 1998, B:3; Elizabeth Mehren, "Going Solo," *Los Angeles Times,* March 28, 1995, E:1; Ginia Bellafante, "Surrogate Mothers' New Niche: Bearing Babies for Gay Couples," *New York Times,* May 27, 2005, A:1; Ragoné (1994).

APPENDIX A

1. Although the California bill under study was vetoed, I contend that the fact that it passed through the legislature indicates comparability with regard to public policy intention. I am not the only one to make such a claim. In their brief to the California Supreme Court, the Calverts, of *Johnson v. Calvert,* also interpreted the legislature's passage of the bill as an expression of California's public policy. Although the court did not accept this argument, they did not reject it either (*Johnson v. Calvert* 1993).
2. Regarding large populations, see Gray (1996) and Rosenthal (1984); regarding politically diverse populations, see Bell (1984), Rosenthal (1984), and P. Smith (1984); regarding prominent surrogacy centers, see U.S. House of Representatives, *Surrogacy Arrangements Act of 1987: Hearing before the Subcommittee on Transportation, Tourism, and Hazardous Materials of the Committee on Energy and Commerce, October 25, 1988* (Washington, DC: U.S. Government Printing Office, 1988); regarding professionalized legislatures, see Bell (1984); regarding strong interest groups, see Bell (1984), Rosenthal (1984), and Smith (1984); regarding highly publicized court cases, see Tong (1995).
3. Gray (1973); Preston (1984); Walker (1969).
4. Articles were found through the use of Lexis-Nexis and the *Los Angeles Times* Web-based search engine. In both electronic search engines, articles were found using the search terms *surrogacy, surrogate mother,* and *surrogate parenting.*
5. The numbers given are for the total number of articles published in each paper's regular edition. To correct for redundancy as well as to keep each sample comparable, I do not include in these totals articles that appeared in other editions (late vs. early, local vs. regional, etc.). These other articles, however, were examined for content.
6. See chapter 4, note 9, for further discussion of the papers chosen for analysis.
7. There were two key informants I was unable to interview, one in each state.

Neither of them responded to my requests for an interview despite my repeated attempts to contact them. Although they might have provided valuable information, particularly since both opposed the policy approach taken in their respective states, I believe I still have a fairly accurate picture of what occurred. In general, the interviews I did conduct were disappointing. Just four years after most of the events in question, I often knew dates, names, and the like better than my informants. But from the almost dozen interviews I did learn to use their accounts with caution. First, since I was mostly interviewing politicians and their aides I was aware that I could only expect a limited degree of candor. Second, even with this small sample I received slightly different versions of events at times. Consequently, any use of interview data should be viewed as an account rather than a factual source per se.

APPENDIX B

1. National Conference of State Legislatures, "Surrogacy Contract Bill Introductions: 1990 Legislative Sessions," November 8, 1990, "Surrogacy Contract Bill Introductions: 1991 Legislative Sessions," November 22, 1991, and "Surrogacy Contract Bill Introductions: 1992 Legislative Sessions," November 30, 1992.
2. The following analysis is on thirty-three of these bills. One bill was introduced by a committee, so I cannot determine the gender of the sponsor. It has therefore been dropped from the analysis. My analysis does include, however, a total of thirty-four sponsors because data from my New York research indicate that one bill introduced by the Assembly Rules Committee in New York was instigated on behalf of two legislators. Because these legislators are both men I only count them once when examining the effect of gender, but because they have different abortion positions I count them separately when analyzing bill success along this dimension.
3. Thomas (1991).
4. Ibid.
5. New York State Assembly Information Office, personal communication, 1997; also see Rosenthal (1990, 121).
6. Christensen and Gerston (1984, 148); Hyink, Brown, and Thacker (1985, 124).
7. For this part of the analysis I added data from 1990. This addition was

necessary so that there would be enough women in each cell for the analysis to have any substantive significance.

8. The abortion positions of the legislators who sponsored surrogacy bills were determined through a variety of methods. These included newspaper articles; phone calls to local NARAL, Planned Parenthood, and other abortion rights groups; and direct calls to the legislator's office.

BIBLIOGRAPHY

Agigian, Amy. 2004. *Baby Steps: How Lesbian Alternative Insemination Is Changing the World.* Middletown, CT: Wesleyan University Press.

Alper, Joseph, et al., eds. 2002. *The Double-Edged Helix: Social Implications of Genetics in a Diverse Society.* Baltimore: Johns Hopkins University Press.

Andrews, Lori. 1989. *Between Strangers: Surrogate Mothers, Expectant Fathers, and Brave New Babies.* New York: Harper and Row.

———. 1992. Surrogacy Wars. *California Lawyer* 12:42–50.

Anspach, Renée. 1993. *Deciding Who Lives: Fateful Choices in the Intensive-Care Nursery.* Berkeley: University of California Press.

Arditti, Rita, Renate Duelli Klein, and Shelly Minden, eds. 1984. *Test-Tube Women: What Future Motherhood?* London: Pandora.

Armstrong, Elizabeth M. 2003. *Conceiving Risk, Bearing Responsibility: Fetal Alcohol Syndrome and the Diagnosis of Moral Disorder.* Baltimore: Johns Hopkins University Press.

Bartels, Dianne M., Reinhard Priester, Dorothy E. Vawter, and Arthur L. Caplan, eds. 1990. *Beyond Baby M: Ethical Issues in New Reproductive Technologies.* Clifton, NJ: Humana Press.

Becker, Gay. 2000. *The Elusive Embryo: How Women and Men Approach New Reproductive Technologies.* Berkeley: University of California Press.

Beisel, Nicola, and Tamara Kay. 2004. Abortion, Race, and Gender in Nineteenth-Century America. *American Sociological Review* 69:498–518.

Bell, Charles G. 1984. California. In *The Politics of the American States,* edited by Alan Rosenthal and Maureen Moakley. New York: Praeger.

Best, Joel, ed. 1989. *Images of Issues: Typifying Contemporary Social Problems.* New York: Aldine de Gruyter.

———. 1991. "Road Warriors" on "Hair-Trigger Highways": Cultural Resources and the Media's Construction of the 1987 Freeway Shooting Problem. *Sociological Inquiry* 61:237–45.

Blake, Judith. 1974. Coercive Pronatalism and American Population Policy. In *Pronatalism: The Myth of Mom and Apple Pie,* edited by Ellen Peck and Judith Senderowitz. New York: Thomas Y. Crowell.

Blank, Robert, and Janna C. Merrick. 1995. *Human Reproduction, Emerging Technologies, and Conflicting Rights.* Washington, DC: Congressional Quarterly Press.

Blankenship, Kim M., Beth Rushing, Suzanne A. Onorato, and Renee White. 1993. Reproductive Technologies and the U.S. Courts. *Gender and Society* 7:8–31.

Blee, Kathleen M. 1991. *Women of the Klan: Racism and Gender in the 1920s.* Berkeley: University of California Press.

Blum, Linda M. 1999. *At the Breast: Ideologies of Breastfeeding and Motherhood in the Contemporary United States.* Boston: Beacon Press.

Bordo, Susan. 1994. *Unbearable Weight: Feminism, Western Culture, and the Body.* Berkeley: University of California Press.

Boris, Eileen. 1994. Mothers Are Not Workers: Homework Regulation and the Construction of Motherhood, 1948–1953. In *Mothering: Ideology, Experience, and Agency,* edited by Evelyn Nakano Glenn, Grace Chang, and Linda Rennie Forcey. New York: Routledge.

Brandel, Abby. 1995. Legislating Surrogacy: A Partial Answer to Feminist Criticism. *Maryland Law Review* 54:488–527.

Brown, Jessica Autumn, and Myra Marx Ferree. 2005. Close Your Eyes and Think of England: Pronatalism in the British Print Media. *Gender and Society* 19 (1): 5–24.

Browner, C. H., and Nancy Ann Press. 1995. The Normalization of Prenatal Diagnostic Screening. In *Conceiving the New World Order: The Global Politics of Reproduction,* edited by Faye D. Ginsburg and Rayna Rapp. Berkeley: University of California Press.

Burstein, Paul. 1991. Policy Domains: Organization, Culture, and Policy Outcomes. *Annual Review of Sociology* 17:327–50.

Casper, Monica J. 1998. *The Making of the Unborn Patient: A Social Anatomy of Fetal Surgery.* New Brunswick: Rutgers University Press.

Center for Genetics and Society. 2004. New Canadian Cloning and Assisted Reproduction Law Could Be Model for the U.S., Experts Say. March 15. www.genetics-and-society.org/resources/cgs/20040315_canadian_press.html (accessed October 3, 2006).

Chesler, Phyllis. 1990. *Sacred Bond: The Legacy of Baby M.* London: Virago.

Christensen, Terry, and Larry N. Gerston. 1984. *Politics in the Golden State: The California Connection.* Boston: Little, Brown.

Colen, Shelle. 1995. "Like a Mother to Them": Stratified Reproduction and West Indian Childcare Workers and Employers in New York. In *Conceiving the New World Order: The Global Politics of Reproduction,* edited by Faye D. Ginsburg and Rayna Rapp. Berkeley: University of California Press.

Collins, Patricia Hill. 1990. *Black Feminist Thought: Knowledge, Consciousness, and the Politics of Empowerment.* New York: Routledge.

———. 1999. Will the "Real" Mother Please Stand Up? The Logic of Eugenics and American National Family Planning. In *Revisioning Women, Health, and Healing: Feminist, Cultural, and Technoscience Perspectives,* edited by Adele E. Clarke and Virginia L. Olesen. New York: Routledge.

Condit, Celeste. 1990. *Decoding Abortion Rhetoric: Communicating Social Change.* Chicago: University of Illinois Press.

Cook, Fay Lomax, Tom R. Tyler, Edward G. Goetz, Margaret T. Gordon, David Protess, Donna R. Leff, and Harvey L. Molotch. 1983. Media Agenda Setting: Effects on the Public, Interest Group Leaders, Policy Makers, and Policy. *Public Opinion Quarterly* 47:16–35.

Corea, Gena. 1985. *The Mother Machine: Reproductive Technologies from Artificial Insemination to Artificial Wombs.* New York: Harper and Row.

Corea, Gena, et al. 1987. *Man-Made Women: How New Reproductive Technologies Affect Women.* Bloomington: Indiana University Press.

Daniels, Cynthia R. 1993. *At Women's Expense: State Power and the Politics of Fetal Rights.* Cambridge, MA: Harvard University Press.

———. 1997. Between Fathers and Fetuses: The Social Construction of Male Reproduction and the Politics of Fetal Harm. *Signs* 22 (3): 579–616.

DaVanzo, Julie, and M. Omar Rahman. 1993. American Families: Trends and Correlates. *Population Index* 59 (3): 350–86.

Davis, Angela. 1981. *Women, Race and Class.* New York: Vintage Books.

———. 1993. Outcast Mothers and Surrogates: Racism and Reproductive Politics in the Nineties. In *American Feminist Thought at Century's End: A Reader*, edited by Linda S. Kaufman. Cambridge, MA: Blackwell.

Dolgin, Janet L. 1997. *Defining the Family: Law, Technology, and Reproduction in an Uneasy Age.* New York: New York University Press.

Duden, Barbara. 1993. *Disembodying Women: Perspectives on Pregnancy and the Unborn.* Cambridge, MA: Harvard University Press.

Duster, Troy. 1990. *Backdoor to Eugenics.* New York: Routledge.

Dworkin, Andrea. 1983. *Right-Wing Women.* New York: Perigee Books.

East Coast Assisted Parenting. 2000. Gestational Surrogacy in Russia. www.russiansurrogacy.com/ (accessed October 3, 2006).

Edelman, Murray. 1988. *Constructing the Political Spectacle.* Chicago: University of Chicago Press.

Ehrenreich, Barbara, and Deirdre English. 1979. *For Her Own Good: 150 Years of Experts' Advice to Women.* Garden City, NY: Anchor Books.

Eisenstein, Zillah R. 1988. *The Female Body and the Law.* Berkeley: University of California Press.

Engels, Frederick. 1884. *The Origin of the Family, Private Property and the State.* Marx/Engels Internet Archive. 2000. www.marxists.org/archive/marx/works/1884/origin-family (accessed September 28, 2006).

Entman, Robert M. 1991. Framing U.S. Coverage of International News: Contrasts in Narratives of the Kal and Iran Air Incidents. *Journal of Communication* 41 (4): 6–25.

Evans, John. 2002. *Playing God? Human Genetic Engineering and the Rationalization of the Public Bioethical Debate.* Chicago: University of Chicago Press.

Faludi, Susan. 1991. *Backlash: The Undeclared War against American Women.* New York: Crown.

Ferree, Myra Marx. 2005. Framing Equality: The Politics of Race, Class, Gender in the US, Germany, and the Expanding European Union. Keynote address at Gender Issues and Women's Movements in the Enlarged European Union Conference, University of Pennsylvania, February 25.

Ferree, Myra Marx, William A. Gamson, Jürgen Gerhards, and Dieter Rucht. 2002. *Shaping Abortion Discourse: Democracy and the Public Sphere in Germany and the United States.* Cambridge: Cambridge University Press.

Field, Martha. 1988. *Surrogate Motherhood.* Cambridge, MA: Harvard University Press.

Finer, Lawrence B., and Stanley K. Henshaw. 2003. Abortion Incidence and Services in the United States in 2000. *Perspectives on Sexual and Reproductive Health* 35 (1): 6–15.

Finkler, Kaja. 2000. *Experiencing the New Genetics: Family and Kinship on the Medical Frontier.* Philadelphia: University of Pennsylvania Press

Fishman, Mark. 1980. *Manufacturing the News.* Austin: University of Texas Press.

Franklin, Sarah. 1993. Making Representations: The Parliamentary Debate on the Human Fertilisation and Embryology Act. In *Technologies of Procreation: Kinship in the Age of Assisted Conception,* edited by Jeanette Edwards et al. Manchester: Manchester University Press.

———. 1995. Postmodern Procreation: A Cultural Account of Assisted Reproduction. In *Conceiving the New World Order: The Global Politics of Reproduction,* edited by Faye D. Ginsburg and Rayna Rapp. Berkeley: University of California Press.

Friedman, Scott E. 1992. *The Law of Parent-Child Relationships: A Handbook.* Chicago: American Bar Association.

Gailey, Christine Ward. 2000. Ideologies of Motherhood and Kinship in U.S. Adoption. In *Ideologies and Technologies of Motherhood: Race, Class, Sexuality, Nationalism,* edited by Helena Ragoné and France Winddance Twine. New York: Routledge

Gamson, William A., and Andre Modigliani. 1987. The Changing Culture of Affirmative Action. *Research in Political Sociology* 3:137–77.

Gamson, William A., and David Stuart. 1992. Media Discourse as a Symbolic Context: The Bomb in Political Cartoons. *Sociological Forum* 7 (1): 55–86.

Gans, Herbert. 1979. *Deciding What's News.* New York: Pantheon.

Garrow, David J. 1994. *Liberty and Sexuality: The Right of Privacy and the Making of Roe v. Wade.* New York: Macmillan.

Georges, Eugenia, and Lisa M. Mitchell. 2000. Baby Talk: The Rhetorical Production of Maternal and Fetal Selves. In *Body Talk: Rhetoric, Technology, Reproduction,* edited by Mary M. Lay, Laura J. Gurak, Clare Gravon, and Cynthia Mynitti. Madison: University of Wisconsin Press.

Ginsburg, Faye D. 1989. *Contested Lives: The Abortion Debate in an American Community.* Berkeley: University of California Press.

———. 1998. Rescuing the Nation: Operation Rescue and the Rise of Antiabortion Militance. In *Abortion Wars: A Half Century of Struggle, 1950–2000,* edited by Rickie Solinger. Berkeley: University of California Press.

Ginsburg, Faye D., and Rayna Rapp, eds. 1995. *Conceiving the New World Order: The Global Politics of Reproduction.* Berkeley: University of California Press.

Gitlin, Todd, ed. 1987. *Watching Television.* New York: Pantheon.

Glendon, Mary Ann. 1989. *The Transformation of Family Law: State, Law, and Family in the United States and Western Europe.* Chicago: University of Chicago Press.

Glenn, Evelyn Nakano. 1994. Social Constructions of Mothering: A Thematic Overview. In *Mothering: Ideology, Experience, and Agency,* edited by Evelyn Nakano Glenn, Grace Chang, and Linda Rennie Forcey. New York: Routledge.

Gómez, Laura E. 1997. *Misconceiving Mothers: Legislators, Prosecutors, and the Politics of Prenatal Drug Exposure.* Philadelphia: Temple University Press.

Gordon, Linda, ed. 1974/1990. *Women's Body, Women's Right: Birth Control in America.* New York: Penguin.

———. 1990. *Women, the State, and Welfare.* Madison: University of Wisconsin Press.

Goslinga-Roy, Gillian. 1998. Naturalized Selves and Cyborg Bodies: The Case of Gestational Surrogacy. In *Biotechnology, Culture and the Body,* edited by Paul Brodwin. Bloomington: Indiana University Press.

Gostin, Larry, ed. 1990. *Surrogate Motherhood: Politics and Privacy.* Indianapolis: Indiana University Press.

Gray, Virginia. 1973. Innovation in the States: A Diffusion Study. *American Political Science Review* 67:1174–93.

———. 1996. The Socioeconomic and Political Context of States. In *Politics in the American States: A Comparative Analysis,* edited by Virginia Gray and Herbert Jacob. Washington, DC: Congressional Quarterly Press.

Greil, Arthur. 1991. *Not Yet Pregnant: Infertile Couples in Contemporary America.* New Brunswick: Rutgers University Press.

Gusfield, Joseph R. 1981. *The Culture of Public Problems: Drinking-Driving and the Symbolic Order.* Chicago: University of Chicago Press.

Harrington, Michael. 1963. *The Other America.* New York: Macmillan.

Harrison, Michelle. 1987. Social Construction of Mary Beth Whitehead. *Gender and Society* 1 (3): 300–311.

Hartouni, Valerie. 1997. *Cultural Conceptions: On Reproductive Technologies and the Remaking of Life.* Minneapolis: University of Minnesota Press.

Hays, Sharon. 1996. *The Cultural Contradictions of Motherhood.* New Haven: Yale University Press.

Heimer, Carol A., and Lisa R. Staffen. 1998. *For The Sake of the Children: The Social Organization of Responsibility in the Hospital and the Home.* Chicago: University of Chicago Press.

Henry, Vickie L. 1993. A Tale of Three Women: A Survey of the Rights and Responsibilities of Unmarried Women Who Conceive by Alternative Insemination and a Model for Legislative Reform. *American Journal of Law and Medicine* 19:285–311.

Herman, Edward, and Noam Chomsky. 1988. *Manufacturing Consent.* New York: Pantheon.

Hevesi, Alan G. 1975. *Legislative Politics in New York State.* New York: Praeger.

Hirsch, Marilyn B., and William D. Mosher. 1987. Characteristics of Infertile Women in the United States and Their Use of Infertility Services. *Fertility and Sterility* 47:618–25.

Hochschild, Arlie. 1989. *The Second Shift.* New York: Avon Books.

Hunter, James Davison. 1991. *Culture Wars: The Struggle to Define America.* New York: Basic Books.

Hyink, Bernard L., Seyom Brown, and Ernest W. Thacker. 1985. *Politics and Government in California.* New York: Harper and Row.

ISLAT Working Group. 1998. ART into Science: Regulation of Fertility Techniques. *Science* 281 (July 31): 651–52.

Joffe, Carole. 1995. *Doctors of Conscience: The Struggle to Provide Abortion before Roe and after Roe v. Wade.* Boston: Beacon Press.

Johnson, John M. 1989. Horror Stories and the Construction of Child Abuse. In *Images of Issues: Typifying Contemporary Social Problems,* edited by Joel Best. New York: Aldine de Gruyter.

Kahn, Susan. 2000. *Reproducing Jews: A Cultural Account of Assisted Conception in Israel.* Durham: Duke University Press.

Kaplan, E. Ann. 1999. The Politics of Surrogacy Narratives: 1980s Paradigms and Their Legacies in the 1990s. In *Playing Dolly: Technocultural Formations, Fantasies, and Fictions of Assisted Reproduction,* edited by E. Ann Kaplan and Susan Squier. New Brunswick: Rutgers University Press.

Kaplan, Temma. 1982. Female Consciousness and Collective Action: The Case of Barcelona, 1910–1918. *Signs* 7 (3): 42–61.

Kepler, Victoria, and Michael Bokelmann. 2000. Surrogate Motherhood: The Legal Situation in Germany. American Surrogacy Center. www.surrogacy.com/legals/article/germany.html (accessed October 3, 2006).

King, Leslie, and Madonna Harrington Meyer. 1997. The Politics of Reproductive Benefits: U.S. Insurance Coverage of Contraceptive and Infertility Treatments. *Gender and Society* 11 (1): 8–30.

Kolker, Aliza, and Meredith Burke. 1994. *Prenatal Testing: A Sociological Perspective.* Westport, CT: Bergin and Garvey.

Ladd-Taylor, Molly, and Lauri Umansky, eds. 1998. *Bad Mothers: The Politics of Blame in Twentieth-Century America.* New York: New York University Press.

Lasch, Christopher. 1977. *Haven in a Heartless World: The Family Besieged.* New York: Basic Books.

Lasker, Judith, and Susan Borg. 1994. *In Search of Parenthood: Coping with Infertility and Hi-Tech Conception.* Philadelphia: Temple University Press.

Laslett, Barbara, and Johanna Brenner. 1989. Gender and Social Reproduction: Historical Perspectives. *Annual Review of Sociology* 15:381–404.

Layne, Linda, ed. 1999. *Transformative Motherhood: On Giving and Getting in a Consumer Culture.* New York: New York University Press.

Leiter, Richard, ed. 1993. *National Survey of State Laws.* Detroit: Gale Research.

Lewin, Ellen. 1995. On the Outside Looking In: The Politics of Lesbian Motherhood. In *Conceiving the New World Order: The Global Politics of Reproduction,* edited by Faye D. Ginsburg and Rayna Rapp. Berkeley: University of California Press.

Linders, Annulla. 1998. Abortion as a Social Problem: The Construction of "Opposite" Solutions in Sweden and the United States. *Social Problems* 45 (4): 488–509.

Litt, Jacquelyn. 2000. *Medicalized Motherhood: Perspectives from the Lives of African-American and Jewish Women.* New Brunswick: Rutgers University Press.

Littleton, Christine A. 1987. Reconstructing Sexual Equality. *California Law Review* 75:1279–1337.

Lorio, Kathryn Venturatos. 1999. The Process of Regulating Assisted Reproductive Technologies: What We Can Learn from Our Neighbors—What Translates and What Does Not. *Loyola Law Review* 45:247–68.

Luker, Kristin. 1984. *Abortion and the Politics of Motherhood.* Berkeley: University of California Press.

———. 1996. *Dubious Conceptions: The Politics of Teenage Pregnancy.* Cambridge, MA: Harvard University Press.

Luppino, Grace A., and Justine Fitzgerald Miller. 2002. *Family Law and Practice: The Paralegal's Guide.* Upper Saddle River, NY: Prentice Hall.

Manoff, Robert Karl. 1989. Modes of War and Modes of Social Address: The Test of SDI. *Journal of Communication* 39 (1): 59–82.

Markens, Susan. 2002. Invisible Women: Gender, Genetics and Reproduction. In *The Double-Edged Helix: Social Implications of Genetics in a Diverse Society,* edited by J. Alper et al. Baltimore: Johns Hopkins University Press.

Markens, Susan, C. H. Browner, and Nancy Press. 1997. Feeding the Fetus: On Interrogating the Notion of Maternal-Fetal Conflict. *Feminist Studies* 23:351–72.

Marshall, Susan 1995. Confrontation and Co-optation in Antifeminist Organizations. In *Feminist Organizations,* edited by Myra Marx Ferree and Patricia Yancey Martin. Philadelphia: Temple University Press.

McAdam, Doug, John D. McCarthy, and Mayer N. Zald. 1988. Social Movements. In *Handbook of Sociology,* edited by Neil J. Smelser, 695–737. Newbury Park, CA: Sage Publications.

McCombs, Maxwell E., and Donald C. Shaw. 1972. The Agenda-Setting Function of the Mass Media. *Public Opinion Quarterly* 36:176–87.

McNeil, Maureen, and Sarah Franklin. 1993. Editorial: Procreation Stories. *Science as Culture* 3 (4): 477–82.

McNeil, Maureen, and Jacquelyn Litt. 1992. More Medicalizing of Mothers: Foetal Alcohol Syndrome in the USA and Related Developments. In *Private Risks and Public Dangers,* edited by Sue Scott, G. Williams, S. Platte, and H. Thomas. Burlington, VT: Ashgate.

Meyer, David S., and Debra C. Minkoff. 2004. Conceptualizing Political Opportunity. *Social Forces* 82 (4): 1457–92.

Michel, Sonya. 1999. *Children's Interests/Mother's Rights: The Shaping of America's Child Care Policy.* New Haven: Yale University Press.

Mills, C. Wright. 1959. *The Sociological Imagination.* New York: Grove Press.

Mink, Gwendolyn. 1990. The Lady and the Tramp: Gender, Race, and the Origins of the American Welfare State. In *Women, the State, and Welfare,* edited by Linda Gordon. Madison: University of Wisconsin Press.

Mintz, Steven, and Susan Kellogg. 1988. *Domestic Revolutions: A Social History of American Family Life.* New York: Free Press.

Misra, Joya, Stephanie Moller, and Marina Karides. 2003. Envisioning Dependency: Changing Media Depictions of Welfare in the 20th Century. *Social Problems* 50 (4): 482–504.

Mitchell, Lisa M., and Eugenia Georges. 1997. Cross-Cultural Cyborgs: Greek and Canadian Women's Discourses on Fetal Ultrasound. *Feminist Studies* 23 (2): 373–401.

Morell, Carolyn M. 1994. *Unwomanly Conduct: The Challenges of Intentional Childlessness.* New York: Routledge.

Morgan, Laura Wish. 2001. The New Uniform Parentage Act (2000): Parenting for the Millennium. *Divorce Litigation* 13 (March 2001): 41.

Mosher, William, and William Pratt. 1990. Fecundity and Infertility in the United States, 1965–1988. *Advance Data* (Vital and Health Statistics of the National Center for Health Statistics) 192:1–8.

———. 1991. Fecundity and Infertility in the United States: Incidence and Trends. *Fertility and Sterility* 56:192–93.

Mulkay, Michael. 1993. Rhetoric of Hope and Fear in the Great Embryo Debate. *Social Studies of Science* 23:721–42.

———. 1997. *The Embryo Research Debate: Science and the Politics of Reproduction.* Cambridge: Cambridge University Press.

Myers, Daniel J., and Beth Schaefer Caniglia. 2004. All the Rioting That's Fit to Print: Selection Effects in National Newspaper Coverage of Civil Disorders, 1968–1969. *American Sociological Review* 69:519–43.

Nelkin, Dorothy, and Susan Lindee. 1996. *The DNA Mystique: The Gene as Cultural Icon.* New York: W. H. Freeman.

Nelson, Barbara J. 1990. The Origins of the Two-Channel Welfare State: Workmen's Compensation and Mother's Aid. In *Women, the State, and Welfare,* edited by Linda Gordon. Madison: University of Wisconsin Press.

Oaks, Laury. 2001. *Smoking and Pregnancy: The Politics of Fetal Protection.* New Brunswick: Rutgers University Press.

Office of Technology Assessment. 1988. *Infertility: Medical and Social Choices.* OTA-BA-358. Washington, DC: U.S. Government Printing Office.

Orloff, Ann. 1991. Gender in Early U.S. Social Policy. *Journal of Policy History* 3:249–81.

Ortiz, Teresa, and Laura Briggs. 2003. The Culture of Poverty, Crack Babies, and Welfare Cheats: The Making of the "Healthy White Baby Crisis." *Social Text* 21 (3): 39–57.

Park, Robert. 1940. News as a Form of Knowledge: A Chapter in the Sociology of Knowledge. *American Journal of Sociology* 45:669–86.

Peirce, Neal R. 1972. *The Megastates of America: People, Politics, and Power in the Ten Great States.* New York: W. W. Norton.

Petchesky, Rosalind Pollack. 1984/1990. *Abortion and Woman's Choice: The State, Sexuality, and Reproductive Freedom.* Boston: Northeastern University Press.

———. 1987. Foetal Images: The Power of Visual Culture in the Politics of Reproduction. In *Reproductive Technologies: Gender, Motherhood and Medicine,* edited by Michelle Stanworth. Minneapolis: University of Minnesota Press.

Pfeffer, Naomi. 1987. Artificial Insemination, In-Vitro Fertilization and the Stigma of Infertility. In *Reproductive Technologies: Gender, Motherhood and Med-*

icine, edited by Michelle Stanworth. Minneapolis: University of Minnesota Press.

Pfohl, Stephen J. 1977. The Discovery of Child Abuse. *Social Problems* 24:310–23.

Pierce, William L. 1985. Survey of State Activity Regarding Surrogate Motherhood. *Family Law Reporter* 11:3001–4.

———. 1987. Surrogate Parenthood: A Legislative Update. *Family Law Reporter* 13:1442–44.

Piven, Frances Fox. 1990. Ideology and the State: Women, Power, and the Welfare State. In *Women, the State, and Welfare,* edited by Linda Gordon. Madison: University of Wisconsin Press.

Pollitt, Katha. 1998. Fetal Rights: A New Assault on Feminism. In *Bad Mothers: The Politics of Blame in Twentieth-Century America,* edited by Molly Ladd-Taylor and Lauri Umansky. New York: New York University Press.

Popenoe, David. 1996. *Life without Father: Compelling New Evidence That Fatherhood and Marriage Are Indispensable for the Good of Children and Society.* New York: Martin Kessler Books.

Preston, Michael B. 1984. *The Politics of Bureaucratic Reform: The Case of California State Employment Services.* Chicago: University of Illinois Press.

Pretorius, Diederika. 1994. *Surrogate Motherhood: A Worldwide View of the Issues.* Springfield, IL: Charles C. Thomas.

Purdy, Laura. 1992. Another Look at Contract Pregnancy. In *Issues in Reproductive Technology,* edited by Helen Bequaret Holmes. New York: New York University Press.

Rae, Scott B. 1994. *The Ethics of Commercial Surrogate Motherhood: Brave New Families?* Westport, CT: Praeger.

Ragoné, Helena. 1994. *Surrogate Motherhood: Conception in the Heart.* Boulder, CO: Westview Press.

———. 1998. "Incontestable Motivations." In *Reproducing Reproduction: Kinship, Power and Technological Innovation,* edited by Sarah Franklin and Helena Ragoné. Philadelphia: University of Pennsylvania Press.

———. 1999. "The Gift of Life: Surrogate Motherhood, Gamete Donation, and Constructions of Altruism." In *Transformative Motherhood: On Giving and Getting in a Consumer Culture,* edited by Linda L. Layne. New York: New York University Press.

Rapp, Rayna. 1999a. Foreword to *Transformative Motherhood: On Giving and Getting in a Consumer Culture,* edited by Linda L. Layne. New York: New York University Press.

———. 1999b. *Testing the Woman, Testing the Fetus: The Social Impact of Amniocentesis in America.* New York: Routledge.

Rapping, Elayne. 1990. The Future of Motherhood: Some Unfashionably Visionary Thoughts. In *Women, Class and the Feminist Imagination: A Socialist-Feminist Reader,* edited by Karen V. Hansen and Ilene J. Philipson. Philadelphia: Temple University Press.

Reese, Ellen. 2005. *Backlash against Welfare Mothers: Past and Present.* Berkeley: University of California Press.

Richard, Patricia Bayer. 1995. The Tailor-Made Child: Implications for Women and the State. In *Expecting Trouble: Surrogacy, Fetal Abuse and New Reproductive Technologies,* edited by Patricia Boling. Boulder, CO: Westview Press.

Richardt, Nicole. 2003. A Comparative Analysis of the Embryological Research Debate in Great Britain and Germany. *Social Politics* 10:86–128.

Rittenhouse, C. Amanda. 1991. The Emergence of Premenstrual Syndrome as a Social Problem. *Social Problems* 38:412–25.

Roberts, Dorothy. 1997. *Killing the Black Body: Race, Reproduction and the Meaning of Liberty.* New York: Random House.

Roberts, Elizabeth F. S. 1998a. Examining Surrogacy Discourses: Between Feminine Power and Exploitation. In *Small Wars: The Cultural Politics of Childhood,* edited by Nancy Scheper-Hughes and Carolyn Sargent. Berkeley: University of California Press.

———. 1998b. "Native" Narratives of Connectedness: Surrogate Motherhood and Technology. In *Cyborg Babies: From Techno-Sex to Techno-Tots,* edited by Robbie Davis-Floyd and Joseph Dumit. New York: Routledge.

Robertson, John. 1994. *Children of Choice: Freedom and the New Reproductive Technologies.* Princeton: Princeton University Press.

———. 2004. Reproductive Technology in Germany and the United States: An Essay in Comparative Law and Bioethics. *Columbia Journal of Transnational Law* 43:187–226.

Rochfort, David A., and Roger W. Cobb. 1993. Problem Definition, Agenda Access, and Policy Choice. *Policy Studies Journal* 21:56–71.

Rogers, Everett M., and James W. Dearing. 1988. Agenda-Setting Research: Where Has It Been, Where Is It Going? *Communication Yearbook* 11:555–94.

Rosenthal, Alan. 1984. On Analyzing States. In *The Politics of the American States,* edited by Alan Rosenthal and Maureen Moakley. New York: Praeger.

———. 1990. *Governors and Legislatures: Contending Powers.* Washington, DC: Congressional Quarterly Press.

Roth, Benita. 2004. *Separate Roads to Feminism: Black, Chicana, and White Feminist Movements in America's Second Wave.* Cambridge: Cambridge University Press.

Roth, Rachel. 1993. At Women's Expense: The Costs of Fetal Rights. In *The Politics of Pregnancy: Policy Dilemmas in the Maternal-Fetal Relationship,* edited by Janna C. Merrick and Robert H. Blank. New York: Haworth Press.

Rothman, Barbara Katz. 1986. *The Tentative Pregnancy: Prenatal Diagnosis and the Future of Motherhood.* New York: Viking Press.

———. 1989. *Recreating Motherhood: Ideology and Technology in a Patriarchal Society.* New York: W. W. Norton.

———. 1998. *Genetic Maps and Human Imaginations: The Limits of Science in Understanding Who We Are.* New York: W. W. Norton.

Ruppe, David. 2003. Global Surrogacy Market. August 23, 2003. Intended Parents Inc. www.intendedparents.com/News/Global_surrogacy_market.html (accessed October 3, 2006).

Saguy, Abigail. 2003. *What Is Sexual Harassment? From Capitol Hill to the Sorbonne.* Berkeley: University of California Press.

Sandelowski, Margarete. 1991. Compelled to Try: The Never-Enough Quality of Conceptive Technology. *Medical Anthropology Quarterly* 5 (1):29–47.

———. 1993. *With Child in Mind: Studies of the Personal Encounter with Infertility.* Philadelphia: University of Pennsylvania Press.

Sawicki, Jana. 1991. *Disciplining Foucault: Feminism, Power and the Body.* New York: Routledge.

Scheper-Hughes, Nancy, and Howard F. Stein. 1998. Child Abuse and the Unconscious in American Popular Culture. In *The Children's Culture Reader,* edited by Henry Jenkins. New York: New York University Press.

Schmidt, Matthew A., and Lisa Jean Moore. 1998. Constructing a "Good Catch," Picking a Winner: The Development of Technosemen and the Deconstruction of the Monolithic Male. In *Cyborg Babies: From Techno-Sex to Techno-Tots,* edited by Robbie Davis-Floyd and Joseph Dumit. New York: Routledge.

Schneider, David. 1980. *American Kinship: A Cultural Account.* Chicago: University of Chicago Press.

Schneider, Joseph W. 1985. Social Problems Theory: The Constructionist View. *Annual Review of Sociology* 11:209–29.

Scritchfield, Shirley A. 1989. The Social Construction of Infertility: From Private Matter to Social Concern. In *Images of Issues: Typifying Contemporary Social Problems,* edited by Joel Best. New York: Aldine de Gruyter Press.

Shaw, Donald, and Maxwell Combs. 1977. *The Emergence of American Political Issues: The Agenda-Setting Function of the Press.* St. Paul, MN: West.

Sigal, Leon V. 1973. *Reporters and Officials: The Organization and Politics of Newsmaking.* Lexington, MA: D. C. Heath.

Skocpol, Theda. 1992. *Protecting Soldiers and Mothers: The Political Origins of Social Policy in the United States.* Cambridge, MA: Harvard University Press.

Smith, Paul A. 1984. New York. In *The Politics of the American States,* edited by Alan Rosenthal and Maureen Moakley. New York: Praeger.

Smith, Tamsin. 2004. Fertility Laws Frustrate Italians. August 9. Intended Parents, Inc. www.intendedparents.com/News/Fertility_laws_frustrate_Italians.html (accessed October 3, 2006).

Solinger, Rickie. 1992. *Wake Up Little Susie: Single Pregnancy and Race before Roe v. Wade.* New York: Routledge.

———, ed. 1998a. *Abortion Wars: A Half Century of Struggle, 1950–2000.* Berkeley: University of California Press.

———. 1998b. Poisonous Choice. In *Bad Mothers: The Politics of Blame in Twentieth-Century America,* edited by Molly Ladd-Taylor and Lauri Umansky. New York: New York University Press.

Spector, Malcolm, and John Kitsuse. 1977. *Constructing Social Problems.* Menlo Park, CA: Cummings.

Stacey, Judith. 1991. *Brave New Families: Stories of Domestic Upheaval in Late Twentieth Century America.* New York: Basic Books.

———. 1996. *In the Name of the Family: Rethinking Family Values in the Postmodern Age.* Boston: Beacon Press.

Stack, Carol. 1974. *All Our Kin: Strategies for Survival in a Black Community.* New York: Harper and Row.

Stanworth, Michelle, ed. 1987. *Reproductive Technologies: Gender, Motherhood and Medicine.* Minneapolis: University of Minnesota Press.

Stevens, Mitchell L. 2001. *Kingdom of Children: Culture and Controversy in the Homeschooling Movement.* Princeton: Princeton University Press.

Strathern, Marilyn. 2002. Still Giving Nature a Helping Hand? Surrogacy: A Debate about Technology and Society. *Journal of Molecular Biology* 319:985–93.

Tarrow, Sidney. 1994. *Power in Movement: Social Movements, Collective Action, and Politics.* New York: Cambridge University Press.

Taylor, Janelle S. 1992. The Public Fetus and the Family Car: From Abortion Politics to a Volvo Advertisement. *Public Culture* 4 (2): 67–80.

Taylor, Philippa. 2003. Surrogacy Arrangements and Payments. Centre for

Bioethics and Public Policy. June. www.bioethics.ac.uk/publications/surrogacy.pdf#search='switzerland%20laws%20surrogacy' (accessed October 3, 2006).

Taylor, Verta. 1996. *Rock-a-by Baby: Feminism, Self-Help and Postpartum Depression.* New York: Routledge.

Teman, Elly. 2001. Technological Fragmentation and Women's Empowerment: Surrogate Motherhood in Israel. *Women's Studies Quarterly* 29:11–34.

———. 2003a. Knowing the Surrogate Body in Israel. In *Surrogate Motherhood: International Perspectives,* edited by Rachel Cook, Shelley Day Sclater, and Felicity Kaganas. Oxford: Hart.

———. 2003b. The Medicalization of "Nature" in the "Artificial Body": Surrogate Motherhood in Israel. *Medical Anthropology Quarterly* 17 (1): 78–98.

Thomas, Sue. 1991. The Impact of Women on State Legislative Policies. *Journal of Politics* 53:958–76.

Thompson, Charis. 2002. Fertile Ground: Feminists Theorize Infertility. In *Infertility around the Globe: New Thinking on Childlessness, Gender, and Reproductive Technologies,* edited by Marcia C. Inhorn and Frank van Balen. Berkeley: University of California Press.

———. 2005. *Making Parents: The Ontological Choreography of Reproductive Technologies.* Boston: MIT Press.

Tong, Rosemarie. 1995. Feminist Perspectives and Gestational Motherhood: The Search for a Unified Legal Focus. In *Reproduction, Ethics, and the Law: Feminist Perspectives,* edited by Joan C. Callahan. Bloomington: Indiana University Press.

Tsing, Anna Lowenhaupt. 1990. Monster Stories: Women Charged with Perinatal Endangerment. In *Uncertain Terms: Negotiating Gender in American Culture,* edited by Faye Ginsburg and Anna Lowenhaupt Tsing. Boston: Beacon Press.

Tuchman, Gaye. 1978. *Making News: A Study in the Construction of Reality.* New York: Free Press.

Van Dyck, Jose. 1995. *Manufacturing Babies and Public Consent: Debating the New Reproductive Technologies.* New York: New York University Press.

Vogel, Lise. 1993. *Mothers on the Job: Maternity Policy in the U.S. Workplace.* New Brunswick: Rutgers University Press.

Walker, Jack L. 1969. The Diffusion of Innovation among the American States. *American Political Science Review* 63:880–99.

Warnock, Mary. 1985. *A Question of Life: The Warnock Report on Human Fertilisation and Embryology.* Oxford: Blackwell.

Weston, Kath. 1997. *Families We Choose: Lesbians, Gays, Kinship.* New York: Columbia University Press.

Wilder, Marcy J. 1998. The Rule of Law, the Rise of Violence, and the Role of Morality: Reframing America's Abortion Debate. In *Abortion Wars: A Half Century of Struggle, 1950–2000,* edited by Rickie Solinger. Berkeley: University of California Press.

Williams, Wendy W. 1984–85. Equality's Riddle: Pregnancy and the Equal Treatment/Special Treatment Debate. *New York University Review of Law and Social Change* 13:325–80.

Willis, Ellen. 1983. Feminism, Moralism, and Pornography. In *Desire: The Politics of Sexuality,* edited by Ann Snitow, Christine Stansell, and Sharon Thompson. London: Virago Press.

Zelizer, Viviana A. 1985. *Pricing the Priceless Child: The Changing Social Value of Children.* New York: Basic Books.

Zimmerman, Joseph. 1981. *The Government and Politics of New York State.* New York: New York University Press.

INDEX

Text:	11/14 Adobe Garamond
Display:	Adobe Garamond, Gill Sans Book
Indexer:	Roberta Engleman
Illustrator:	Bill Nelson
Compositor	Integrated Composition Systems
Printer and binder:	Sheridan Books, Inc.